COMPASSIONATE SOCRATES

COMPASSIONATE SOCRATES

READINGS ON WISDOM ACROSS THE CULTURES AND DISCIPLINES

FIRST EDITION

Edited by Jung Kwon

California State University—Dominguez Hills

cognella®
SAN DIEGO

Bassim Hamadeh, CEO and Publisher
Mieka Portier, Acquisitions Editor
Tony Paese, Project Editor
Alia Bales, Production Editor
Emely Villavicencio, Senior Graphic Designer
Michael Skinner, Senior Licensing Specialist
Natalie Piccotti, Director of Marketing
Kassie Graves, Vice President of Editorial
Jamie Giganti, Director of Academic Publishing

3970 Sorrento Valley Blvd., Ste. 500, San Diego, CA 92121

CONTENTS

PREFACE

Those who know what humanity does, use what they know to nurture what they do not know.

Chuang Tzu

We are living in a world marked by rapid changes at an unprecedented scale. It is my humble desire to create a philosophy anthology that can help college students to reflect on a growing sense of chaos and uncertainty we are living with. As a philosopher trained primarily in the Western philosophy, I started to question the potency of the Western philosophy as a source of wisdom in this tumultuous time. I was drawn to the ancient wisdom traditions born out in the Eastern soil as a fountain of resources that are nowhere found in the Western mind. I firmly believe in the unbeatable force that the Socratic tradition exerts on the history of philosophy. I came to a realization however that the Socratic pillars of the Western thinking may not be adequate to address many questions we face in our time. Socrates urges us to examine life using the instrument of reason and logical inference to reveal the pitfalls of doxastic opinions and dogmatic creeds. Western philosophy for the past 2,500 years has greatly contributed to developing the rational, executive function of the human brain, entrenching the anthropo-centric attitude as an indubitable stock of leitmotif of human civilization. Such a single-minded promulgation of human reason while gravely ignoring the rest of the living world, I claim, can be redirected to a wholehearted promotion of the welfare of all the sentient beings of which humans are only a part. I propose compassion should be an essential companion of reason if we hope to see a turning point in the Western philosophy in this direction. Compassion is never a sentimentalized pity but a sincere intent to experience and act selflessly. Socratic reason and Cartesian ego alone are not a balanced philosophical diet. Selfless compassion, I believe, will make human being whole and flourishing.

This anthology takes the form of an interdisciplinary dialogue on human experiences in religion, art, science, as well as philosophy. If philosophy aspires to offer a cross-cultural wisdom on the whole humans, it must embrace all the subjects in humanities as the limbs of human experiences. It is essential for students of philosophy to be acquainted with prominent ideas that arise in diverse subjects in humanities in order to understand that philosophy is hardly an autonomous discipline, but a system of reflection and criticism built on those ideas. I chose religion, art, and science as the perennial source of philosophical inspiration and reflection. Each subject accentuates a specific dimension of human experience. Religion accentuates our experience of vulnerability and frailty albeit a highly evolved conscious creature. Art accentuates our experience of expressive urge and joy of creation in the image of our most cherished qualities. Science accentuates our experience of puzzles and wonders at objectified nature waiting to be explained by confident reason. I selected historical conspicuous figures in the Western philosophy that represent philosophical responses to seismic epochs in human intellectual history. Religion, art, science, and philosophy in this regard together form a humanist quartet, so to speak. My interest in a cross-cultural and interdisciplinary dialogue necessitates a concluding part of the anthology in which the ancient Eastern wisdom opens a vista to a radically new way of thinking and living in this uncertain and chaotic time of the twenty-first century.

I am greatly indebted to the Cognella Academic Publishing in getting my project on a very different kind of philosophy textbook taking a shape and coming into existence. I could not have dreamed of teaching a class with my own anthology, had it not been for a serendipitous encounter with the Cognella staff. I feel I can best return their excellent support by inspiring my students with the spirit of compassionate Socrates and helping them cultivate the whole humanity and steer their way through whatever weather they are living under.

INTRODUCTION

Humanities subject as an academic study looks at human experiences and records the ways in which we make sense of them. What is a philosophical way of looking and recording? Questioning and seeing things from a certain frame of questions are a fundamentally philosophical way of understanding human experiences. Philosophy intrinsically is a questioning discipline. The gist of philosophical study is to articulate questions. Philosophy in this regard can be called an art of questioning. The emphasis is equally on "art" and "questions," because it is crucially important to raise a question in an appropriate frame—not just a random question. Philosophy treats questions as a key chain that can unlock and open the door for a new way of thinking and seeing the world and ourselves. This is because questions themselves reveal unstated assumptions, unspoken opinions, unproven beliefs about how things are, and even underlying interests and preferences about how things should be. Formulating a question is in a sense analyzing a question. By carefully analyzing the implicit claims nascent in a question as if treating a question like a densely packed information cluster, we questioners gain self-knowledge. Our questions make known to us what we assume, believe, favor, and hope. This is the spirit of Socratic method adequately captured in the exhortation, "The unexamined life is not worth living." Human life is a life of a conscious actor who acts and reacts in an unceasing chain of endeavors. We act and react with little effort to look into our assumptions and preferences that motivate and fuel our endeavors. Certainly, Socratic reason cannot help frowning upon such a dangerous complacency. Actions and reactions leave a permanent impression that is indelible and inevitably brings us to their unpredictable outcomes. We want to examine our life by examining everything that keeps us going as conscious agents. This is not possible without questioning. Questioning reveals and initiates a critical thinking and responsible action and reaction. This is a philosophical way of understanding human experiences.

Why then a humanist quartet in a philosophy anthology, with readings that present religious thoughts, significant art forms, and scientific development, beside prominent philosophers? The rationale for such an interdisciplinary interest is that philosophy as a branch in humanities is rooted in religion, art, and science. Pre-Socratic philosophers were natural philosophers in the sense that Galileo and Newton were. Platonic philosophy unmistakably bears the mark of the religious aspirations of the Pythagorean school that was itself inspired by the Upanishadic vision for the ultimate reality. Kant's monumental turn in his critical philosophy was a reaction to the medieval dogmatic theology-philosophy as well as a deference to the modern empirical way of knowing. Ancient or modern, systematic philosophers such as Aristotle and Kant wrestle with the problem of reconciling emotions or feelings—aesthetic organs—with the rational order of thinking. Their theories of art are still canonical and a must-read for anyone with theoretical interest in art. I am indeed picturing an organic system of understanding, of which the branches are religion, art, science, and philosophy. They develop together to record ways in which we make sense of human experiences.

There is another reason for an interdisciplinary anthology. I want to embrace distinct methods and paths each of the four subjects takes. Questioning as a philosophical method opens a path to critical reasoning. What can be a principal method of religion, art, and science and what types of paths are in view? I appreciate religious traditions in that they offer the most ancient sources of wisdom that are still highly influential. I selected Hinduism, Buddhism, Christianity, and Islam—four of the most practiced religions in the world—in this anthology to examine their philosophical and spiritual underpinnings. Religion appeals to the aspects of human experience that are not neatly understood in terms of reason and logic. Some of these experiences can best be understood in terms of meaning or purpose of human life. If it is an intelligible concept that human life serves a certain goal, then what can tell us which direction our life should take? I believe it is the religious aspiration to answer this question. This quest for meaning guided by religion accompanies a profound emotion of human finitude and vulnerability. How can we ever study religion as a subject in humanities without engaging ourselves with religious imagination that accompanies viscerally experiential dimension? What is it to feel finitude? What is it to be aware of vulnerability? Such an experiential understanding will certainly give philosophical questioning and reasoning an affective undertone. This enriches philosophy.

The term "art" is a nebulous vocabulary that does not have a fixed boundary of meaning, thus placed to a vast range of human creations with varying purpose in view. I chose a Greek tragedy, a study on a modern system of fine art applied to music, a psychological-philosophical account of the layers of meaning in painting, and a literary sensation in the twentieth century that revolves around the absurd as an unnerving existential sentiment. This part of the anthology is a survey of art forms and each chapter investigates distinct ways of creation, interpretation, and appreciation that each art form has. My interest in selecting a tragic drama is to understand the ancient social and political context in which ethical questions arise and are answered. Music, especially purely instrumental music, deserves a special attention as it helps us probe the possibility of pure musical experience that is autonomous and meaningful in its own way without an association or affinity with other human experiences. Philosophers in modern times onward recognize the musical autonomy ground in the purity of the musical sound and proposed sophisticated aesthetics and metaphysics with aesthetical backdrop. In contrast, painting as principally a visual medium offers complex layers of meaning that paintings communicate with the viewers. It is the task undertaken by Wollheim to distinguish different ways in which paintings appeal to the viewers. I selected a reading on the literary provenance of the mid-twentieth century existentialist novel to understand the social unrest and political turbulence out of which the protagonist was created. Dramatic, musical, visual, and literary medium creates its own world of meaning that is not always translated into discursive and logical language. Artistic modalities of communication and expression are for this very reason essential components of human experiences that philosophy must appreciate.

Science has always given the greatest momentum in the advancement of philosophical thoughts. Hard facts of science demand philosophical theories to be adequately representing the material world, regardless of the philosophical reflections made onto the scientific theories. Scientific evidence can work like a stumbling block to a contemplative philosophy or a clarifying token of philosopher's conviction. For the anthology, I started with the modern scientific upheaval of humanly possible experiences and new ways of thinking about the material world. I moved to another upheaval in the way we see human nature and the entire life forms by selecting a portion of Darwin's book. I then included a biographical sketch of the two most notable quantum physicists—Einstein and Schrödinger—to understand the tension and resonance in the profound scientific intelligence of the turn of the century. Natural world is certainly shared by all humans and the ways of understanding the material nature is not a sole occupation of the Western mind. Philosophy, while paying due attention to the scientific explanation of the world, tends to ignore the ways of understanding the natural world by indigenous people, who nonetheless have developed an insightful system of knowledge. This is why I selected a reading on indigenous scientific knowledge. Are there really such things as scientific hard facts? Is the distinction between the knower and the knowable a valid assumption or a questionable scheme of the thinking mind that has no basis in reality? I want readers to ponder on these questions and make the best effort to understand the human experiences and endeavors behind the scientific reason.

It is a difficult task to line up several philosophers to represent an epochal significance in the history of philosophy. Every philosopher signifies something in an unbroken stream of human intellectual development. Socrates firmly establishes the spirit of philosophy in a devout pursuit of wisdom that puts human knowledge as "nothing" with little value except one mark of wisdom regarding profound ignorance. It is indeed a truly liberating, even therapeutic, voice of Socrates, freeing us from the compulsive desire to know the truth and to be right and urging us instead to embark on an inward journey to self-knowledge. "Knowledge" directed to self is not really knowledge that can be true or false, but instead a practice of making and remaking of oneself with the aspiration to be an excellent human being. I call this Socratic freedom, which is nourished by Socratic spirit of questioning and examination of all the assumptions and beliefs that underlie questions. In this regard, Socrates already planted the seed of spiritual practice in the Western philosophical soil. He was not a logical reason fanatic, despite his unmistakable belief that logical reason is an essential instrument for questioning and reflection. He pointed us to the abysmal deficiency of human reason and inspired us to be confident in one's humanness, for being human is more than knowing. Spinoza, the great early modern philosopher, inherited exactly this spirit of human freedom. Philosophical understanding does not add anything novel to the world, nor does it change anything outside human life. What it does is to increase the level of freedom within us and help attain contentment and happiness as a human being. A soaring modern thinker and deeply spiritual philosopher, Spinoza, offers us an insight into a philosophical way of overcoming human sufferings and achieving freedom from them. Kant is presented as a critically (contra pathological) skeptical philosopher who carefully probes the possibility of adequate and justified human knowledge. He marks a momentous turning point in the Western philosophy, and subsequent philosophical development can hardly be understood without Kantian revolution. Wittgenstein made another turning point by shifting philosophical attention to the propositions per se to the ways in which propositions are constructed and used. My own philosophical career indeed began with studying Wittgenstein's philosophy, and I can hardly express my appreciation of his austere and frugal outlook (as the epigraph above suggests) on what philosophy can do. Philosophy does not moralize in a way Kant does with reference to an indubitable moral law, nor does it increase our knowledge in ways natural philosophers do with laws of physics and systems of deductions. Philosophy at its best points us to the ways in which language is used to communicate questions and exchange responses to the questions. Without investigating the linguistic medium we convey philosophical "stuffs" in, we are forever stuck and never find a way out. It is this trenchant insight I want readers to capture in the reading from his *Philosophical Investigations*.

The selection from the ancient Chinese philosophy of change may appear a unique component of an anthology for an undergraduate philosophy course. The choice is deliberate. In conceiving an anthology from a different direction that resonates with a growing sense of dystopia and uncertainty, I cannot help but include the first two chapters of the Book of Changes (known as *I Ching*) to introduce the readers to the oldest Eastern wisdom on change and invariables. What follows is an ancient Greek philosopher, Aristotle's, philosophy on fulfilling human life. How much weight does it bear to seek a way to fulfill a human potential in the way Aristotle sees in this age of unpredictability and collective incapacity to face challenges? This is the question I want to share with anyone interested in "refreshing" human reason and finding the extent to which it promotes lasting happiness and well-being. For next, I chose a reading on Marx and his diagnosis of alienation to counter Aristotelian look on human potential presented as a time-less placeholder, which is, from the Marxist perspective, only a historical contingency. The last selection brings us back to the ancient Eastern wisdom tradition of Taoism. I cannot think of a better reading for the concluding chapter of the anthology than a general introduction to Taoism, a religion without God or deities and philosophy without propositions or theories. There are some elements of Taoism that became popular among Westerners and students of philosophy, such as yin-yang complementarity and the dynamic reversal-support of opposing forces that underlie changes. I intend this chapter to suggest an open-ended, amorphous character of the philosophy as an academic discipline from now onward.

UNIT I

MAKING SENSE OF RELIGION

In the first chapter on Hinduism, Ray Billington introduces fundamental beliefs in Hinduism by presenting key ideas and concepts in a lucid and ordered way. In the second chapter, Damien Keown introduces fundamental Buddhist teachings in his typical style of lucid and compelling presentation as a renowned scholar of Buddhist Ethics. In chapter three, William Shepard presents some of the central aspects of the Qur'an to guide us to the second largest religion of the world. In the fourth chapter, Robert Harrison examines an intriguing difference between the Islamic and Christian conception of the Garden of Eden, in a way to contrast the Islamic perspective on heaven as a peaceful earthly Eden and the Christian outlook on celestial heaven remote from the primordial earthly Garden.

Hinduism II

Its basic teaching

Ray Billington

As the preceding chapter should have indicated, there are many ramifications in Hinduism, both philosophical and religious, which have well-nigh overwhelmed many a novice in the field. To explore its labyrinthine paths comprehensively requires both a fixed resolve and virtually a lifetime of study and experience: here we can only assume the former and anticipate the latter. It is nonetheless possible to extrapolate some central ideas to which most, if not all, who call themselves Hindus are likely to subscribe; between them, they give Hinduism its essential and unique character.

The central drive of Hinduism, its view of the underlying aim of all life's activities, decisions, relationships and commitments, is the attainment of **moksha**. This word literally means 'enlightenment', in the sense of 'seeing the light'. It is the moment when scales are removed from the eyes, so that one recognises as real what had always been there to be seen, but to which one had previously been blind.

There are two parallel revelations which lead to *moksha*, one negative, the other positive (what Taoists would describe as *yin* and *yang*). The negative is the realisation that the world and all it has to offer is an illusion, **maya**: not in the sense that it does not really exist, but because its ability to satisfy human needs can never be other than temporary. Material objects will either decay or lose their appeal; skills and talents will decline with advancing years; relationships will either fall apart or end in death; not even the pursuit of scholarship can last for ever. As the Hebrew text Ecclesiastes, written in the second century BC, states repeatedly: 'All is vanity'; and the writer's words are echoed in an ancient Hindu saying: 'This world is a bridge: pass over it, and do not build your house upon it.'

This philosophy may sound pessimistic, but to those whose goal is *moksha* this would be a blinkered assessment, arrived at only by cushioning oneself from reality and living in a permanent state of delusion; as artificial and transitory as the euphoria gained from a bottle or a needle. *Maya* is held to be so all-pervasive that any goal in life that seeks to overcome its threat must be seen in a positive light. Of the four goals that Hindus recognise, *moksha* alone achieves this absolutely. This becomes apparent when it is compared with the other three goals: **artha** (wealth), **kama** (pleasure) and **dharma** (duty). None of these is viewed as reprehensible *per se,* but if they become ends in themselves (which, as experience shows, they tend to do), *maya* triumphs.

It is important to be clear about the Hindu attitude here, since otherwise we might be identifying it, wrongly, with the ultra-asceticism and world-hating self-denial of the Jains (to be discussed in Chapter 5). The pursuit of *artha* is viewed as natural and, if it does not involve the destruction of other people in the process, even laudable. Wealth is neither good nor evil in itself: used for the benefit of others, it may be spiritually advantageous to its possessor. Only when it induces greed and leads its owner to lose sight of the ultimate end does it become a hindrance on the religious path: and, sadly, this is its propensity.

The fact that Hindus can make the same concession about *kama* is more significant. The word (not to be confused with *karma,* action, a concept that will feature later in this account) means pleasure, the outcome of sensual desire; in particular, it means sexual delight. We have noted (page 23) how sexual intercourse is used in Tantrism as a foretaste, if not actual experience, of the divine: and this is indicated in the *Rigveda,* which describes *kama* as the first stage by which the Absolute reveals itself:

> Desire [*kama*] arose in him who is the source of consciousness, whom the sages by examination have found in their hearts and who unites absolute being with the manifest world.

This seems to be making explicit what is implicit in the description of Jesus as 'the Son of God': to have a son, there must be *kama* on the part of the father. But Hindus are no less aware than are the Jains that the pursuit of *kama,* even more than *artha* (which is often directed toward *kama*), can divert people from the spiritual path. As in many religions, there is considerable ambivalence on this issue.

The third goal, *dharma,* refers to the basis of moral behaviour in the world, its underlying principles, such as justice, righteousness, benevolence. So far as the individual is concerned, it means the kind of behaviour that is viewed as a person's religious duty. Even more than *artha* and *kama,* it may be recognised that *dharma* can be observed without being deceived by *maya*; but, just as obviously, it can become an end in itself, so that *moksha* remains remote, eclipsed by the myopia often found among believers in duty for duty's sake. For Hindus, the extent to which *dharma* might lead to *moksha,* rather than be obscured by *maya,* depends on the individual's karmic situation, that is, his or her current position on the spiritual quest (see pages 37–40).

Maya is, then, a condition of cosmic ignorance (**avidya**), which is reflected in any individual who is deceived by it. It is the equivalent of what is known in Sanskrit as **ajnana,** the state of one whose eyes have yet to be opened by attaining *moksha.* Its opposite is **vidya,** or knowledge (equivalent, **jnana**), which can be interpreted both at a low level, in the sense of garnering information and experience, and at a higher, intuitive level, as a faculty that leads to liberation from *maya* and the acquisition of spiritual enlightenment. So far as Hindus of the Advaita Vedanta school are concerned, however, even *vidya* needs to be transcended, since, like its opposite, *avidya,* it operates in the sphere of time, place and causality, and is consequently, and inevitably, an aspect of the world of the relative, not of the absolute. What this means brings us to the heart of Hinduism.

We could condense the positive aspect of *moksha* (positive, that is, in the sense of what is turned to, or embraced, rather than what is turned away from, or rejected—though the one, of necessity, cannot occur without the other) into the single succinct statement that may be made by anyone who has reached the state of *moksha*: *I am God.* For any Western reader, however, (and for not a few Hindus) the baldness of this assertion is likely to jar, and it must be tempered with an account of Hindu ontology, with particular reference to the teachings of Advaita Vedanta.

The key words are, as we have seen, **atman** and **brahman,** and it is necessary both to understand their meanings and to appreciate how they differ in implication from their Western counterparts. *Atman* is often translated as 'the soul', and, in the sense that it refers to an immortal element in human beings, contrasted with the mortal body, it is a reasonable starting point. In the West, however, the word 'soul' is used in so wide a range of senses that its meaning is often (and no pun is intended here) nebulous. Sometimes it means an alternative self to that represented by the body, as in Wordsworth's 'Ode on the Intimations of Immortality':

> The Soul that rises with us, our life's Star,
> Hath had elsewhere its setting,
> And cometh from afar.

Sometimes it means a human being, no more, no less, as when we describe a person as a 'poor soul', or in David Lodge's description of the British postgraduate student as 'a lonely, forlorn soul'. In other expressions the word implies the basic 'real' self, exemplified in Simone Weil's words in *The Need for Roots*: 'To be rooted is perhaps the most important and least recognised need of the human soul.'

Because of the confusion that is therefore inevitable if we translate *atman* as 'soul', it seems preferable to use the word 'self', in the sense of the underlying person represented by his or her physical actions, mental deliberations and spiritual reflections; however, since all of these, including the last, are likely to be subject to *maya,* the word 'represented' could well be replaced by 'camouflaged'. The *atman* is the essential self, universally acknowledged to be a mystery, in the literal sense of 'that which is waiting to be unfolded, or revealed'. Hindus would argue that this condition is inevitable in the pre-*moksha* stage because only with enlightenment and the release from *maya* comes awareness of who or what one basically is.

The other key word, *brahman,* occurs throughout the Vedas and describes a number of related but contrasting ideas. Derived from a verb meaning 'to grow' or 'to expand', it literally means 'vast expanse', but is commonly translated as 'the Absolute' (note the upper-case: having no capitals, Sanskrit transliterations into European languages may be found with or without them). In the earliest Upanishads, the word refers to the primal creative (or procreative) source of the cosmos, the world that is made manifest. In this sense, there is little to distinguish *brahman* from the Creator God of other religions. Later, a pantheistic element was introduced, when it was taught that the universe and *brahman* were identical: 'All this is the brahman', it is stated (Chandogya-Upanishad III.14); *brahman* subsists in everything 'as a razor is hidden in a razor case' (Brihad-Aranyaka-Upanishad I.4.7).

The ultimate and essential theme of Upanishadic literature, however, gives a new and unique perspective to the debate: *brahman is identified with atman.* As the air inside a jar is substantially the same as that on the outside, though separated artificially by the glass, so the absolute ground of being is one with the basic self of every individual, but seemingly separated because of the blinkers brought about by *maya.* Once those blinkers have been removed through the experience of *moksha,* it becomes possible to make, with absolute assurance, the great affirmation (*mahavakya*) from the third Veda, '*Tat tvam asi*': 'Thou art that.' Each of the four Vedas contains a similar *mahavakya*; the other three are: 'I am that' (or 'I am *brahman*'); 'Consciousness is *brahman*'; and 'This self is *brahman*' (*Ayam atman Brahma*). All have overtones of the Hebrew word for God, Yahweh, meaning 'I am that I am', but they diverge from the Hebrew affirmation by discarding the implicit dualism of that word (since it refers only to God, not to human beings) in favour of *advaita,* or non-dualism. '*Tat tvam asi*' can be addressed to both the *brahman* and the *atman* because, as salt dissolved in water flavours all the water, so does *atman* pervade *brahman:*

> That which is the finest essence—this whole world has that as its soul. That is reality. That
> is *Atman.* That art Thou.

> (Shvetashvatara Upanishad VI.9.4.)

As we shall see in Chapter 9, there is a parallel here with the teaching of Taoism: the *Tao* is the 'Way', the equivalent of *brahman*; and the *Te* is the manifestation of the *Tao* in the life of any individual human being.

The affirmation '*tat tvam asi*' can be made authentically (that is, with the authority which comes from experience) only after the attainment of *samadhi,* the final limb of Yoga. In order to give those—and there are, of course, many of them—who are still on the path towards this an idea of what to expect when they arrive, Vedanta uses the phrase *sat-chit-ananda,* literally 'Being-consciousness-bliss'. It is an attempt to put into words what is ultimately inexpressible: the bliss referred to is not that which can be enjoyed through worldly activities since, worthy though these often are, they are inevitably clouded by *maya.* Rather, it is the unaffected absolute bliss found only when one is free from thoughts, anxieties, hopes, fears and suffering: in other words, as the word *samadhi* indicates, only when one has experienced divine consciousness. For this reason, every member of a certain monastic tradition in Vedanta who has become a *sannyasin* (that is, has surrendered all worldly concerns in the pursuit of *moksha,* and, having attained it, spends the rest of his or her days facilitating the path for others) is given a name ending in -ananda, such as (and probably the most famous) Vivekananda (1863–1902).

The 'certain tradition' referred to is that of **Adi Shankara** (788–820), who, more than any other Hindu teacher, drew out the teaching of *advaita* from the Upanishads and expounded it with wisdom and deep insight. Tradition has it that, from a very early age, he exhibited such deep spirituality that he was seen as the incarnation of Shiva, after whom his name is derived. He founded numerous monasteries, several of which still survive, and was a man of great versatility, being not only a mystic and a saint but also a philosopher, a poet, a scholar and a reformer (an earlier Martin Luther, perhaps, with saintliness added).

It was Shankara who first used the image of the air and the jar, mentioned earlier. The state of non-dual unity that this image illustrates was described by Shankara as the final state to which all human beings aspire, if not at present, then eventually. He was referring to one of the most famous sections of the Vedas, the Mandukya-Upanishad, where the view is propounded that human beings experience four states of consciousness (*avasthas*): the waking state (**jagrat**, or **vaishvanara**); dreaming sleep (**svapna**); deep, or dreamless sleep (**sushupti**); and **turiya**, which means, quite literally, 'the fourth'. *Jagrat* is the normal state of consciousness, both of oneself as subject and of the outside world as object: it is therefore a dualistic state. *Svapna* is also dualistic: in dreams, one is conscious still of oneself as subject and of the dream's characters as objects of that consciousness. With *sushupti*, however, we enter into a different state of consciousness, in which there is no longer mind or ego, and we cease to be aware either of ourselves or of the universe; it should accurately be described as a state in which all thought has ceased, rather than one of unconsciousness.

Turiya is also non-dualistic, but in a way quite different and, in Shankara's view, infinitely beyond *sushupti*. It is a state of absolute consciousness that defeats any attempt at description; effectively (though this statement is tautologous) only those who have known *turiya* can know it. Even the verb 'to know', with its connotation of *jagrat*, the dualistic state of awareness, is misleading. It must be understood in terms of *jnana* or *vidya*: knowledge that springs from insight, closer to intuition than to reasoning. The Mandukya-Upanishad is in fact more comprehensible when describing what it is not than what it is:

> Neither subjective nor objective experience, neither knowledge of the senses, nor relative knowledge, nor derived knowledge ... [it is] pure, unified consciousness, unspeakable peace, nondualistic [*advaitam*] ... the nature of the *atman*.

This fourth state is also described as **brahma-chaitanya**, '*brahman*-consciousness', and, whatever may happen afterwards to one who has attained it, he or she can never be disabused about its reality. Shankara, in a famous image, describes the situation before and after achieving *moksha* as like a man in a darkened room who spends his time in terror because he believes a deadly poisonous snake to be over by the window. A moment arrives, however, when a gleam of light reveals to him that it is no snake, but simply the window-sash. From that moment his terror evaporates and will never return. Others may call out to warn him that he is risking his life by remaining in that room, but their fear does not touch him. He can laugh at his former terror for he now knows, absolutely, that it was based on an illusion. Now he has experienced *moksha*, and *maya* can no longer deceive him.

The first three states are symbolised in Vedanta by the letters A, U and M, making the sound 'OM'. This indicates that the *atman* combines the waking state, the dreaming state and the state of dreamless sleep. But the *atman* is more than these, since they do not include *turiya*, the fourth, the state of enlightenment. This is a state of silence, so no sound needs to be added to the A, U and M: OM therefore represents all four states of consciousness, and together they describe the *atman*. Ultimately, according to the Upanishad, the silence of the fourth state makes the other three redundant, so that the sound of OM can no longer be heard:

> The fourth is soundless: unutterable, a quieting down of the differentiated manifestations, blissful-peaceful, nondual. Thus OM is *atman,* verily. He who knows thus merges his Self in the Self—yea, he who knows thus.

OM is referred to in the Maitrayaniya-Upanishad as 'the sound of the soundless Absolute', and for this reason it is the most fundamental of all Hindu (and Buddhist) **mantras**: words or phrases repeated (or, in the case of OM, hummed) in meditation in order to bring the *yogin* or *yogini* (male or female practitioners of yoga) to a state beyond that of finite consciousness. Because the aim is to experience the numinous, the sound of OM has no literation; it is written as a symbol which, rightly understood, expresses and reinforces the meaning of the four states. OM, both as a sound and as a symbol, represents the Absolute, beyond time and space. As the Upanishad states:

> The past, the present, and the future—everything is but the sound *om.* And whatever else that transcends triple time—that, too, is but the sound *om.*

The sacred sentence *OM tat sat*—'OM, that is Being', where 'that' refers to *brahman*—is found at the beginning of many books, and is written at the end of every chapter in the *Bhagavad-Gita.*
The poet Shelley, in his 'Adonais', already quoted, expresses a similar idea:

> The one remains, the many change and pass;
> Heaven's light forever shines, Earth's shadows fly;
> Life, like a dome of many-coloured glass,
> Stains the white radiance of Eternity.

It should be emphasised that entry into the fourth state does not mean that thereafter the *yogin/yogini* excludes the other three from his or her life. Most of them carry out their daily work, often, but not exclusively, as teachers: their entry into *turiya* is then a continual reminder of what, to them, eternity has in store. Heinrich Zimmer, in *The Philosophies of India* (p.376) states:

> The self-transforming change of emphasis becomes a well-known and controllable experi-ence for the skilled practitioner of yoga. He can make the states come and go, their spheres appear and disappear, according to his will ... he can produce the subtle, fluid forms of the inward state of vision whenever he likes, fix them and retain them as long as he requires, and after that, again according to his wish, come temporarily back into touch with the exterior world. Such a virtuoso is not subject and exposed helplessly to the waking state, but enters it only when and as he wishes—his real abode, or homestead, meanwhile, being the 'fourth' at the opposite end of the series.

KARMA AND REINCARNATION

Having attempted to describe the significance of *moksha,* we need now to examine how Hindus perceive the hindrances to the arrival at this state, and the life-long, or, to be more accurate, lives-long process by which progress is generally made. One concept here is central, and we shall not understand the Hindu mind until we have come to terms with it: that of *karma,* or *karman.*

Its basic meaning is 'deed', or 'action'. It can mean ritualistic actions, but in Hindu thought it refers typically to the accumulated effect of moral behaviour, and the intentions that direct it. Everything we do creates *karma,* which we bear with us as part of an inexorable cycle of cause and effect, extending from the past through the present and into the future. What we do now has been affected by previous deeds, because the situations in which we now find ourselves, with their broad or narrow range of options, are themselves the product of earlier decisions, as they in their turn were products of decisions before them, and so on. Similarly, what we do now will fix the range of options open to us in the future, and, according to the action then taken, those available in situations beyond that, and so on. Furthermore, because the thoughts and actions that produce *karma* relate to concerns of the material world, the world of *maya,* it follows that, while the notion of 'good' *karma* versus 'bad' is not unheard-of, all *karma* is ultimately bad because it binds us to this world of illusion: it is the mechanism by which conditional existence maintains itself: existence, that is, which gains meaning only through activities characterised by *maya,* and therefore, by definition, ultimately unrewarding; so long as anyone remains subject to *maya,* this binding mechanism continues to operate.

The name for this process is **samskara,** meaning 'impression' or 'consequence'. It describes the tendencies in each person's character that have arisen as a result of thoughts, intentions and related actions throughout his or her existence: and for Hindus this includes not only this present life but also an indeterminate number of previous lives, or cycles of experience. That is to say, the concept of *karma* is linked with what Western theology describes as the transmigration of souls; in Hinduism the word is **samsara** (not to be confused with *samskara,* mentioned above). So long as one is subject to *karma,* the process of *samsara* is inevitable.

The word literally means 'journeying' and refers to the journey through many incarnations that is the lot of everyone until he or she achieves deliverance (see below). The view is that everyone experiences birth, or rebirth (the Sanskrit word is *punar-janman*) with the *karma* he or she accumulated in previous existences; throughout this present life, either deliverance is found or further *karma,* 'good' or 'bad', is added: and this in turn determines the starting conditions for the next cycle of experience. Thus *samsara* may be described as the domain of *karma:* the Varaha-Upanishad characterises it as 'a long dream (*svapna*), a delusion of the mind, a sea of sorrow' (II.64); the Maitrayaniya-Upanishad states that 'those who are liberated look down upon the samsara as upon a dizzily revolving wheel' (VI.28). *Samsara* is a state similar to that of drug dependency, with *karma* the drug on which it feeds: and as with many people so dependent, it is possible to have an attitude of mind that not only does not look beyond this state for what passes as fulfilment, but has no desire to do so.

Karma, then, spreads its tentacles timelessly, over the past, present and future, working itself out according to the laws of causality. These laws are illustrated by the three types of *karma* identified in the Vedas. The first of these is **prarabda-karma**, literally, *karma* that is the consequence of deeds (*karma*) begun (*arabdha*) before (*pra*): that is, *karma* borne in this life as a result of deeds performed in an earlier existence, the consequences of which are still working themselves out. As the arrow that has left the bow cannot be recalled, so, by a similar natural law, the effects of the earlier deed cannot be wiped out. (Our bodily constitution is a good example of this type of *karma*.)

Second, there is **sanchita-karma**, the accumulated *samskaras* or 'karmic deposits' (*ashaya*) that we built up in past lives and await fruition in some future life: these deposits are the network of subliminal *samskaras* (or activators) that form the subconscious or depth memory (*smriti*). This may or may not be the equivalent of the 'collective unconscious' described by the Western psychologist (and amateur orientalist) C. G. Jung, but Hindu teaching is that it affects our life span and life experience.

The third type of karma is **agami-karma**. This is the *karma* arising from actions in this present life, which will work themselves out, according to the same inexorable natural law of cause and effect, in some future existence. A distinction can be made between this and the other two types of *karma*: with them, there is absolutely nothing that can be done to bring about change: the natural law is operating, based on earlier decisions and inherited predilections. So far as *agami-karma* is concerned, however, we are dealing with future effects of present actions: actions, that is, which have either not yet been taken, or are only at the initial process of being taken. This means something that is absolutely basic and philosophically pivotal: we can influence our futures by our choice of present actions.

On the face of it, that statement sounds banal rather than pivotal, but the pivot is the word 'choice', which is redolent of implications for the whole theory. The doctrine of *karma* is often represented as deterministic, even fatalistic, and there are certainly elements of fatalism in the teaching. We are dealt a certain hand—through our parents, our genes, even our social background—and there is nothing we can do to change this. It is a harsh thing to say, but the sins, or the virtues, of one generation can be seen to have worked their way through 'unto the third and fourth generation', as the Old Testament frequently puts it: we simply have no choice over what we inherit from parents and grandparents. But at every point where we make a decision between alternative courses of action there is, according to the teachings of *karma,* genuine choice, and the same was true in the past when we made the decisions whose consequences we are experiencing now. The *karma* we get is the *karma* we have freely chosen, and nobody but ourselves is responsible for where or what we are. In Kierkegaard's words, we are, then, 'free to choose, free to be': the *agami-karma* we are about to accumulate will be the direct result of the choices we are about to make.

So there is both determinism and free will in this Hindu teaching, expressed succinctly by the first prime minister of independent India, Pandit Nehru, with the words, 'It's like a game of cards: determinism is the hand you're dealt: free will is how you play it.' Natural law fixes the hand: the rest is up to us. Just as Western existentialism, with its emphasis on libertarianism, or freedom of the will, emphasises our personal responsibility for the decisions we make by stressing our autonomy and the need for authenticity, so Hinduism affirms that where we are and what we are is the consequence, not of fate, but of our own freely made choices throughout aeons of existence. Thus an existentialist carries his own can, a Hindu his own *karma*.

This reflection may help to modify the critical attitude that Westerners usually adopt towards the Hindu **caste** system. This system, (in Sanskrit, ***varna***) was first mentioned in the *Rigveda* and divides Hindus from birth into fixed social groups. The highest of these is the ***brahmans*** (*brahmanas*), or priestly caste; this comprises the educated class of religious and academic leaders: priests, scholars, philosophers. Then comes the caste of warriors (***kshatriyas***), comprising both military people and politicians and civil authorities. Third are the merchants and farmers (***vaishyas***): those who produce the nation's financial and economic resources, hence also known as the providers. The lowest of the four major castes is the ***shudras***, the workers and servants. Lower than these, however, are the untouchables, or outcasts (***pariahs***), who are outside the caste system: they are generally left to perform the most menial and undesirable tasks.

If this were a treatise on the sociology of India, a broad excursion would be needed here, along quite obvious lines. How rigidly the system still operates is a matter for considerable (and often vituperative) debate. If it is becoming less rigid in its application (and the fact that an outcast became prime minister of independent India suggests that it may be) then it could be said that the system is returning to the original Vedic tradition, designed to order a complex society and to minimise rivalry and competition. The rigidity that we tend to associate with the system came about only after the Mogul invasion of India in the sixteenth century, with its introduction of stricter Islamic teaching, and it was not modified by subsequent colonial authorities. A reform movement in the nineteenth century set about dismantling the system gradually, and modern Indians such as Mahatma Gandhi have supported this process.

It is worth pausing to wonder, independently of the rights and wrongs of the system, whether there is any other country in the world that places its scholars and religious leaders in a higher category than that of its soldiers, politicians and businessmen: an affirmation of values that merits some reflection. Furthermore, while any defence of the system on the basis of the doctrine of *karma* may seem, on the face of it, to be an example of buck-passing, Vedanta teaches that *moksha* can be achieved by everybody, including the outcast. And even if enlightenment is not found in this present cycle of existence, the message is that all, of whatever background, will eventually find it: there is to be no final Day of Judgment, where the sheep are divided from the goats.

HINDU PHILOSOPHY—HINDU RELIGION

One final issue remains for consideration. Anyone who has visited India may feel justified in believing that the above, basically philosophical, outline of Hindu thought takes little account of the more popular expressions of Indian beliefs to be seen throughout the subcontinent, with individuals praying to their own private god or gods, and ritualistic acts taking place in temples and elsewhere, including rivers, streets and numerous other 'holy' places. We may start with the concept of the *avatara,* or avatar, meaning literally a 'descent', or incarnation of divine consciousness on Earth. An *avatara,* it is believed, occurs not because of *karma* (as we have seen to be the case with ordinary human beings) but through the free choice of one who, though enlightened, and therefore released from *samsara,* enters the world from time to time in order to give spiritual impetus to those struggling on the path to *moksha.* Precisely when an *avatara* has occurred is not a matter of chance but is related to the special needs arising from the circumstances of the time.

The traditional view is that only Vishnu, one of the Hindu trinity, or **trimurti** (alongside Brahma and Shiva: see below), is incarnated, and has appeared in ten forms, each relating to the era of the appearance: (1) Matsya, the fish; (2) Kurma, the tortoise; (3) Varaha, the boar; (4) Narasimha, the man—lion; (5) Vamana, the dwarf; (6) Parashu-Rama, or Rama the Axe-Wielder; (7) Rama of the Ramayana (see page 22); (8) Krishna; (9) Buddha; (10) Kalki, who has not yet appeared. A separate tradition includes Jesus as an *avatara*—a point that will be followed up in Chapter 18.

The other two divinities in the Hindu trinity are Brahma and Shiva. Brahma symbolises the principle of creation and the ontological necessity of being. Vishnu symbolises the sustaining force of the universe; hence it is logical that he should be seen as the one whose *avatara* is necessary when particular needs arise. Shiva, with his consort Shakti, or Kali, functions as the god of dissolution and destruction (that is, of *avidya,* or ignorance.) All three are interdependent, since everything in creation, after a period of sustained existence, experiences the process of destruction, to be followed by further creation, and so on. (We are again not far from the Chinese philosophy of *yin* and *yang,* to be discussed in Chapter 11.) The important point that links this more theistic approach with the non-dualism of Vedanta is that all three gods are viewed as manifestations of the One, with whom all Hindus expect ultimately to be united.

Modern Hindu worship divides itself into three main groupings, concentrated in different parts of India, and each of them holding different sections of the Vedas as central to its beliefs. On the one hand is Vaishnavism, followers of Vishnu, and subdivided according to which aspect of the god they worship. The followers of Shiva are the Shaivists, while the third group, believers in Shaktism, take their name from Shiva's consort, Shakti. This school is also called Tantrism, which was discussed on page 23. While Western writers often mention Brahmanism, after the third god in the trinity, it plays only a minor role in modern-day Hinduism.

In addition to the *avataras* there are Vedic hymns and prayers addressed to numerous *devas,* or minor gods, each with a special area of responsibility: thus there is Indra, the god of rain and thunder, Varuna, the god of sky, Usha, the goddess of dawn, Agni, the god of fire, and so on. Many of them are mentioned in the Vedas, and both Indra and Agni (for example) are described in different places as the greatest of all the gods. How can this be, and how does one accommodate the *devas* into the schema of the Six Systems?

It must be emphasised that, in a nation as large as India and a religion as widespread as Hinduism, it would be surprising to the point of miraculous if there were not a wide range of understanding of metaphysical issues between those with scholarly training at one extreme, and simple peasants at the other. There is a similar world of difference in Christianity between, say, Catholics in rural South America and Quakers in urban Britain.

I am grateful to Professor Sushanta Sen of Visva-Bharati University for the clarification he makes concerning the *devas* in relation to *brahman*. (*Concepts of the Ultimate,* ed. L.J. Tessier, ch. 11). He makes three points. The first is that the Vedas themselves acknowledge all gods and all *devas* to be no more than names or manifestations of *brahman,* the ground of being. For example: 'That which exists is one: sages call It by different names' (Rigveda I.90.3). Even more explicitly, a later Upanishadic text states: 'There is but One Being, not a second' (*op. cit.* p.91).

Sen's second argument is also aimed at dispelling the charge of polytheism sometimes made against Hinduism. He suggests that the *devas* are in fact presented as human beings who have built up such good *karma* (although without having yet attained *moksha*) that no earthly rebirth can compensate adequately; so 'after physical death he or she is reborn as a god [*deva*] in heaven to enjoy uninterrupted heavenly bliss'. Sometimes, when the saintliness of the individual on Earth has been exceptionally awe-inspiring, his or her reward may be to become the chief of these gods: Indra, Agni, or any other who had achieved that status at that time.

> But the lives of all these gods including Indra come to a definite end when their accumulated merits become exhausted by the enjoyment of heavenly pleasures and privileges; and after that they have to die from heaven as gods and be reborn again on earth as ordinary human beings within the process of ... samsara.
>
> (*ibid.* p.89)

This explains, Sen suggests, why no god or *deva* remains as king of gods throughout the Vedas; and why Hinduism should not be equated with the polytheism of, say, the Greek or Roman theodicy.

Sen's final point is that the furthest the Vedas stray from monotheism is not into polytheism but to henotheism (see page 13). Whether this label fits a religion that hardly lends itself to Western delineations is a moot matter. The fact is that, so far as Hindus themselves are concerned, theirs is, quite simply, **sanatana-dharma,** 'the eternal religion': a claim to be tested in the latter part of this book.

Discussion Questions

1. What are the four main goals of human life that Hinduism recognizes?
2. What are the four states of consciousness that human beings experience? How does Shankara explain his view on non-dual unity in reference to these states?
3. Do you agree that Atman or the ultimate reality runs through in each individual?
4. It is believed in Hinduism that karma (action) engenders samskara (impression or consequence), which fuels samsara (cycles of life). How do we make sense of this belief in karmic impression that turns the wheel of life?
5. Many people think that the Hindu view of rebirth (reincarnation) is a form of life after death, ignoring the teaching that rebirth is fueled by ignorance and that we should all strive to be enlightened and put an end to rebirth. Is this a possible desirable goal as a human being?

The Dharma

Charles S. Prebish and Damien Keown

In this chapter

Dharma is one of the 'three jewels' (*triratna*)—namely the Buddha, the *Dharma*, and the *Sangha* (the monastic community)—which collectively comprise the essence of the Buddhist religion. *Dharma* denotes the teachings and doctrines set forth by the Buddha, and it is one of the words by which Buddhists refer to their religion. The most fundamental Buddhist doctrines are known as the Four Noble Truths, and these are discussed in this chapter in turn, along with an explanation of the Buddhist theory of causation known as 'dependent origination'. Another important doctrine explained here is 'no self' (*anātman*). This is the Buddhist teaching that has fascinated Westerners more than any other but which has given rise to much misunderstanding. The material in this chapter is important for both the early teachings of Buddhism and the doctrinal developments in later centuries which will be explored in subsequent chapters.

Main topics covered

- The First Noble Truth: Suffering (*duḥkha*)
- The Second Noble Truth: Arising (*samudaya*)
- Dependent origination (*pratītya-samutpāda*)
- The Third Noble Truth: Cessation (*nirodha*) or nirvana
- The Fourth Noble Truth: the Path (*mārga*)
- Holy persons
- The doctrine of no-self (*anātman*)

The Four Noble Truths

We saw in the last chapter that on the night of his awakening the Buddha apprehended the Four Noble Truths, and that when he gave his first sermon in the deer park at Sarnath he made specific reference to them. His audience consisted of five ascetics with a background in religious discipline and familiarity with philosophical notions, and the teaching the Buddha gave was of an advanced kind, comparable to a postgraduate class. In other sermons when speaking to ordinary layfolk, the Buddha does not generally mention these points of doctrine, and instead delivers a 'gradual talk' (*anupūrvikā kathā*) in which he encourages the practice of generosity (*dāna*) and morality (*śīla*) as the way to a heavenly rebirth.

> Monks, it is through not understanding, through not penetrating the Four Noble Truths that this long course of birth and death has been passed through and undergone by me as well as by you. What are these four? They are the noble truth of suffering (*duḥkha*); the noble truth of the origin of suffering; the noble truth of the cessation of suffering; and the noble truth of the way to the cessation of suffering. But now, monks, that these have been realized and penetrated, cut off is the craving for existence, destroyed is that which leads to renewed becoming, and there is no more re-becoming (D.ii.90)

The Noble Truths (*ārya-satya*) thus provide a sophisticated and advanced formulation of Buddhist teachings. They form the cornerstone of Buddhist doctrine, and encapsulate the Buddha's understanding of the human predicament and its solution. The Four Truths assert that:

1. life is suffering.
2. suffering is caused by craving.
3. suffering can have an end.
4. there is a path which leads to the end of suffering.

The Four Truths provide a kind of diagnosis of the ills which affect humanity, and a remedy for the 'sickness' that afflicts all sentient life. The Buddha was often compared to a physician, and his teachings (*Dharma*) to a medicine. The formulation of the Four Truths is like that of a medical examination: first, the condition is diagnosed; second, its cause is sought; third, the physician makes a prognosis for recovery; fourth and finally, a course of treatment is prescribed.

The First Noble Truth: Suffering

The word translated as 'suffering' in the above extract is *duḥkha*. *Duḥkha* is a term with a spectrum of meanings, all denoting circumstances or situations that are in some way unsatisfactory, or not as we would wish them to be. According to context, it can be translated as 'suffering', 'pain', 'ill', 'unsatisfactoriness', 'anguish', 'stress', 'unease', and a range of other synonyms. *Duḥkha* is the opposite of *sukha*, which means 'pleasure', so one of its basic meanings is certainly 'pain'. But just as in English 'pain' can refer not just to physical but also to psychological or emotional distress, and also to situations which are bothersome or inconvenient ('it was a pain having to go to work today'), so *duḥkha* can also have a more generalized range of meaning and a more nuanced translation is often required.

> This, monks, is the Noble Truth of Suffering (*duḥkha*). Birth is suffering, sickness is suffering, ageing is suffering, death is suffering. Sorrow, grief, pain, unhappiness and despair are suffering. Association with what one dislikes is suffering, being separated from what one likes is suffering. Not to get what one wants is suffering. In short, the five aggregates which are grasped at (*upādāna-skandha*) are suffering (Vin.i.10; S.v.421).

Some of the biological aspects of suffering mentioned in the First Noble Truth—such as old age, sickness and death—were things the Buddha himself had seen at first hand on his visits outside the palace with his charioteer. The problem that concerned the Buddha was not just the unwelcome nature of these experiences, but the fact that they would be repeated over and over in life after life, and would happen not just to oneself but to everyone one loved. Individuals are powerless in the face of these circumstances, regardless of what progress is made in science and medicine. Though we may live longer, we will never be immune from the risk of accidents, and death will inevitably separate us again and again from family and friends.

In addition to mentioning the biological aspects of human suffering that the Buddha had himself observed, the First Noble Truth broadens out to include other aspects of suffering as well. There is a reference to psychological states such as 'sorrow' and 'despair', and psychological afflictions like depression can sometimes be more debilitating and difficult to cope with than physical ones.

Next, the Buddha goes on to speak about the emotional pain of being separated from what is dear to one, such as from the things or people one loves, and being forced to endure experiences, places, or situations which one dislikes. This is followed by a reference to the general feeling of frustration that can arise when things don't work out as we planned, and ambitions go unfulfilled. Clearly, this is at several removes from physical pain, but often the effect can be such as to sour our whole outlook on life and leave a lingering and pervasive feeling of disappointment or failure.

Finally, the First Noble Truth ends with a cryptic reference to the 'five aggregates which are grasped at'. This introduces a Buddhist doctrine known as *anātman*, or the 'no-self' teachings, which will be examined further below. This claims that our nature as human beings is constituted in such a way that makes it impossible for us ever to find complete happiness or fulfillment in *saṃsāra*.

The various kinds of suffering identified above are classified by Buddhist sources into three categories. The first of these is '*duḥkha-duḥkha*', which means suffering 'plain and simple', as we might say. This includes all the examples of suffering due to biological causes (birth, sickness, ageing, death) mentioned in the First Noble Truth. Next comes *vipariṇāma-duḥkha*, which means 'suffering due to change'. It is a basic tenet of Buddhist thought that everything that arises will cease—in other words, things are impermanent and constantly changing. Given this fundamental instability we can never know what will come next, and so cannot guarantee that our happiness will endure. The fact that in *saṃsāra* nothing is permanent means that it is impossible to find lasting satisfaction or fulfilment. Finally, the third aspect of suffering is 'duḥkha as formations' (saṃskāra-duḥkha). This kind of suffering arises because everything in saṃsāra is made up of component parts, like a package of self-assembly home furniture: you never find a bookcase or a chair in the box, just an assemblage of bits and pieces. Buddhism teaches that the whole world is like this, and that since everything is made up of component parts it will sooner or later be reduced to them. In other words, everything (including us) will fall apart, just like that bookcase we assembled.

Many people approaching Buddhism for the first time find the analysis provided in the First Noble Truth pessimistic and wonder whether the bad news isn't being overdone. The translation of duḥkha as 'suffering' helps reinforce this impression, and can make the First Noble Truth sound as if the Buddha believed that human life was constant agony. This is not what he intended, and he was certainly aware from his own comfortable childhood inside the palace that life could have its pleasant moments. Buddhists generally reject the charge of pessimism and claim that their religion is neither optimistic nor pessimistic, but realistic. They point out that few lives are untouched by sorrow, whether caused by physical suffering, psychological disorders, death, or more existential causes such as frustration, disappointment, and disillusionment. In their view, the First Noble Truth simply 'tells it how it is', and if it sounds negative this is because there is a natural inclination for people to suppress or ignore the unpleasant realities of life.

THE PARABLE OF THE TRAVELER

An ancient Indian story recounts how a traveler slips on a precipice and falls over the edge. As he tumbles down he grasps hold of a creeper and manages to stay his fall. At first he feels relieved, but looking down sees that beneath him is a pit of poisonous snakes. To add to his alarm, he notices that two mice, one black and one white, are nibbling away at the creeper he is holding onto. In this moment of despair he sees that honey is trickling down the creeper from a beehive that was overturned when he fell. As it reaches his lips he relishes the sweet taste and exclaims 'Oh, how wonderful is the taste of that honey!'

The story depicts the Buddhist view of the human predicament. We are like the traveler, with death (the pit of snakes) staring us in the face. The black and white mice (night and day) are constantly whittling away at our lifespan. Yet in spite of this dire situation we, like the traveler, are captivated by pleasure (the honey) and forget all about the perils that surround us.

A Buddhist might also maintain, reverting to the medical analogy which began this section, that there is also a more positive aspect to the First Noble Truth, just as when we go to the doctor to find out what is wrong with us. While it may be unwelcome to be told we have a condition of some kind, it is certainly better to find out and be treated than live in ignorance until the disease is so far advanced that nothing can be done. It takes courage to take the first step, but since we can look forward to good health and happiness when we are well, the message is ultimately one of hope. Those who heed the Buddha's call and take up the religious life, furthermore, are said to experience joy (prīti) and happiness, as well as an inner calmness and serenity.

The Second Noble Truth: Arising

If suffering is an inevitable part of life, how does this suffering come about? The Second Noble Truth explains that the cause of suffering is due to craving (*tṛṣṇā*). Just as with *duḥkha*, we have to be careful how we translate the word *tṛṣṇā*. It is quite common to translate this as 'desire', but this can lead to the mistaken idea that Buddhism sees all desire as wrong, and thus to the paradoxical conclusion that we must somehow seek nirvana without desiring it. A common reason for this misunderstanding is that in English 'desire' can be for good things as well as bad things: for example, one can desire to give up smoking, take exercise and eat healthy food (good things); and one can also desire to smoke cigarettes and to eat junk food (bad things). The Sanskrit word *tṛṣṇā*, however, has a more limited semantic range and refers only to negative desires and addictions (another word, '*chanda*', is reserved for good or wholesome desires). For this reason 'craving' is a better translation for *tṛṣṇā*, since it reminds us that the Second Noble Truth is referring to desire that is of an excessive, selfish, or morbid nature, and usually directed towards unwholesome objects or ends. Whereas craving tends to be repetitive, limiting, and cyclic, desire for wholesome things is liberating and enhancing. For example, the desire of a chain-smoker to give up cigarettes breaks a compulsive habit and enhances the health and quality of life of that person.

THE TRUTH OF ARISING (*samudaya*)

This, O Monks, is the Truth of the Arising of Suffering. It is this thirst or craving (*tṛṣṇā*) which gives rise to rebirth, which is bound up with passionate delight and which seeks fresh pleasure now here and now there in the form of (1) thirst for sensual pleasure, (2) thirst for existence, and (3) thirst for non-existence.

Craving is like sticky glue that makes us become attached to things, and once attached we cannot easily let go, as in the case of bad habits that are hard to break. Giving up craving is akin to weaning oneself off an addiction, such as to cigarettes or drugs, and is no easy thing to do. The Buddha's favorite metaphor for craving was fire. In the Fire Sermon (S.iv.19), he said that all our experience was 'ablaze' with desire. Just like fire, craving spreads rapidly from one thing to another and seems to destroy what it feeds on without ever being satisfied. After one cigarette we soon want another, and so it goes on. There is no end to desires of this kind, and the satisfaction they provide is short-lived. The Buddha compared the pleasure gained through satisfying such desires to the temporary relief of scratching a boil.

The Second Noble Truth makes reference to three forms of craving, and the first of these is craving for sensual pleasures (*kāma*). (The word *kāma* is the same word found in the title of the ancient Indian treatise on erotic pleasure, the *Kāma Sūtra*.) Sensual craving (*kāma*) is any kind of desire for gratification that comes by way of the senses, such as the desire to experience plea-surable sensations of touch, taste, smell, sight, or sound. Since Indian psychology includes the mind as one of the senses (thus counting six senses instead of the usual five), this also includes pleasurable fantasies and daydreams (M.i.51). The second kind of craving refers to the desire for existence (*bhava*). This is a kind of instinctual urge, a deep yearning to be, which propels us from one life to another and brings us back again and again to seek new pleasures and experiences. The third aspect of craving is an inverted form of desire, of the kind that drives us not towards things but away from what we do not like. This is desire that manifests itself in a negative way and which seeks to destroy (*vibhava*) rather than possess. Such destructive desires can be directed towards both self and others. When directed towards the ego they manifest themselves in self-harming behavior, and, in extreme cases, suicide. They are typically seen in self-deprecatory remarks and other instances of low self-esteem in which people 'put themselves down'.

In the formulation of the Second Noble Truth *tṛṣṇā* is picked out as the single cause of the arising of suffering. Elsewhere, however, the cause of suffering is said to be threefold in nature, consisting of greed (*rāga*), hatred (*dveṣa*) and delusion (*moha*). Other formulations again, such as in the doctrine of dependent origination (see text box), explain the arising of suffering as a twelvefold chain that includes ignorance as its first link and craving as its eighth. In spite of the different formulations, it is clear that the root problem is a complex involving both cognitive error (such as ignorance or delusion), and inappropriate affective dispositions or emotional responses (such as excessive attachment or aversion). The problem is therefore one which affects both the head and the heart, and needs to be addressed through a program of retraining or therapy which develops insight and understanding as well as eliminating stubborn emotional attachments to unwholesome things.

DEPENDENT ORIGINATION (Skt.: *pratītya-samutpāda*; Pāli: *Paṭicca-samuppāda*)

The doctrine of dependent origination is a fundamental Buddhist teaching on causation. It holds that all phenomena arise in dependence on causes and conditions, and as a consequence lack intrinsic being of their own. The doctrine is expressed in its simplest form in the Sanskrit phrase *idaṃ sati ayaṃ bhavati* ('when this exists, that arises'), a proposition that can be expressed in the logical form A→B (when condition A exists, effect B arises), or as its negation—A→—B (where condition A does not exist effect B does not arise). The important corollary of this teaching is that there is nothing that comes into being through its own power or volition, and there are therefore no entities or metaphysical realities—such as God or a soul (*ātman*)—that transcend the causal nexus. In this respect the doctrine dovetails with the teaching of no self (*anātman*), discussed later in this chapter. Early sources indicate that the Buddha became enlightened under the Bodhi Tree when he fully realized the profound truth of dependent origination, namely that all phenomena are conditioned (*saṃskṛta*) and arise and cease in a determinate series.

There are various formulations of the doctrine in early sources, but the most common one illustrates the soteriological implications of causality in a series of twelve stages or links (*nidāna*) showing how the problem of suffering (*duḥkha*) and entrapment in *saṃsāra* arises due to craving (*tṛṣṇā*) and ignorance (*avidyā*). The twelve links in the process (often depicted around the rim of the wheel of life or *bhavacakra*) are:

(1) Ignorance (*avidyā*)

(2) Compositional factors (*saṃskāra*)

(3) Consciousness (*vijñāna*)

(4) Name and form (*nāma-rūpa*)

(5) Six sense spheres (*ṣaḍ-āyatana*)

(6) Contact (*sparśa*)

(7) Feelings (*vedanā*)

(8) Craving (*tṛṣṇā*)

(9) Grasping (*upādāna*)

(10) Becoming (*bhava*)

(11) Birth (*jāti*)

(12) Old age and death (*jarā-maraṇa*).

The significance of the individual links is open to interpretation, but one popular understanding is that of the fifth-century commentator Buddhaghosa in terms of which the series extends over three lives. Thus (1)–(2) relate to the previous life, (3)–(7) to the conditioning of the present existence, (8)–(10) to the fruits of the present existence, and (11)-(12) to the life to come. Various later schools came to their own, sometimes radical, understanding of the doctrine. Chief among these is that of the Mādhyamika, for whom dependent origination came to be synonymous with the concept of emptiness (*śūnyatā*), as explained in Chapter Six.

The Third Noble Truth: Cessation

The Third Noble Truth is a corollary of the Second. If craving (*tṛṣṇā*) is the cause of suffering (*duḥkha*), it follows that once craving is removed, suffering will cease. This is exactly what the Third Noble Truth proclaims. This state of being free from suffering is known as nirvana, and is the supreme goal of the Buddhist path. Nirvana literally means 'blowing out', in the way that the flame of a candle is blown out. What is blown out are the three 'fires' (also known as the 'three poisons') of greed, hatred and delusion which are the components of craving. The simplest definition of nirvana is 'the end of greed, hatred, and delusion' (S.38.1). So long as these three 'fires' continue to burn, the individual will remain trapped in *saṃsāra*, going round and round in the wheel of rebirth which is driven by his or her own craving for pleasurable experiences.

Someone who embarks on the Buddhist path seeks to reverse this process. Over the course of many lifetimes, as the negative forces of craving and ignorance are slowly weakened through following Buddhist teachings, an individual can begin to cultivate positive states of mind and to undergo a spiritual transformation in which virtuous qualities come to predominate over negative ones. Such individuals become empowered, growing stronger, freer, and happier as they leave behind negative states such as fear, doubt, worry and anxiety. Eventually they evolve into saints (either as *arhants* or Buddhas) who have developed their capacities far beyond the limits of ordinary folk.

When recounting the story of the Buddha's life it was mentioned that he 'attained nirvana' while seated under the Bodhi tree at the age of thirty-five, and that then he attained 'final' nirvana on his death at the age of eighty. It is important to distinguish clearly these two kinds of nirvana. The first refers to the destruction of greed, hatred, and delusion by a living human being, and denotes essentially an ethical and spiritual transformation. Having achieved nirvana in this sense—often referred to as 'nirvana in this life' or 'nirvana with remainder' (*sopadiśeṣa-nirvāṇa*) since the body continues to exist afterwards—the Buddha lived on for forty-five years giving religious teachings. When he died at the age of eighty he entered 'final nirvana' (*parinirvāṇa*) or 'nirvana without remainder' (*anupādiśeṣa-nirvāṇa*), a discarnate or disembodied state from which he would never more be reborn.

THE TRUTH OF CESSATION (*nirodha*)

This, O Monks, is the Truth of the Cessation of Suffering. It is the utter cessation of that craving (*tṛṣṇā*), the withdrawal from it, the renouncing of it, the rejection of it, liberation from it, non-attachment to it.

The first kind of nirvana is relatively easy to understand. Here, we see an outstanding human being, a person displaying qualities of the kind we are familiar with from the biographies of saints, heroes, and role models from various backgrounds. The second kind of nirvana, however, is more problematic, for it is not clear what has happened to the Buddha once his mortal body has been left behind. We know the Buddha will not be reborn, but where has he gone? There is no definitive answer to this question in the early texts. The Buddha said that it was a bit like asking where a flame has gone once the candle is blown out. Of course, it has not actually gone anywhere, all that has happened is that the process of combustion has ceased. Likewise, when craving and ignorance are eliminated rebirth ceases, just like a flame goes out when deprived of oxygen and fuel. The Buddha's point here was that the question about what happens to a Buddha in final nirvana is based on a misconception, and since the question is in some sense misconceived, it is difficult to answer in a straightforward way. However, there are two possibilities at least that can be eliminated. These are known as the 'two extremes', and are the views that final nirvana means a) the total annihilation of the subject, or b) the eternal existence of a personal soul. Both these alternatives give a distorted idea of final nirvana since they presuppose the existence of a self or soul (*ātman*) that is either destroyed or continues to exist after death. As we shall see below, the Buddha's teaching on the nature of the self made no allowance for such an entity, so these explanations of nirvana had to be rejected.

In general, the Buddha was not keen for his followers to explore questions of the above kind, and discouraged speculation about things which could only be known through personal experience. He compared idle speculation about the nature of final nirvana to a man who was out walking one day when he was struck by a stray arrow. The man insisted that he would not have the arrow removed until his curiosity had been satisfied on a number of points, such as the identity of the archer, his name and clan, where he had been standing, and a host of other trivial details (M.i.246). The Buddha urged his followers not to behave like this foolish man and waste their lives in idle speculation when there was a clear need to take urgent practical action to pluck out the arrow of suffering from their bodies.

There is a famous verse which refers to the situation of an enlightened being (*arhant*) after death. The verse reads:

> There exists no measuring of one who has gone out (like a flame). That by which he could be referred to no longer exists for him. When all phenomena (*dharmas*) are removed, then all ways of describing have also been removed.
>
> (*Suttanipāta* v.1076)

This suggests there are no reference points by which an enlightened person can be known after death. In keeping with this, the sources generally speak of nirvana using negative terminology such as 'blowing out', 'cessation', 'the absence of desire', and 'the extinction of thirst', although occasionally more positive terms are encountered, such as 'the auspicious', 'the good', 'purity', 'peace', 'truth', and 'the further shore'. Certain passages seem to suggest that nirvana is a transcendent reality which is 'unborn, unoriginated, uncreated and unformed' (*Udāna* 80), but it is difficult to know how to interpret such statements. Thinkers in some later schools would speculate further on the nature of final nirvana, interpreting it in various ways in the light of their own philosophical views, while others were happy to leave the subject as mysterious and elusive, seeing final nirvana as a transcendent realm whose nature could only be known by those who had experienced it.

The Fourth Noble Truth: the Path

The Fourth Noble Truth—that of the Path or Way (*mārga*)—explains how suffering is to be brought to an end and the transition from *saṃsāra* to nirvana is to be made. The Eightfold Path is known as the 'middle way' because it steers a course between a life of indulgence and one of harsh austerity. It consists of eight factors divided into the three categories of Morality (*śīla*), Meditation (*samādhi*), and Wisdom (*prajñā*) (M.i.301).

Let us describe the eight factors briefly.

1. **Right View**, in essence means seeing and accepting the Four Noble Truths. A complete understanding is not envisaged in the preliminary stages, simply an initial acceptance of—and confidence or faith (*śraddhā*) in—the Buddha and his teachings. This initial confidence will be confirmed through personal experience over the course of time, and nothing has to be believed purely as an article of faith. Right View (*samyag-dṛṣṭi*) is also explained in the *Mahācattārīsaka Sutta* in terms of a traditional religious outlook on life involving belief in the moral law of karma, respect for parents and religious teachers, and in the possibility of personal spiritual progress.

THE TRUTH OF THE PATH (*mārga*)

This, O Monks, is the Truth of the Path which leads to the cessation of suffering. It is this Noble Eightfold Path, which consists of (1) Right View, (2) Right Resolve, (3) Right Speech, (4) Right Action, (5) Right Livelihood, (6) Right Effort, (7) Right Mindfulness, (8) Right Meditation.

THE NOBLE EIGHTFOLD PATH

1. Right View
2. Right Resolve   WISDOM (*prajñā*)

3. Right Speech
4. Right Action   MORALITY (*śīla*)
5. Right Livelihood

6. Right Effort
7. Right Mindfulness   MEDITATION (*samādhi*)
8. Right Meditation

2. **Right Resolve (*samyak-saṃkalpa*)** means developing right attitudes such as freedom from desires, friendliness, and compassion. It includes making a serious commitment to attaining a state of contentment (*naiṣkāmya*) and freedom from sensual desires (*kāma*), abandoning hatred (*avyābādha*) and abstaining from causing any injury to others (*ahiṃsā*).

3. **Right Speech (*samyag-vāc*)** means not telling lies, avoiding 'divisive speech' (such as making remarks that can cause enmity among people), avoiding harsh speech (speech which is aggressive or hurtful to others), and frivolous talk (such as gossip and idle chatter).

4. **Right Action (*samyak-karmanta*)** means abstaining from wrongful conduct through the body such as killing, stealing, or behaving inappropriately with respect to sensual pleasures.

5. **Right Livelihood (*samyag-ājīva*)** means not engaging in an occupation which causes harm or suffering to others, whether human or animal. This involves being honest in one's business affairs and not cheating one's customers (M.iii.75). It also involves avoiding certain trades and professions that cause death or harm such as 'trade in weapons, living beings, meat, alcoholic drink, or poison' (A.iii.208).

6. **Right Effort (*samyag-vyāyāma*)** means developing one's mind in a wholesome way by practicing mindfulness and mental cultivation as in meditation. It involves slowly transforming one's mind by replacing negative thoughts with positive and wholesome ones.

7. **Right Mindfulness (*samyak-smṛti*)** means developing constant awareness in four areas: in relation to the body, one's feelings, one's mood or mental state, and one's thoughts. It also involves eliminating negative thought patterns such as the 'five hindrances' (*nīvaraṇa*), namely (desire for sensual pleasure, ill-will, sloth and drowsiness, worry and agitation, and nagging doubts).

8. **Right Meditation (*samyak-samādhi*)** means developing clarity and mental calm by concentrating the mind through meditational exercises. By such practices the practitioner

is able to enter states like the four *dhyānas*, the lucid trances which played such an important part in the Buddha's quest for awakening. The various techniques of meditation used to concentrate the mind and integrate the personality will be explained more fully in Chapter Seven.

As noted, the eight factors of the Path fall into three areas, and these can be pictured in the form of a triangle. Morality (*śīla*) forms the baseline and is the foundation of religious practice since without self-discipline and virtuous behavior it is difficult to make progress in any endeavor. Meditation (*samādhi*) denotes the process of calming and self-integration that takes place at the deepest levels of the psyche, while wisdom (*prajñā*) relates to knowledge and understanding of the nature or reality and the ability to see clearly how awakening can be achieved. These three brace and support one another like the sides of a triangle, and each is in constant contact with the other two. Thus just as morality is the foundation for meditation and wisdom, it is also strengthened by them in turn, since inner calm and clear understanding produce a heightened moral sensibility which helps us distinguish more clearly between right and wrong. Meditation boosts the intellectual faculties and makes wisdom stronger and more penetrating, and wisdom supports meditation by making clearer and more intelligible the experience of the meditative states.

It is important to realize that the Noble Eightfold Path is not like a series of stages one passes through on the way to nirvana, in the way that a traveller making a journey might pass through various towns before reaching his destination. The eight factors are not objectives to be reached and then left behind; rather the Path is a continuous program in which the eight factors are developed cumulatively. Another misleading interpretation is to think of the eight factors of the Path as rungs on a ladder which is climbed in order to reach nirvana as a ninth rung at the top. In fact nirvana is not mentioned in the Path at all, the reason being that it is the lived experience of the Path itself that constitutes nirvana. In following the Path one acts like a Buddha, and by acting like a Buddha one progressively becomes one. The Path is essentially a means of self-transformation, a remodeling project or spiritual makeover, which turns the ordinary unenlightened person into a Buddha.

Holy persons

Not all who practice the Eightfold Path do so at the same level. The sources distinguish various kinds of practitioners who are more or less advanced in their spiritual practice. First of all comes the category of the 'worldly person' (*pṛthagjana*) or non-Buddhist, who does not follow the Path at all. Such people will continue to wander in *saṃsāra* until such time as they hear and respond to Buddhist teachings. Next come ordinary Buddhists, who follow a basic form of the Path, in contrast to the more advanced practitioners who follow the 'Noble' (*ārya*) form. The distinction here relates to the degree of insight into Buddhist teachings one possesses. At a higher level come what we might term the 'saints' of Buddhism, or holy people who are close to nirvana and destined to attain it in the near future.

THE FOUR HOLY PERSONS (*ārya-pudgala*)

1. Stream Winner (*śrotāpanna*)
2. Once-Returner (*sakṛdāgāmin*)
3. Non-Returner (*anāgāmin*)
4. *Arhant*

Four categories of 'holy person' (*ārya-pudgala*) are distinguished, the first being that of the 'stream winner' (*śrotāpanna*). Such a person, through deep meditation on the 'three marks' of suffering (*duḥkha*), impermanence (*anitya*) and 'no-self' (*anātman*), has gained a glimpse of nirvana and has entered the 'stream' that will carry him or her inexorably towards it within seven lives at the most. All of these lives will be as either a human or a god. Next comes the 'once-returner' (*sakṛdāgāmin*), who will return at most one further time to the human world, with any further rebirths taking place in the higher heavens. Third is the 'non-returner' (*anāgāmin*), who will never again be reborn in the human realm.

Having freed himself entirely from craving and hatred, he no longer has any attachment to the realm of sense-desires (*kāma-loka*) and so will not be reborn there, but still lacks sufficient insight to put an end to rebirth. Such a person will be reborn in one of the five 'pure abodes', which are the five highest heavens reserved especially for *anāgāmins*. The last of the four noble persons is the *arhant*, one who has freed himself from any belief in a self (*ātman*), eliminated all ignorance and spiritual defilements, and destroyed all desire for rebirth at any level of existence. For the *arhant* all suffering (*duḥkha*) is at an end, and at death he will attain final nirvana and never more be reborn, like the Buddha.

The doctrine of no-self

Buddhism sees the human subject as made up of two parts, one spiritual (*nāma*), the other material (*rūpa*). In recognizing that there is both a spiritual (*nāma*) and material (*rūpa*) side to human nature the Buddha was not saying anything new in the context of Indian philosophy. He went on, however, to extend the analysis and to define five categories in terms of which human nature can be analyzed. This further analysis is referred to towards the end of the First Noble Truth in the phrase 'the five aggregates which are grasped at (*upādāna-skandha*) are suffering'. This teaching of the five aggregates was elaborated on by the Buddha in his second sermon, the *Anattalakkhaṇa Sutta* (Vin.i.13), preached five days after the first. The five aggregates are collectively known as the 'aggregates of attachment' (*upādāna-skandha*) because as the means to pleasurable experiences they are themselves objects of desire or craving (*tṛṣṇā*) and are grasped at in life after life.

Before looking at the five aggregates individually, the important point to note is not so much what the list of the five includes as what it does not. Specifically the doctrine makes no mention of a soul or self, understood as an eternal and immutable spiritual essence. By adopting this position the Buddha set himself apart from the orthodox Indian religious tradition known as Brahmanism, which claimed that each person possessed an eternal soul (*ātman*) which is either part of, or identical with, a metaphysical absolute known as *brahman* (a sort of impersonal godhead). He also rejected the views of other contemporary teachers, such as the Jain leader Mahāvīra, who taught that at the core of each individual was an eternal and unchanging spiritual principle known as the *jīva*, or life principle.

The Buddha said he could find no evidence for the existence of either the personal soul (*ātman*) or its cosmic counterpart (*brahman*), and he also rejected the Jain and similar teachings concerning the *jīva*. Instead his approach was practical and empirical, more akin to psychology than theology. He explained human nature as constituted by the five factors much in the way that an automobile is constituted by its wheels, transmission, engine, steering, and chassis. Unlike science, of course, he believed that a person's moral identity survives death and is reborn.

In stating that the five factors of individuality are suffering, however, as he did in the First Noble Truth, the Buddha was pointing out that human nature cannot provide a foundation for permanent happiness because the doctrine of the five aggregates shows that the individual has no real core. Because human beings are made up of these five constantly shifting components it is inevitable that sooner or later suffering will arise, just as an automobile will eventually wear out and break down. Suffering is thus engrained in the very fabric of our being.

The five aggregates

Let us now consider the five aggregates in turn. The first and simplest of the five is form (*rūpa*). Although not exactly equivalent to 'matter' this may be thought of as denoting the physical substance of the body. The second of the five categories is feeling (*vedanā*), and this denotes the capacity to respond affectively to a stimulus. Feelings are classified as pleasant, unpleasant, or neutral, and the most basic kind of feelings are simple sensations of the stimulus–response kind. An example of an unpleasant sensation might be to be pricked by a pin; a pleasant one would be a hot relaxing bath on a cold day. In addition to the capacity for feeling, human beings also have the power of perception and conceptual thought, and this constitutes the third category, known as *saṃjñā*. This includes the capacity to discern and discriminate between things, for example to name and distinguish different colors.

THE FIVE AGGREGATES

1. Material form (*rūpa*)
2. Feelings and sensations (*vedanā*)
3. Perceptions (*saṃjñā*)
4. Mental formations (*saṃskāra*)
5. Consciousness (*vijñāna*)

The picture sketched so far is abstract and two-dimensional, and lacks any reference to the features which distinguish one person from another. These are the elements which constitute the fourth category. Granted the power to think and feel, individual development will be shaped by personal experiences and reactions to them. From these reactions are built up particular tendencies, traits and habits, and eventually the complex pattern of dispositions which is referred to as 'character'. It is the particular configuration of these traits and characteristics which defines people as the individuals they are. Buddhist commentators drew up long lists of virtues, vices, and other mental factors in order to provide an exhaustive account of this fourth category, which we have called 'mental formations' (saṃskāra). A central role here is played by the will or volition (cetanā), the mental faculty through which we deliberate and take decisions, and through which karma is produced. Retrospectively, the fourth category is the sum of the karma or moral choices made in previous lives.

The fifth category, vijñāna, is usually translated as 'consciousness', but this term can be misleading as a translation since it is usually taken to mean the mental 'stream of consciousness'. The experience of vijñāna as a stream of mental awareness, however, is merely one of its many modes. It is better understood as functioning at a deeper level as that which animates an organism. It is by virtue of vijñāna that we have bodily sensations, that we see, hear, taste, touch and think. The translation 'sentiency' may be preferable to 'consciousness' since it is not restricted to the mental sphere in quite the same way. Vijñāna has an important function in relation to death and rebirth. Following death, vijñāna fuses with a new biological form giving rise to a being with a new physical body but a karmic profile carried over from a previous life. Buddhist sources refer to vijñāna in this transitional phase as the 'gandharva'.

According to Buddhism, then, the human subject can be deconstructed into these five aggregates without remainder, and since the five make no reference to an eternal soul Buddhism is said to teach a doctrine of 'no-self' (anātman). In terms of this doctrine, the common but fallacious belief in an eternal soul is really a case of mistaken identity whereby one or more of the skandhas is mistaken for a soul.

So, in the doctrine of 'no-self' is the Buddha denying that individuals exist or have any unique personality or identity? No, the ego is not denied by this teaching. As explained above, the particular traits and characteristics which go to make up an individual (as when we say 'that was typical of him') are explained as belonging to the fourth skandha, the saṃskāra-skandha. Here are [there] found the various tendencies and patterns of behavior which collectively give shape to an individual character. The doctrine of anātman is not taking away anything: it is simply recognizing that the concept of an eternal and unchanging soul is redundant, and is not required to explain how human beings function.

Discussion Questions

1. What does the parable of the traveler purport to convey?
2. Why are the seemingly natural biological aspects of human experience, such as old age, sickness, and death, dissatisfactory and unfulfilling?
3. Buddha's teaching on dependent origination holds that all phenomena arise in dependence on causes and conditions. What are the twelve links of dependent arising?
4. Do you think that individual human being is made up with five aggregates and thus is empty of essential nature?
5. How can you employ the Noble Eightfold Path in your daily life to use it as a practical guide to live suffering-free?

The Qur'an

God speaks

We have revealed it as an Arabic Qur'an so that you may understand.

(Qur'an 12:2)

The Qur'an is the Muslim scripture and the primary authority for Muslim life. It is comparable in some respects to the Christian and Jewish scriptures. An English-speaking non-Muslim who first approaches it will probably find some of the content familiar, but the form and the style will often seem strange. This chapter will focus on how Muslims understand their scripture and the influence it has on their life and culture.

In this chapter

- What is the Qur'an?
- The Qur'an in Muslim culture
- The main teachings of the Qur'an on God, faith, prophecy, other spiritual beings, the Last Day, social teachings
- Interpretation of the Qur'an
- Modern critical approaches to the Qur'an

What is the Qur'an?

For Muslims the Qur'an consists of the verbatim words of God, conveyed in the Arabic language to the Prophet **Muhammad** by the Angel Gabriel, and not modified by Muhammad's personality. The Qur'an commands Muhammad to say, "It is not for me to change it of my own accord. I follow only what is revealed to me" (10:16). The messages were conveyed in relatively short sections over the twenty-three years of his prophetic mission in response to his needs and those of the *umma*. Muhammad's own words and deeds are also important for Muslims and will be discussed in the next chapter, but the distinction between his words and God's words is kept clear. This view is held by virtually all Muslims today although a few modernists have sought ways to say that the Qur'an is human as well as divine (see chapter 20). Non-Muslims usually treat the Qur'an as Muhammad's words, but this can be offensive to Muslims. When quoting the Qur'an, it is best to say, "The Qur'an says ... " rather than "Muhammad said ... ".

As passages of the Qur'an were revealed to Muhammad, whom most Muslims believe to have been illiterate, he recited and memorized them and others wrote them down on materials that were available. It is claimed that from time to time Muhammad reviewed with Gabriel the content of what had been revealed, but at the end of his life it was still scattered on "pieces of papyrus, flat stones, palm-leaves, shoulder-blades and ribs of animals, pieces of leather and wooden boards, as well as [in] the hearts of men" (Watt, 1970, 40), as one source puts it. The "hearts of men" refers to the fact that many had memorized part or all of it. From the beginning the Qur'an was transmitted both in written form and in memorized form. The memorized form was the more important since the society of the time was one in which literacy was limited and which therefore relied mainly on memory. The heritage of pre-Islamic poetry was also memorized and was only written down much later. Moreover, the Arabic script of the time was very primitive and did not distinguish all of the letters (e.g. *b*, *t*, *th*, and sometimes *y* and *n* were written the same way), so that it was mainly useful as an aid to memory. It would take two centuries before it was to be fully adequate to record the Qur'an.

The best known account of the compilation of the Qur'an is as follows. In a battle the year after Muhammad's death a number of those who had memorized the Qur'an were killed and **Abu Bakr**, the first caliph, decided that the whole should be collated and recorded. This was done by Zayd ibn Thabit, who had been one of Muhammad's secretaries, and the text was eventually passed to Hafsa, the daughter of **'Umar** and widow of Muhammad. Under the third caliph, **'Uthman**, as the *umma* spread geographically, it became evident that different people were writing and reciting the Qur'an in slightly variant ways. This he considered a threat to the unity of the *umma* and so he had Zayd and others produce a definitive edition and sent copies of it to the main centers, ordering all others to be destroyed. In this edition there are 114 chapters, or *suras*, of quite unequal length, the shortest having three and the longest 286 verses, or *āyas*. Except for the short first *sūra* (quoted below), the *suras* are placed roughly in order of length, from the longest to the shortest, not in the order in which they were revealed nor in any clear thematic arrangement. Many Muslims believe that at least two of these copies still exist, one in Tashkent and one at the Topkapi museum in Istanbul. Most critical scholars, however, doubt the authenticity of these. In spite of 'Uthman's effort, there came to be some seven to ten different "readings" of the Qur'an that vary in details but are all judged to be acceptable. Some hold that all of these were revealed to Muhammad, possibly to accommodate different dialects of Arabic. Muslims do not consider that these variations compromise the integrity of the text, which they believe has been protected by God from distortion. In recent years most printed editions of the Qur'an follow the edition authorized by the Egyptian government in 1925.

If the Qur'an is the verbatim speech of God, it can only be so in the Arabic language, in which it was revealed. A "translation" into any other language is merely an imperfect effort to convey some of its meanings. Therefore, the Qur'an is always recited in Arabic and serious study of it is done in Arabic. Even apart from this "theological" point, it is a fact that Arabic generally is difficult to translate into English and the Qur'an, with its particular style, is even more so. It is usually not possible to render all of the ideas, allusions and emotions present in a Qur'anic passage adequately into English.

In fact, Muslims insist that the Qur'an is a literary miracle that cannot be equalled as literature. The Qur'an, indeed, makes this claim for itself (2:23–24) and Muslims have devoted a considerable literature to elaborating this claim. It is said that 'Umar, who was to be the second caliph, had been a bitter opponent of Muhammad but was converted after reading a page of the Qur'an. It is believed that every prophet's mission was confirmed by a miracle from God and Muhammad's main miracle, according to many his only miracle, was the Qur'an. The miraculous aspect is heightened by the fact that he is believed to have been illiterate.

This literary claim is not easy for the outsider to appreciate. The parts of the Bible Westerners most often read have a fairly straightforward narrative, poetic or doctrinal line and the whole has a fairly clear organization. The Qur'an by contrast often jumps unexpectedly from one topic to another, tells only part of a story and elliptically omits words and phrases. (It should be noted, though, that some of the prophetic books of the Bible are closer to the Qur'an in this respect.) Apart from the decreasing length of the *suras* it is hard to discern any overall principle of organization. Thomas Carlyle, who was one of the first writers in English to write favorably of Muhammad, spoke for many who approach the Qur'an for the first time when he described it as "a wearisome confused jumble, crude, ... endless iterations, long-windedness, entanglement ... ", though he also went on to say that in it "there is a merit quite other than the literary one. If a book [comes] from the heart, it will contrive to reach other hearts; all art and authorcraft are of small amount to that" (Carlyle, 1910, 86–87). One problem, of course, was that he had to read the Qur'an in English, and in a poorer translation than those available today. Even in Arabic, though, the Qur'an's style and organization often appear fragmented. It is important, however, to bear in mind that the Qur'an is more recited and listened to than read and is mostly recited in relatively short sections, so that the power of the words and the immediate content is more important than the logical coherence of the larger context in which it is set. Muslim scholars have devoted considerable attention to the rhetorical features of the Qur'an. Many have also claimed to discern coherent organization in the text though this may be a different sort of coherence from what Westerners look for. In any case, incoherence can be only apparent, for God has undoubtedly given the Qur'an the form it has for a good reason.

Since Muslims view the Qur'an as the actual speech of God, it is for them the point where God is most fully present in the mundane world. The significance of this can be underlined by a comparison with Christianity. It would seem obvious to compare the Qur'an with the Bible, but on closer reflection we may conclude that the person of Christ provides a closer parallel.

For orthodox Christians it is not the Bible but the person of Jesus Christ, the incarnation of God (God "in the flesh"), who is the point where God is most fully present in the world. There is a confirmation of this point in the history of Muslim theology, where the debates over whether the Qur'an was created or uncreated (see chapter 11) resemble the Christian debates over the nature of Christ (see chapter 2). Orthodox Jews, on the other hand, will find that the Muslim view of the Qur'an is fairly close to their own of the written Torah (first five books of the Bible) given to Moses on Mount Sinai.

Being the speech of God, the Qur'an has *baraka*, a spiritual or almost magical power (we shall see this term again later). This is illustrated at the popular level by such practices as putting a passage of the Qur'an into a small container and hanging it around one's neck as an amulet to ward off bad luck or evil forces or writing a passage on paper and dissolving the ink in water to drink as a medicine. There are stories such as one that the horse of a Companion of the Prophet bolted when someone recited the Qur'an. One should be ritually pure before touching a copy of the Qur'an or reciting it. Arabic copies of the Qur'an usually have on the title page the following, which comes from the Qur'an: "a well guarded book which none may touch except the purified" (56:78–80). It is also worth noting that the word *āya*, used for a verse of the Qur'an, also means sign or even miracle. It is used in the Qur'an for God's activity in creation, e.g. the rain, the winds, the alteration of day and night (2:164), for a victory in battle such as Badr (3:13) and for "miracles" such as Moses' rod turning into a serpent (7:106, cf. Exodus 4:3 and 7:10 in the Bible). All of these are signs of God and so is, pre-eminently, each *āya* of the Qur'an.

The Qur'an in Muslim culture

The Qur'an penetrates Muslim cultures to a degree even greater than that to which the Bible used to penetrate Western, especially Protestant, cultures. Muslim names are commonly drawn from the Qur'an, as we shall see later. Phrases such as *al-ḥamdu li-llāh* (praise be to God), *inshā'allāh* (if God wills) and *Allāhu a'lam* (God knows best) are constantly on people's lips. Muslims recite a portion of the Qur'an in their regular prayers (*salah*) and on many other occasions during the day. The *Fātiḥa*, the opening chapter of the Qur'an, is recited on many occasions, such as the closing of marriage contracts. The Qur'an also generates what Westerners would call "art forms". One of these is calligraphy. The Arabic script, which has been developed in several styles, lends itself particularly well to graceful presentation. One finds Qur'anic calligraphy often on the walls of mosques and other public buildings, as well as on posters and in pictures in people's homes and elsewhere (see chapter 14).

Since the Qur'an is primarily a book to be recited and listened to, recitation also gives rise to something like an art form. Until modern times recitation of the Qur'an, along with its use in learning to read and write, was the mainstay of Muslim primary education. Many people memorize and recite the Qur'an even though they don't know Arabic and cannot understand the words; they and their listeners still benefit from the *baraka*. Those who memorize the whole of the Qur'an are called *ḥāfiz* and have considerable prestige. For some, recitation becomes a profession. They will be called on to recite at weddings, funerals, and various other religious, civic and family occasions. (See *Online Resources for Qur'an Recitation* under Further Reading at the end of this chapter and also on the website.) For purposes of recitation and also learning, the Qur'an is divided into thirty "parts" of equal length and each of these into two *ḥizb*; this is separate from the division into *suras* and *ayas*. There are two styles of recitation, *tartīl*, which is fairly plain, and *tajwīd*, which is more ornamental and "musical" (Qur'anic recitation is in fact not considered "music" by Muslims) and more difficult to master. It may be said that a leading Qur'an reciter has a status comparable to a leading opera singer in the West and evokes an intensity comparable perhaps to a rock star. Kristina Nelson describes a dramatic moment in the public recitation of the Qur'an in Cairo in terms that suggest both art and *baraka*:

> Suddenly the power of the phrase seizes the scattered sensibility of the crowd, focusing it, and carrying it forward like a great wave, setting the listeners down gently after one phrase and lifting them up in the rising of the next. The recitation proceeds, the intensity grows. A man hides his face in his hands, another weeps quietly. Some listeners tense themselves as if in pain, while, in the pauses between phrases, others shout appreciative responses to the reciter. Time passes unnoticed.

> (Nelson, 1985, xiii)

The main teachings of the Qur'an

God

The main teachings of the Qur'an relate, of course, to God, **Allah**. The Qur'an does not introduce Allah, since the Arabs already knew of Him, but it has much to say about Him. First and foremost, He is One and has no partner. "Say: He is Allah, One, Allah, the Eternal; He has not begotten nor has he been begotten, and none is equal to Him." (Qur'an 112). The recognition that Allah is one is called **tawhīd** (literally, considering [Allah] to be one), a very important term in the Muslim lexicon. Moreover, Allah is the creator and sustainer of everything. He created the universe in six days and "settled on the throne" (32:4 and elsewhere). He did not rest on the seventh day, as the Bible claims, but immediately took charge of His universe. He created humans to praise and obey Him and He guides them. On the Last Day He will dramatically bring the universe to an end and judge humankind.

Most of these themes are captured in the *Fātiḥa,* the opening *sura*, and the one most often recited by Muslims.

> In the name of Allah, the Merciful, the Compassionate.
> Praise be to Allah, Lord of the worlds
> The Merciful, the Compassionate
> Master of the Day of Judgment

You only do we serve; to You only do we turn for help
Guide us in the straight path,
The path of those whom You have blessed,
Not of those with whom You are angry,
Nor of those who are astray.

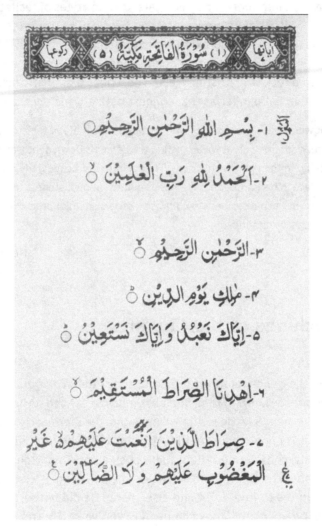

FIGURE 3.1   Calligraphy of the opening sura of the Qur'an, the Fatiha

The Qur'an has a number of epithets or names for Allah, and from these Muslims have compiled lists of ninety-nine names (they vary slightly), of which the first two are the Merciful (*Raḥmān*) and the Compassionate (*Raḥīm*), mentioned in the *Fatiha*. These names are often recited and appear in calligraphy in pictures and posters. They also appear in Muslim names, such as ʿAbd al-Rahman, servant of Merciful One, ʿAbd al-Nāṣir, servant of the Helper (name of the former president of Egypt, usually known in the West as Nasser), and of course, 'Abd Allah (usually transliterated Abdullah), servant of God.

The opposite of *tawhid* and the most serious sin humans can commit is *shirk* (commonly and slightly inaccurately translated "polytheism"), meaning to ascribe partners or associates to Allah, something the Meccans did with three of their pagan goddesses, whom they considered to be daughters of Allah, as the following passage indicates:

> Have you considered al-Lat and al-'Uzza,
> and that other, Manat, the third?
> Are you to have sons, and He only daughters?
> That would be a most unfair division!
> They are naught but names you have named,
> you and your fathers.
> Allah has sent no warrant for them.
> They follow only their own ideas and desires,
> Even though sound guidance
> has come to them from their Lord.

> (53:19–23)

It is interesting to note that this is the site of the so-called "Satanic verses", made famous by Salman Rushdie's novel. According to some reports Muhammad was overly anxious to convince the **Meccans** to accept his message and Satan took advantage of this to suggest the following verses as a compromise: "They are the exalted swans whose intercession is to be desired" (after the second line, above). The Meccans were so happy they joined him in prayer, but soon Gabriel appeared and told him these were not from God and replaced them with the present text. The Meccans turned away. Gabriel guaranteed that nothing inspired by Satan would be allowed to stand. Most Muslims today deny the historicity of this account. While *shirk* in its most obvious form involves the worship of other gods, most Muslims would say that it also includes giving anything, whether pleasure, wealth, career, family, or nation, equal place in one's life with God.

Faith

The most important requirement for humans is faith, *īmān*. In fact, the word *mu'min* (believer) is the most common word used in the Qur'an to denote Muhammad's followers, the word *muslim* being comparatively rare. Even today, *mu'min* is preferred by many. The term *iman* became the subject of considerable theological discussion and we will return to it in chapter 11. The opposite of *iman* is *kufr*, unbelief or, more precisely, the refusal to recognize and act on the blessings of Allah. It carries the strong connotation of ingratitude and is perhaps the most forceful negative term in the Islamic vocabulary.

Prophecy

Allah's power and mercy can be perceived in the universe by those with eyes to see but He conveys his commands and moral standards to humans primarily by way of prophets (*nabī*) and messengers (*rasūl*) (the relation between these terms is too complex to enter into here). The Qur'an names some twenty-five of these and makes it clear that there are many it does not mention. Muslim traditions suggest that there have been as many as 124,000 prophets over the whole course of history. Most but not all of those named correspond to Biblical figures. In most cases the accounts of each prophet are scattered through the Qur'an with each account giving part of the story from a particular perspective. We will consider a few here.

Although Adam, the first man, is not specifically called a prophet or messenger in the Qur'an, Muslims have generally taken him to be such. Adam was created to be God's *khalīfa*, or deputy, on earth (2:30–39 and elsewhere). This is the same term that is used in a different context for the later leaders of the *umma*, in their case commonly transliterated "caliph". Adam and his wife, not named in the Qur'an, are placed in paradise (called "the garden", *janna*) and told not to eat of a certain tree, but they disobey and are therefore expelled to the earth. There is no indication that Eve first disobeyed and then tempted Adam; they appear to have disobeyed together. Adam then repented and was forgiven and received "words of guidance". While they are put on earth where they will face temptation and difficulty, sin consists of specific acts of disobedience to God, not the corruption of their moral nature (as in the Christian doctrine of original sin). They have the ability to obey.

Nuh (Noah) and several other prophets, including Arabian prophets such as Hud and Salih, who are not in the Bible, convey a warning from Allah to their communities (*ummas*), most of whose members reject the message and are destroyed by Allah, while only the prophet and a few followers escape. The story of Nuh's ark is presented in the Qur'an and fits this pattern (11:25–48 and elsewhere).

Ibrahim (Abraham) is particularly important. The Qur'anic Ibrahim was raised in an idolatrous family, discovered the truth of *tawhid* while observing the heavens (6:75–80), destroyed his father's idols (21:51–67), was thrown into a fire from which Allah saved him and migrated to Palestine (29:24–26 and elsewhere, the term **Hijra** is used here). After this, among other things, he was commanded by God to sacrifice his son, who was ransomed at the last minute (37:102–11). The Qur'an does not say which of his sons this was but Muslims believe it was Isma'il (Ishmael), not Ishaq (Isaac). He also traveled with Isma'il to Mecca where they built, or rebuilt, the **Ka'ba** (2:125–28) (some think it was built originally in Adam's time). Ibrahim's descendants, Ishaq, Isma'il, Ya'qub (Jacob) and Yusuf (Joseph), were all prophets. The people of Israel (Banu Isra'il) were descended from Ishaq, Ya'qub and Yusuf, and the Arabs from Isma'il, though the Qur'an is not explicit on the latter point.

The story of Musa (Moses) has much in common with the Biblical account. He is saved from death as a baby (28:4–13 and elsewhere), flees after killing a man (28:15–21), is called to by God from a burning bush (20:9–24 and elsewhere), and sent to confront Pharaoh, who is more consistently evil than in the Biblical account, and who is drowned as Musa's people escape (2:50

and elsewhere). Musa receives the Torah from God, but the people worship the calf and prove disobedient in other ways (2:51–54 and elsewhere).

'Isa (Jesus) is understood to be a messenger sent to the people of Israel and is explicitly stated not to be Son of Allah or part of a Trinity (19:35; 5:73–78). He is born of a virgin and there are accounts of the annunciation and the birth that differ considerably from the Biblical ones (3:42–47; 19:16–34). He receives a scripture, the *Injīl* (Gospel), preaches, performs miracles, and raises the dead. His enemies try to crucify him but fail as Allah raises him to Himself (4:157–58 but see 19:33).

The Qur'an calls Jews and Christians "People of the Book" (*ahl al-kitāb*) and in some places seems to put their faith on the same level as that preached by Muhammad, whose message is said to be the same as theirs and as all the other prophets (2:136; 42:13 and elsewhere). Elsewhere they are criticized for disobedience, for changing their scriptures (4:46 and elsewhere) and for rejecting Muhammad. Though critical of both, the Qur'an is more consistently critical of Jews while having some favorable things to say about Christians (5:82). The Qur'an says, "No compulsion in religion" (2:256), but it also calls on Muslims to fight the People of the Book until they are humbled and pay *jizya*, a special tax (9:29).

Many of the elements in the accounts of the prophets that are not found in the Bible are found in other Jewish and Christian sources, one example being Ibrahim breaking the idols. This has led many Western scholars to speak of Jewish and Christian influence on Muhammad and even to speculate whether Muhammad was more influenced by Judaism or Christianity. For Muslims all these stories come from Allah. They and others were undoubtedly circulating in the environment; otherwise the Qur'anic versions, which are usually highly elliptical, would not have been understood. God in the revelation confirmed what was true in the material being circulated and discarded what was false, as well as adding new material.

These stories are still very much alive in Muslim societies, just as Old Testament stories are alive in Christian circles. "Stories of the prophets" is and always has been a very popular literary genre. These works collate the Qur'anic accounts of each prophet and fill in the gaps. In the process, a considerable amount of Biblical and other Jewish and Christian material is often included. For example, in these works, contrary to the Qur'an, usually Eve's name is given (Ḥawā' in Arabic) and she is first tempted and then tempts Adam, as in the Bible. Many Muslims are named after these prophets and allusions are often made to events in their lives. Khomeini, the leader of the Islamic revolution in Iran, was given the epithet "idol breaker", alluding to Ibrahim's action. Several rulers, including the Shah of Iran and President Sadat of Egypt, have been labeled "Pharaoh" by their enemies (see chapters 17 and 18 on these).

Other spiritual beings

In addition to Allah, the Qur'an speaks of other spiritual beings. Angels are servants and messengers of Allah who praise Him and do His bidding. *Jinn* (singular: *jinnī*) are beings made of invisible fire who may harm or help humans and may be believers or unbelievers. The Qur'an gives an account of a group of *jinn* who were converted by hearing it recited (46:29–31). *Jinn* are, of course, the "genies" who supposedly are let out of bottles and grant three wishes. Among the *jinn* is Iblis (devil) or Shaytan (satan), who was commanded along with the angels to bow down to Adam, after he was created, but refused. For this he was thrown out of heaven, but has been allowed to tempt human beings (17:61–65).

The Last Day

Some of the most dramatic passages of the Qur'an deal with the Last Day. For example:

> When the heaven is split open,
> When the stars are scattered,
> When the seas are poured forth,
> When the tombs are overturned,
> Then a soul shall know what it has done,
> And what it has left undone.

(82:1–5)

Descriptions of Paradise and the Fire (hell) are likewise vivid, including the heavenly maidens (*houris*) who will attend those in Paradise (no number is given in the Qur'an). Feminists complain that the description of Paradise is very male oriented. Interestingly, it is reported that some of the women of the time thought so, too, and complained to Muhammad. Following this he received the following verses: "Muslim men and women, believing men and women, obedient men and women ... for them God has prepared forgiveness and a mighty wage" (33:35). In this worldly life social rights and duties differ but in the final accounting gender, like other social distinctions, falls away.

Social teachings

Many of the Qur'an's social and moral teachings will be dealt with in later chapters, but it is worth mentioning three that underline the contrast between the Qur'anic ethos and the *jahili* ethos of the pre-Islamic Arabs.

As mentioned in chapter 3, the highest loyalty of the pre-Islamic Arabs was given to the tribe. The *jahili* poet Durayd ibn Simma sang:

> I am of Ghaziyyah: if she be in error, then I will err;
> And if Ghaziyyah be guided right, I go right with her.

(Nicholson, 1969, 83)

By contrast, the Qur'an says:

> O, humankind,
> Surely, We have created you from a male and a female,
> and made you into nations and tribes
> so you may know each other.

Surely, the most noble of you in God's sight
Is the most pious.

(49:13)

That the *jahili* attitude of Durayd lives on is suggested by the following statement of the American Stephen Decatur in 1816: "Our country! In her intercourse with foreign nations may she always be in the right; but our country, right or wrong!" This supports the view of many Muslims today that modern nationalism is the moral equivalent of *jahili* tribalism and is *shirk*. The same Qur'anic passage also signals a shift in what it means to be noble (*karīm*). For the *jahili* Arabs nobility meant having noble ancestry and demonstrating this by noble deeds such as bravery in battle and generosity. For the Qur'an nobility is piety, which requires no ancestry.

As also mentioned in chapter 3, *jahiliyya* meant not so much ignorance as a glorying in extreme behavior, as illustrated by the accounts of Imru al-Qays, with his drinking, womanizing and then persistent quest for vengeance and Hatim al-Tayyi giving away all of his father's camels as an act of hospitality. The Qur'an, by contrast forbids fornication, gambling and wine drinking, and calls for the limitation of vengeance or, preferably, forgiveness (5:45). As for generosity, "be neither miserly nor prodigal" (17:29).

For the *jahili* Arabs the motive of ethical action was essentially honor, especially the honor of the tribe. Hatim says to his father,

> Oh my father, by means of [the camels] I have conferred on you everlasting fame and honor that will cleave to you like the ring of the ringdove and men will always bear in mind some verse of poetry in which we are praised. This is your recompense for the camels.

(Nicholson, 1969, 86)

As for a future life, the Qur'an quotes them as saying, "There is this life and no other. We live and die; nothing but Time destroys us!" (45:24). For the Qur'an, on the other hand, the primary motive is precisely the "mighty wage" of the future life:

> Say: "It is God who gives you life and later causes you to die. It is He who will gather you all on the Day of Resurrection. Of this there is no doubt. ... As for those who have faith and do good works, their lord will admit them to His mercy. Theirs shall be a glorious triumph. To the unbelievers. ... The evil of their deeds will manifest itself to them and the scourge at which they scoffed will encompass them...."

(45:27–33)

Out of fear for honor or fear of poverty *jahili* Arabs would sometimes bury their girl babies (16:58–60). The Qur'an forbids this, "Do not kill your children, fearing poverty. We shall provide for them and for you. Killing them is a great sin" (17:31).

Interpretation of the Qur'an

Like all scriptures, the Qur'an needs interpretation. Indeed, some interpretation is involved in the material presented above. A basic level of interpretation has been the effort to determine the temporal order of the Qur'anic material. Muslim scholars have distinguished between *suras* revealed in Mecca and those revealed in Medina. In general the first group are shorter and more poetic while the latter are longer, more prosaic and more likely to deal with legal material. Beyond this there has been an effort to determine the order of the *suras* within each group and this appears in the chapter headings of the Egyptian edition. It is recognized, though, that in some cases a *sura* includes material from different periods. One reason the temporal order is important is the idea that sometimes a later passage abrogates an earlier one. This is one explanation of apparent contradictions and is also important for applying the Qur'an in practice. In such cases it is important to know which is the later passage. For example, Qur'an 2:219 says that wine is of some value but greater evil but Qur'an 5:90, which is later, unreservedly forbids it.

An important part of interpretation is the effort to determine the "occasions of revelation" (*asbāb al-nuzūl*), that is the specific circumstances under which a passage was revealed and the issues that were being addressed. Much of the Qur'an cannot be understood without this information, since the Qur'an usually does not provide the context of its statements or at most alludes to it without giving the details. The case of the women questioning about paradise is an example of this.

The commentaries to the Qur'an that follow the order of the text are called *tafṣīrs* and a considerable number have been written. These are sometimes divided into those based on transmission (especially of *hadiths*, statements of the Prophet, see the next chapter) and those that make greater use of rational opinion. The most famous of the first group is that of Ibn Jarir al-Tabari (d. 922) and of the second that of al-Zamakhshari (d. 1144), condensed and edited by al-Baydawi (d. c. 1286). These and other traditional *tafsirs* usually contain a considerable amount of linguistic analysis and other technical material, as well as discussion of "occasions of revelation" and stories of the prophets, and much else. *Tafsirs* continue to be produced in modern times, some of them ideological in character, such as those of Mawdudi and Sayyid Qutb (see chapters 15 and 17 respectively) and some especially concerned to relate the Qur'an to modern science, such as that of Tantawi Jawhari (1940). These are generally less technical and more accessible to the general reader. A distinction is also often made between *tafṣīr* and *ta'wīl*. The former is a straightforward, exoteric interpretation, while the latter seeks hidden, esoteric meanings. An example of *tafsir* is the interpretation of "Lord" in the *Fatiha* as meaning not only master but also nurturer, based on the root of the Arabic word. An example of *ta'wil* would be the interpretation of the first letter of the same *sura* as symbolizing the beginning of creation and also 'Ali, the first Shi'i *Imam*.

One can see that the scholarly interpreter of the Qur'an faces a considerable task. He or she must master the various approaches just described as well as the fine points of the Arabic language and sciences related to the *Hadith* described in the next chapter.

Modern critical approaches to the Qur'an

Most Western scholars accept that the present text of the Qur'an is essentially what Muhammad presented as divine revelation, though they raise some questions at particular points and question the traditional accounts of its compilation. The German scholar Nöldeke (1836–1930) developed an analysis of the *suras* that divided them into three Meccan stages and one Medinan. This analysis has been extremely influential though more recent scholarship questions whether the *sura* can be the unit of analysis, since many *suras* contain material from different periods. Indeed, many doubt whether the temporal sequence of the Qur'anic material can in fact be determined. In a refined form, though, Nöldeke's approach is still used by most Western scholars and many Muslims. A Muslim scholar has recently developed a highly sophisticated analysis of stylistic elements, discerning seven chronologically ordered groups of material.

Western scholars have also come up with different interpretations from traditional Muslims on specific points. For example, traditionally the word *ummī* when applied to Muhammad is taken to mean "illiterate". Westerners, by contrast, generally take it to mean something like "gentile", i.e. belonging to a community that has not received a scripture.

Since the 1970s the "revisionists" mentioned at the end of chapter 3 have developed a much more radical criticism. John Wansbrough and others have applied to the Qur'an methods of literary criticism that have long been applied to the Bible. Denying any historical value to the traditional accounts of the compilation of the Qur'an and stressing the piecemeal and, in their view, contradictory nature of its contents, they conclude that the Qur'an was authored and edited over a period of some two centuries before it reached its present form and does not all come from Muhammad. Less radically, others note that the earliest surviving written passages of the Qur'an date from the late seventh century and often have wordings that are not standard (e.g. in the Dome of the Rock and a large number of ancient Qur'an fragments discovered in Yemen in 1972). Even though these variations are minor they are significant in a text whose wording is supposed to be sacrosanct and they suggest that the text was still developing long after the Prophet's death. If, as is commonly held, the orally transmitted version was (and is) the most authoritative minor written discrepancies would not prove much. These critics, however, claim a greater role for the written text even in the early period and argue that the existence of the discrepancies makes the existence of an authoritative oral version unlikely. Some critics argue that much of the Qur'an is in, or closely related to, the Aramaic language. One, going under the pseudonym of C. Luxenberg, has gained considerable media attention by claiming on this basis that the *houris* are not heavenly virgins but really white grapes, a view hardly accepted by other scholars. Other scholars, however, have argued on critical grounds that the Qur'an as we have it substantially goes back to Muhammad and question the idea of 'Uthman's compilation.

These various revisionist views are not accepted by most Western scholars, much less by Muslims, but they have had some influence and have to be taken seriously. For the purposes of this book, however, it will usually be appropriate to assume that the Qur'an is at least from Muhammad.

References

Carlyle, Thomas (1910) *On Heroes and Hero Worship*, London: Ward, Lock & Co. First published 1841 under the title *Heroes, Hero Worship and the Heroic in History*.

Lester, Toby (1999) "What Is the Koran?" *The Atlantic Monthly* 283/1 (January 1999): 43 (passim). Also online: http://www.theatlantic.com/doc/199901/koran (accessed 17 August 2013).

Nelson, Kristina (1985) *The Art of Reciting the Qur'an*, Austin, TX: University of Texas Press.

Nicholson, R.A. (ed.) (1950) *Rumi, Poet and Mystic*, London: Allen and Unwin.

——— (1969) *A Literary History of the Arabs*, Cambridge: Cambridge University Press, first edition, 1907.

Watt, W. Montgomery (1956) *Muhammad at Medina*, Oxford: Clarendon Press.

——— (1970) *Bell's Introduction to the Qur'an*, Edinburgh: Edinburgh University Press.

Discussion Questions

1. How does the Qur'an depict God? What are the most common epithets of God?
2. The Qur'an is believed to be a literary miracle, not a human-authored text, and to have a beneficial effect when recited even if meaning is not intelligible. What is the evidence, if any, of this Islamic belief?
3. The most important requirement for humans is faith. Absolute submission to Allah is the most important Muslim virtue. Do you think faith is the supreme human virtue?
4. How do you think the five pillars of the Islam—formula of witness, prayer, fasting during *Ramadan*, offering, pilgrimage to Mecca—support the Islamic faith?
5. What do you think makes Islam the second-most practiced religion with many followers around the world?

The Paradise Divide

Islam and Christianity

Robert Pogue Harrison

It is worthwhile to cite one more passage from Tournier's novel *Gemini*, where one of the narrators, pondering the wisdom of Japanese gardens, contrasts the Eastern cult of serenity with our Western courting of stress, tumult, and danger. Here is what he says:

> The balance which the Japanese had created between human and cosmic space, these gardens situated at their point of contact, constituted a wiser, more ordered undertaking in which failures were fewer—theoretically even impossible. This balance—which is called serenity when it wears a human face—seems to me, in fact, to be the fundamental value of Eastern religion and philosophy. It is extraordinary that this idea of serenity should have so small a place in the Christian world. The story of Jesus is full of crying, weeping and sudden dramas. The religions that have sprung from it have wrapped themselves in a dramatic atmosphere which makes serenity look lukewarm, like indifference or even stupidity. The failure and discrediting of Madame Guyon's quietism in the seventeenth century provides a good illustration of Western contempt for all values that do not relate to action, energy and emotional tension.... The forty-five-foot-high bronze figure [of the Buddha statue in Kamakura], standing in the middle of a wonderful park, radiates gentleness, protective power and lucid intelligence.... Children laugh and play in the Founder's shadow. Whole families have themselves photographed in front of him. Who would ever think of having his picture taken in front of Christ crucified? (Tournier, 379–80)

For the cultural historian, Tournier's remarks are astonishingly perceptive. Peace and quietude have never been dominant ideals in Western culture, whether in ancient times, Christian times, or modern times. The only notable exception to the long tradition of Western contempt for serenity is Epicureanism, although one could say that even Epicureanism was at bottom a polemical rather than a peaceful philosophy (much of its energies went into denouncing the Platonists, for example, and vying with rival philosophies). Where does it come from, this hypertension of the West—this inability of ours to sit still, as if stillness were a prelude to death rather than beatitude?

Modernity has no doubt exasperated our disquiet, has even rendered it pathological, but the roots of this condition lie deep in the premodern past. No one will deny that there is a strong monastic strain in Christian spirituality, with its silent cloisters of contemplation, yet Tournier is onto something essential when he points to the tumultuous *drama* of the Christian narrative. If Christianity is part of the history and etiology of Western restlessness, as I believe it is, it is because of its "unquiet heart," as Saint Augustine called it, which finds no repose until it reaches some impossible place outside of space and time where God, in a way that is never fully explained, finally puts an end to its otherwise endless yearnings. No matter how post-Christian we may have become in the West, the unquiet heart of the Christian past still agitates inside us.

Our spiritual restlessness marks one the great divides not only between Eastern and Western philosophies, as Tournier claims, but between Christianity and Islam as well. This is not to suggest that Islam and Buddhism, for example, are on one side of the divide and Christianity on the other. The divide between the former two religions is no doubt as great as the one between Islam and Christianity, yet in this chapter my intention is to focus exclusively on the latter, and to do so from a very specific point of view: the two religions' visions of paradise. I believe that by comparing and contrasting these respective visions, one can reveal the true depth and extent of the divide that separates the two traditions. While one could of course stress the elements held in common by Islam and Christianity, what interests me here the most are the differences.

For someone acquainted with the Hebrew and Christian scriptures, there is much in the Qur'an that is familiar, to be sure, yet a striking aspect of the Qur'an that distinguishes it from its predecessors is its abundant references to the afterlife, as well as its vivid descriptions of the delights and rewards that the righteous may expect in paradise. Astonishingly enough, there are no explicit mentions of paradise in the Hebrew Bible. In the New Testament—and this despite an obsession with the afterlife in Christian theology, poetry, and iconography—there are extremely few, mostly fragmentary, references to paradise. Where the Hebrew Bible remains largely silent on the topic and the Christian Bible remains vague and reticent, the Qur'an does not shrink from evoking time and again both the agonies of hell and the pleasures of paradise.

Another significant difference between Islam and Christianity is the fact that Islam boldly identifies paradise with the Garden of Eden. Indeed, in Islam the two poles of the afterlife are hell and the earthly paradise. In the Christian afterlife, by contrast, Eden is a kind of halfway place between hell and heaven, insofar as the Christian abode of the blessed is not an earthly but a heavenly paradise. Much is at stake in this distinction, not only theologically but culturally, and in the pages that follow I will try to show that a religion that points to a celestial paradise is far more restless in its soul than one that envisions Eden as the ultimate dwelling place of the blessed.

If Islam is indeed a "religion of peace," as its defenders keep insisting, it's not so much because it rejects war (the history of the Islamic world belies any such proposition, as does the history of Christendom) but because its paradise is a place of repose, where the righteous "shall be lodged in peace together amidst gardens and fountains." It is to this preexisting Eden of serenity, abundance, and harmony with the cosmic order that the faithful shall come after death: "They shall enter the gardens of Eden, together with the righteous among their fathers, their wives, and their descendants. From every gate the angels will come to them, saying: 'Peace be to you for all that you have steadfastly endured. Blessed is the reward of Paradise'" (13:21–24). It is difficult for us in the West to understand how the religion in whose name so much violence is unleashed these days can have peace as its highest ideal. Even more challenging is to fathom how *the demand for peacefulness* in Islam might be behind the great upheavals. One of the major challenges we face in this regard is the fact that in the West we are driven by desires very different from the desire for peace. That difficulty is compounded by our naive assumption that the desires that drive us are universally shared, whereas they are in fact anything but universal in nature. One day we will hopefully overcome this limitation and realize that it is not so much our modern Western values (freedom, democracy, gender equality, etc.) but rather the unconstrained frenzy of the West—our relentless demand for action, change, innovation, intervention, and a systematic transgression of limits—that offends the very core of Islam in the eyes of the extremists. Where paradise is imagined as a garden of perfect tranquillity, our incurable Western agitation takes on a diabolical quality.

One of the problems that confront a non-Muslim reader of the Qur'an (I do not presume to speak for Islam's adherents) is how to interpret its beautifully sensuous descriptions of Eden. In the book's first evocation of the earthly paradise, it seems that Eden is indeed a place of inward grace and spiritual peace: "Theirs shall be gardens watered by running streams, where they shall dwell forever: spouses of perfect chastity, and grace from God" (3:16–17). Yet in the vast majority of subsequent passages about the earthly paradise, it is difficult if not impossible to read the language of fruits, fountains, virgins, and silk as merely symbolic or figurative, if only because the endless repetition of the same motifs places a heavy emphasis on the literal referent as the true substance of God's gift to the faithful. Here are some examples:

> As for the righteous, they shall be lodged in peace together amidst gardens and fountains, arrayed in rich silks and fine brocade. Yes, and we shall wed them to dark-eyed houris. Secure against all ills, they shall call for every kind of fruit; and, having died once, they shall die no more. (44:45–57)
>
> They shall recline on jeweled couches face to face, and there shall wait on them immortal youths with bowls and ewers and a cup of purest wine (that will neither pain their heads nor take away their reason); with fruits of their own choice and flesh of fowls that they relish. And theirs shall be the dark-eyed houris, chaste as hidden pearls: a guerdon for their deeds.

There they shall hear no idle talk, no sinful speech, but only the greeting, "Peace! Peace!" (56:19–26)

> But the true servants of God shall be well provided for, feasting on fruits, and honored in the gardens of delight. Reclining face to face upon soft couches, they shall be served with a goblet filled at a gushing fountain, white, and delicious to those who drink it. It will neither dull their senses nor befuddle them. They shall sit with bashful, dark-eyed virgins, as chaste as the sheltered eggs of ostriches. (37:46–49)

> Theirs shall be gardens and vineyards, and high-bosomed maidens for companions: a truly overflowing cup. (78:31)

> God will deliver them from the evil of that day, and make their faces shine with joy. He will reward them for their steadfastness with Paradise and robes of silk. Reclining there upon soft couches, they shall feel neither the scorching heat nor the biting cold. Trees will spread their shade around them, and fruits will hang in clusters over them. (76:10–14)

Even in translation these passages, taken from different sections of the Qur'an, convey the incantatory effect of the Qur'an's descriptions of paradise. Time and again the book evokes the rewards that await the faithful in reiterative verses whose exquisite musicality gives the reader a foretaste, as it were, of the sensuous enchantments of Eden. The effect is mesmerizing. We in the rain-abundant modern West may fail to appreciate the meaning of fountains in a waterless place, the meaning of green in a desert, the meaning of rich clothing and physical comfort under the intense sun of the Middle East. And certainly this paradise seems made for men rather than women: it seems to represent a particular male fantasy of satisfied appetites, where the houris are of the same ontological order as fruits and ostrich eggs. The Westerner who knows little about Islam is immediately inclined to wonder where Islamic women go after death—what sorts of rewards await *them*? A fruitless speculation, no doubt, but an irresistible one nonetheless. The Qur'an calls on the believer to trust God's infinite wisdom, even when—or especially when—it leaves certain questions unanswered.

Certainly such passages as those cited above confirm the *terrestrial* quality of the Islamic paradise. The garden is a place where no material or sensuous pleasure is denied. Fruits, soft couches, dark-eyed virgins, and gushing fountains are ready at hand, immediately available, ready for endless consumption. In short, Islam is not about the denial, repression, or sublimation of desire, as some believe; it is all about pleasure's postponement to the afterlife. Earthly life calls not so much for self-overcoming or the struggles of moral reformation; it calls rather for patience. Eden is where abeyance will give way to gratification, where waiting will give way to having, where the desert will give way to the garden. If death is a welcomed prospect for so many would-be Islamic jihadists, it is because death marks the end of deferral and the beginning of delectation. Or so they believe.

The verses cited above suggest, if not confirm, that the Islamic paradise is a place where enjoyment and repose reinforce one another rather than work against one another. An apt figure or image of this synergy between enjoyment and repose is the Edenic tree whose fruits hang in clusters over the blessed, who recline in its shade. In the West, by contrast, a veritable *gaudium* is almost antithetical to any homeostatic state of repose, as we will see shortly.

I have raised the question whether the language in which the Qur'an articulates its vision of the afterlife is to be understood literally or in some other more figurative or spiritual way. My comments so far—which are those of a lay reader—favor a literalistic interpretation of the text's figures of speech (fruits, rivers, virgins, reclining couches, etc.). I tend in this literal direction not because I wish to exclude a figurative interpretation, à la Sufism, but because I believe the Qur'an explicitly warns its readers not to doubt the veracity of its letter. Unlike the inscrutable and often unreliable God of both the Hebrew and Christian scriptures, the God of the Qur'an is absolutely trustworthy. He does not play games with his servants. He does not promise one thing and deliver another. He does not remain silent or absent at the most critical moments (Jesus on the cross, for example). He is a lucid, fair, and unwhimsical God. This is especially the case when it comes to the promises he makes to the faithful about the rewards they may look forward to in paradise. At least that how I interpret the insistent reiteration of the phrase "Which of your Lord's blessings would you deny?" in the following passage:

But for those that fear the majesty of their Lord there are two gardens (which of your Lord's blessings would you deny?) planted with shady trees. Which of your Lord's blessings would you deny?

Each is watered by a flowing spring. Which of your Lord's blessings would you deny?

Each bears every kind of fruit in pairs. Which of your Lord's blessings would you deny?

They shall recline on couches lined with thick brocade, and within reach will hang the fruits of both gardens. Which of your Lord's blessings would you deny?

Therein are bashful virgins whom neither man nor jinnee will have touched before. Which of your Lord's blessings would you deny?

Virgins as fair as corals and rubies. Which of your Lord's blessings would you deny?

Shall the reward of goodness be anything but good? Which of your Lord's blessings would you deny?

And beside these there shall be two other gardens (which of your Lord's blessings would you deny?) of darkest green. Which of your Lord's blessings would you deny?

A gushing fountain shall flow in each. Which of your Lord's blessings would you deny?

Each planted with fruit trees, the palm and the pomegranate. Which of your Lord's blessings would you deny?

In each there shall be virgins chaste and fair. Which of your Lord's blessings would you deny?

Dark-eyed virgins sheltered in their tents (which of your Lord's blessings would you deny?) whom neither man nor jinnee will have touched before. Which of your Lord's blessings would you deny?

They shall recline on green cushions and fine carpets. Which of your Lord's blessings would you deny? (55:49–70)

Who would deny that these are literal promises and not just sensuous images of abstract, disembodied blessings? Would God dare to say to the faithful, upon their entry into the afterlife, "That is not what I meant, that is not what I meant at all"? In the final analysis, the very real yet abstract gardens of Islamic art seem far more chaste in their symbolic spirituality than the imaginary carnal plenitude of the Qur'an's earthly paradise (see appendix 4).

By the same token, there is no denying the *basso continuo* of chastity, sobriety, and spiritual peace in these same passages. Those who say that the rewards promised by the Qur'an have *only* a literal referent are probably as mistaken as those who would see them as purely figurative. This fault line between the sensual and the spiritual, between the literal and the metaphorical, between the sign and its referent runs straight through the gardens of paradise described by the Qur'an. Or perhaps it is not a fault line at all but rather a harmonization of possible contradictions. Gardens after all are never either merely literal or figurative but always both one and the other.

Certainly the same ambiguity (between the literal and figurative) pervades the whole concept of jihad, about which so much is made today. Does it mean a literal holy war against the enemies of Islam, or does it mean rather the inward moral struggle of the soul to attain self-mastery? Perhaps every great religion draws its energy from the tension it creates between the literal and metaphorical poles of its proclamation. If Islam has given us some of the most beautiful, formal, and serene gardens in the world, it is no doubt thanks to the way their designers brought that tension into sublime harmony—the harmony between spiritual abstraction on the one hand and radiant sensuality on the other, or between the beauty of form and its contemplative content. Perhaps that fusion is what gives those gardens their foretaste of things to come, or not to come, as the case may be (see appendix 4).

It is difficult to compare the Islamic vision of paradise with the Christian vision, for as I mentioned earlier, the Christian scriptures, unlike the Qur'an, offer only scant allusions to, and even fewer images of, the kingdom of God. Beatitude in the Christian scheme of things is an altogether enigmatic, elusive, almost unimaginable state, precisely because the Christian heaven is not an earthly but a celestial paradise that by definition defies representation. But even calling it a "celestial paradise" is saying too much, for it is not clear whether the kingdom of God is located in the celestial heavens at all, except by analogy. It could be all around us, or it could be beyond the universe of space and time altogether. It could be in one's inward and invisible heart or it could be in one's resurrected body. To dwell in the presence of the Lord in heaven—how does one describe something as vague as that except through generic evocations of radiant luminosity and musical harmonies?

In the Christian tradition there is only one person who dared undertake an extended representation of the Christian paradise, and that person was Dante. Dante's *Paradiso* is the most heroic work of literature ever written—heroic because the poet from the start is fully aware of the impossibility of his task, yet he undertakes it nonetheless, without ever shrinking from the challenges of representing the unrepresentable, saying the unsayable, imagining the unimaginable. Thus it is to that exceptional yet quintessentially Christian canticle of the *Divine Comedy* that we will now turn our attention, in order to gauge just how much is at stake in the difference between a religion that envisions paradise as an earthly garden and one that envisions it as a transterrestrial heaven.

When one considers the "plot" of the *Divine Comedy*, the journey undertaken by Dante's pilgrim should, by all narrative rights, end in the Garden of Eden at the top of the mountain of Purgatory. The journey begins in a state of sin (the dark wood of canto 1). The pilgrim descends through the nine circles of Hell (in so doing he sees the consequences of sin). He then climbs the seven terraces of Purgatory (in so doing he understands the causes of sin, namely misdirected love). By the time he passes through the ring of fire and enters Eden, he is poised to shed his human guilt and recover his original innocence. As Virgil tells him, his once fallible will (the seat of sin) is now *libero, dritto e sano*, free, straight, and sound. All that was lost through the fall has now been regained. End of story. But we know that the story does not end there. Eden is not a destination but only a temporary stop on the way to Paradise. "Qui tu sarai con me poco tempo silvano" (Here you will be a forester for a little while with me), says Beatrice to Dante in Eden. After spending only a few hours in Eden, Dante ascends to the celestial spheres with Beatrice, leaving the garden behind. Why?

Because it seems that Dante's will, even after its complete reformation, is not really at home in the everlasting peace of the earthly paradise. There is a desire in that Christian will of his which remains unrequited. It is a desire for ecstasy, not serenity; for self-transcendence, not self-possession; for heaven, not Eden. As Dante depicts it, beatitude is not a homeostatic state of reconciliation but a dynamic, intoxicating process of self-surpassing. Where the will demands ecstasy, the self-contained happiness of Eden cannot satisfy it. In Eden the "new wine" dies on the vine. Indeed, the realm of Paradise in *Dante's Divine* Comedy is so beyond the human and the earthly, so indescribable in its bliss, that its beatitude can be understood only as rapture. Dante in fact tells his reader in the first canto of *Paradiso* that the region he is now entering is altogether ecstatic in nature—that is, it stands outside the poem's capacity to represent it in word, image, or concept. If Dante nonetheless proceeds to "write paradise," he does so in a highly charged language of fervor, ardor, inebriation, and self-transcending desire. Anyone who has read *Paradiso* can attest to the fact that its narrative register is altogether preorgasmic and that there is intensification of the rhetoric of ecstasy as the journey proceeds through the celestial spheres.

The Qur'an may speak of virgins "fair as corals and rubies" and "chaste as hidden pearls" or "the sheltered eggs of ostriches," but the *mood* of Eden in the Qur'an is altogether reposeful, free from the violent compulsion of desire, while in Dante's *Paradiso* the mood is one of heightened sexual excitement. Consider, for example, the erotic intensity of the imagery and language in the following verses—especially in the words uttered by Beatrice to her pilgrim lover in the last tercet. The two of them are gazing at a swarm of angels who, like bees in a flower bed, enter and exit the great river of light in *Paradiso* 30:

> E vidi lume in forma di rivera
> fulvida di fulgore, intra due rive
> dipinte di mirabil primavera.

Di tal fiumana uscian faville vive,
e d'ogni parte si mettien ne' fiori,
quasi rubin che oro circumscrive;
poi, come inebriati da li odori,
riprofondava sé nel miro gurge,
e s'una intrava, un'altra n'uscia fori.

"L'alto disio che mo t'infiamma e urge,
d'aver notizia di ciò che tu vei,
tanto mi piace più quanto turge ..."

(*Paradiso* 30.61–72)

And I saw light that took a river's form—
light flashing, reddish-gold, between two banks
painted with wonderful spring flowerings.

Out of that stream there issued living sparks,
which settled on the flowers on all sides,
like rubies set in gold; and then, as if
intoxicated with the odors, they
again plunged into the amazing flood:
as one spark sank, another spark emerged.

"The high desire that now inflames and incites
you to grasp mentally the things you see,
pleases me more as it swells more ..."

No English translation can properly convey the erectile ardor of the original, where visionary ecstasy before the river of light takes on an explicitly tumescent character in the verbs *urge* and *turge*. In Dante's paradise, *all* of the saints (and not only the pilgrim) find their joy in a breathless transport. Their gaze is forever directed toward an ever-higher principle of transcendence; they yearn for things to come (the resurrection of their bodies, for instance, or Christ's appearance within their midst). While Dante looks into Beatrice's eyes, her eyes always look into the beyond. In this paradise the saints are projected beyond themselves, in anticipation of something imminent but still out of reach. Not so in the earthly paradise of the Qur'an, where the righteous recline on couches face to face and where fruits hang overhead, ready for the picking. If Islam's paradise is a place of contentment, Dante's is a place of desire's intensified expectation.

The rapture of Dante's heaven is as removed as can be from the placid tranquillity of Eden, either as Dante describes it at the end of *Purgatory* 27 or as the Qur'an describes it in the passages quoted earlier. The *Paradiso's* "dramatic atmosphere" indeed seems to share in that "western contempt for all values that do not relate to action, energy and emotional tension," to recall the words of Tournier quoted at the beginning of this chapter. There is no question that the *Paradiso's* atmosphere is thoroughly dramatic. The pilgrim's experience in celestial spheres consists of a continuous series of excesses, blackouts, sensorial overloads, and orgasmic releases, all culminating in the great fulmination of the last canto's face-to-face vision of God. The pilgrim's "doors of perception" are constantly being cleansed, expanding ever wider with each new planetary sphere, until they are blown open altogether by the infinite. Meanwhile the poet whose task it is to describe this ecstatic experience continues to struggle against impossible odds. From start to finish, *Paradiso* totters on the brink of disaster. As the poem reaches higher and higher, the possibility of failure—failure to describe the indescribable—becomes more and more imminent. This extremely high risk of failure gives the canticle an almost unbearable tension and drama, of the sort we in the West have come to expect from our greatest poets. Nor would anything less satisfy us.

I am not suggesting that the antagonism between Islamic extremism and Western modernity can be traced back to the fact that in the Christian imaginary Eden lies somewhere between the turmoil of history and the rapture of heaven, while in Islam paradise is envisioned as Eden. Yet one could say that there is at least something symptomatic about Dante's impatience with Eden, just as there is something *symptomatic* about the televangelist's intoxication with the kingdom of God on Sunday mornings. It reveals the existence of a craving in the Western soul that cannot be fulfilled by the ideal of serenity or the self-contained contentment of Eden.

In the West we tend to speak of "Islamic extremism" as if the West were the measure of moderation. Yet the paradox is that Islamic extremists long for a garden where all is moderation and temperance, while we in the modern West are driven by the need to constantly act, contend, achieve, overcome, transform, and revolutionize—in other words, we are driven by compulsions that assume any number of extreme manifestations. What philosophy has traditionally claimed about happiness as the goal of all human action and aspiration is at best only a half-truth. We in the West may hanker for happiness, as long as it eludes us, but somewhere deep inside of us the prospect of happiness—like that of Eden—fills us with dread. This spiritual restlessness is the source of many virtues, as well as many vices, and the least one can say about the modern era that swept away Dante's medieval world order without surrendering its unquiet heart is that it has rendered our spiritual restlessness far more virulent—and far more destructive—in nature, as we will see in what follows.

Works Cited

Dante Alighieri. *The Divine Comedy of Dante Alighieri*, vol. 1, *Inferno*. Translated by Robert M. Durling and Ronald L. Martinez. Oxford: Oxford University Press, 1993.

———. *The Divine Comedy of Dante Alighieri*, vol. 2, *Purgatorio*. Translated by Robert M. Durling and Ronald L. Martinez. Oxford: Oxford University Press, 2004.

———. *Paradiso*. Translated by Allen Mandelbaum. New York: Bantam, 1986.

Tournier, Michel. *Gemini*. Translated by Anne Carter. Garden City, NY: Doubleday, 1981.

Discussion Questions

1. How does Harrison compare the visions of paradise between Christianity and Islam? Why is Christianity lacking in descriptions of the afterlife in more detail?
2. How does Dante in the *Divine Comedy* treat heaven, according to Harrison?
3. According to Harrison, Eden in Christianity is a kind of halfway between hell and heaven, with heaven far from earthly delight. Why is the eventual human abode not the Eden but a heavenly paradise, if it's the Eden that human ancestors come from?
4. Harrison sees that Christian heaven is not an earthly but a celestial paradise that defies representation. Is it worth living the whole human life with the heavenly life in view, when we do not even know what the heaven will be like?
5. How free can humans be from the Christian perspective? What is valuable about the capacity to choose between faith and disobedience when humans are doomed to be in a restless moral battleground with little hope of repose and tranquility?

UNIT II

MAKING SENSE OF ART

In the fifth chapter, a brief excerpt from Sophocles' *Antigone* was presented to provide readers with the sense in which the ancient Greek drama offers a philosophical dialogue on a par with the critical spirit of Socrates. In the sixth chapter, Richard Wollheim discusses, in a deeply enchanting style, the way in which a painting can have a metaphoric meaning by being a metaphor of body or corporeality, with Titian as a prime example. In the seventh chapter, Larry Shiner describes a social context throughout the nineteenth century in which music gained an autonomous and distinct status as a fine art and became a form of leisure for the ascending bourgeoisie class. In the eighth chapter, Alice Kaplan describes the features of the narrative from the first chapter of Camus' *The Stranger* that highlights the theme of the absurd.

Antigone

Sophocles; trans. David Grene and Richmond Lattimore

GUARD

> This is the woman who has done the deed.
> We caught her at the burying. Where's the king? 385

> *(Enter Creon from the palace.)*

CHORUS LEADER

> Back from the house again just when he's needed.

CREON

> What must I measure up to? What has happened?

GUARD

> Lord, one should never swear off anything.
> Afterthought makes the first resolve a liar.
> I could have vowed I wouldn't come back here 390
> after your threats, after the storm I faced.
> But joy that comes beyond the wildest hope
> is bigger than all other pleasure known.
> I'm here, though I swore not to be, and bring 395
> this girl, We caught her burying the dead.

This time we didn't need to shake the lots;
mine was the luck, all mine.
So now, lord, take her, you, and question her
and prove her as you will. But I am free.
And I deserve full clearance on this charge.   400

CREON

Explain the circumstance of the arrest.

GUARD

She was burying the man. You have it all.

CREON

Is this the truth? And do you grasp its meaning?

GUARD

I saw her burying the very corpse
you had forbidden. Is this adequate?   405

CREON

How was she caught and taken in the act?

GUARD

It was like this: when we got back again
struck with those dreadful threatenings of yours,
we swept away the dust that hid the corpse.   410
We stripped it back to slimy nakedness.
And then we sat to windward on the hill
so as to dodge the smell.
We poked each other up with growling threats
if anyone was careless of his work.
For some time this went on, till it was noon.   415
The sun was high and hot. Then from the earth
up rose a dusty whirlwind to the sky,
filling the plain, smearing the forest leaves,

clogging the upper air. We shut our eyes,   420
sat and endured the plague the gods had sent.
Then the storm left us after a long time.
We saw the girl. She cried the sharp and shrill
cry of a bitter bird which sees the nest
bare where the young birds lay.   425
So this same girl, seeing the body stripped,
cried with great groanings, called out dreadful curses
upon the people who had done the deed.
Soon in her hands she brought the thirsty dust,
and holding high a pitcher of wrought bronze   430
she poured the three libations for the dead.
We saw this and rushed down. We trapped her fast;
and she was calm. We taxed her with the deeds
both past and present. Nothing was denied.   435
And I was glad, and yet I took it hard.
One's own escape from trouble makes one glad;
but bringing friends to trouble is hard grief.
Still, I care less for all these second thoughts
than for the fact that I myself am safe.   440

CREON

You there, whose head is drooping to the ground,
do you admit this, or deny you did it?

ANTIGONE

I say I did it and I don't deny it.

CREON   *(To the Guard.)*

Take yourself off wherever you wish to go
free of a heavy charge.   445

                                                             (To Antigone.)

You—tell me not at length but in a word.
You knew the order not to do this thing?

ANTIGONE

I knew—of course I knew. The word was plain.

CREON

And still you dared to overstep these laws?

ANTIGONE

For me it was not Zeus who made that order. 450
Nor did that Justice who lives with the gods below
mark out such laws to hold among mankind.
Nor did I think your orders were so strong
that you, a mortal man, could overrun
the gods' unwritten and unfailing laws. 455
Not now, nor yesterday's, they always live,
and no one knows their origin in time.
So not through fear of any man's proud spirit
would I be likely to neglect these laws,
and draw on myself the gods' sure punishment.
    I knew that I must die—how could I not?— 460
even without your edict. If I die
before my time, I say it is a gain.
Who lives in sorrows many as are mine
how shall he not be glad to gain his death?
And so, for me to meet this fate's no grief. 465
But if I left that corpse, my mother's son,
dead and unburied I'd have cause to grieve
as now I grieve not.
And if you think my acts are foolishness
the foolishness may be in a fool's eye. 470

CHORUS LEADER

The girl is fierce. She's her father's child.
She cannot yield to trouble; nor could he.

CREON

These rigid spirits are the first to fall.
The strongest iron, hardened in the fire, 475
most often ends in scraps and shatterings.
Small curbs bring raging horses back to terms:
enslaved to his neighbor, who can think of pride?
This girl was expert in her insolence 480

when she broke bounds beyond established law.
Once she had done it, insolence the second,
to boast her doing, and to laugh in it.
I am no man and she the man instead
if she can have this conquest without pain.   485
She is my sister's child, but were she child
of closer kin than any at my hearth,
she and her sister should not so escape
a dreadful death, I charge Ismene too.
She shared the planning of this burial.   490
Call her outside, I saw her in the house,
maddened, no longer mistress of herself.
The sly intent betrays itself sometimes
before the secret plotters work their wrong.
I hate it too when someone caught in crime   495
then wants to make it seem a lovely thing.

ANTIGONE

Do you want more than my arrest and death?

CREON

No more than that. For that is all I need.

ANTIGONE

Why are you waiting? Nothing that you say
fits with my thought. I pray it never will.   500
Nor will you ever like to hear my words.
And yet what greater glory could I find
than giving my own brother funeral?
All these would say that they approved my act
did fear not mute them.   505
A king is fortunate in many ways,
and most, that he can act and speak at will.

CREON

None of these others see the case this way.

ANTIGONE

They see, and do not say. You have them cowed.

CREON

And you are not ashamed to think alone?   510

ANTIGONE

It is no shame to serve blood relatives.

CREON

Was not he who died on the other side your brother?

ANTIGONE

Full brother, on both sides, my parents' child.

CREON

Your act of grace, in his regard, is crime.

ANTIGONE

The corpse below would never say it was.   515

CREON

When you honor him and the criminal just alike?

ANTIGONE

It was a brother, not a slave, who died.

CREON

Died to destroy this land the other guarded.

ANTIGONE

Death yearns for equal law for all the dead.

CREON

Not that the good and bad draw equal shares.   520

ANTIGONE

Who knows but this is holiness below?

CREON

Never is the enemy, even in death, a friend.

ANTIGONE

I cannot share in hatred, but in love.

CREON

Then go down there, if you must love, and love
the dead. No woman rules me while I live.   525

(Ismene is brought from the palace under guard.)

CHORUS [*chanting*]

Look there! Ismene is coming out.
She loves her sister and mourns,
with clouded brow and bloodied cheeks,
tears on her lovely face.   530

CREON

You, lurking like a viper in the house,
who sucked me dry, while I raised unawares
a twin destruction planned against the throne.
Now tell me, do you say you shared this deed?
Or will you swear you didn't even know?   535

ISMENE

I did the deed if she agrees I did.
I am accessory and share the blame.

ANTIGONE

> Justice will not allow this, You did not
> wish for a part, nor did I give you one.

ISMENE

> You are in trouble, and I'm not ashamed   540
> to sail beside you into suffering.

ANTIGONE

> Death and the dead, they know whose act it was.
> I cannot love a friend whose love's mere words.

ISMENE

> Sister, I pray, don't fence me out from honor,
> from death with you, and honor done the dead.   545

ANTIGONE

> Don't die along with me, nor make your own
> that which you did not do. My death's enough.

ISMENE

> When you are gone what life can I desire?

ANTIGONE

> Love Creon. He's your kinsman and your care.

ISMENE

> Why hurt me, when it does yourself no good?   550

ANTIGONE

> I also suffer, when I laugh at you.

ISMENE

What further service can I do you now?

ANTIGONE

To save yourself. I shall not envy you.

ISMENE

Alas for me. Am I outside your fate?

ANTIGONE

Yes. For you chose to live when I chose death.   555

ISMENE

At least I was not silent. You were warned.

ANTIGONE

Some will have thought you wiser. Some will not.

ISMENE

And yet the blame is equal for us both.

ANTIGONE

Take heart. You live. My life died long ago.
And that has made me fit to help the dead.   560

CREON

One of these girls has shown her lack of sense
just now. The other had it from her birth.

ISMENE

Yes, king. When people fall in deep distress
their native sense departs, and will not stay.

CREON

You chose your mind's distraction when you chose   565
to work out wickedness with this wicked girl.

ISMENE

What life is there for me to live without her?

CREON

Don't speak of her. For she is here no more.

ISMENE

But will you kill your own son's promised bride?

CREON

Oh, there are other furrows for his plough.

ISMENE

But where the closeness that has bound these two?   570

CREON

Not for my sons will I choose wicked wives.

ISMENE°

Dear Haemon, your father robs you of your rights.

CREON

You and your marriage trouble me too much.

ISMENE

You will take away his bride from your own son?

CREON

Yes. Death will help me break this marriage off.   575

CHORUS LEADER

It seems determined that the girl must die.

CREON

You helped determine it. Now, no delay!
Slaves, take them in. They must be women now.
No more free running.
Even the bold will flee when they see Death   580
drawing in close enough to end their life.

(Antigone and Ismene are taken inside.)

CHORUS [*singing*]

STROPHE A

Fortunate they whose lives have no taste of pain.
For those whose house is shaken by the gods   585
escape no kind of doom. It extends to all the kin
like the wave that comes when the winds of Thrace
run over the dark of the sea.
The black sand of the bottom is brought from the depth;   590
the beaten cliffs sound back with a hollow cry.

ANTISTROPHE A

Ancient the sorrow of Labdacus' house, I know.
Dead men's grief comes back, and falls on grief.   595
No generation can free the next.
One of the gods will strike. There is no escape.
So now the light goes out
for the house of Oedipus, while the bloody knife   600
cuts the remaining root,° in folly and the mind's fury.

STROPHE B

What transgression of man, O Zeus, can bind your power?
Not sleep can destroy it who governs all,°   606
nor the weariless months the gods have set. Unaged in time
monarch you rule in Olympus' gleaming light.   610
Near time, far future, and the past,
one law controls them all:
any greatness in human life brings doom.

ANTISTROPHE B

Wandering hope brings help to many men.
But others she tricks with giddy loves,   616
and her quarry knows nothing until he has walked into flame.
Word of wisdom it was when someone said,   620
"The bad looks like the good
to him a god would doom."
Only briefly is that one free from doom.   625

                                  (Haemon enters from the side.)

[*chanting*]
Here is Haemon, your one surviving son.
Does he come in grief at the fate of his bride,
in pain that he's tricked of his wedding?   630

CREON

Soon we shall know more than a seer could tell us.
Son, have you heard the vote condemned your bride?
And are you here, maddened against your father,
or are we friends, whatever I may do?

HAEMON

My father, I am yours. You keep me straight   635
with your good judgment, which I shall ever follow.
Nor shall a marriage count for more with me
than your kind leading.

CREON

There's my good boy. So should you hold at heart

and stand behind your father all the way.   640
It is for this men pray they may beget
households of dutiful obedient sons,
who share alike in punishing enemies,
and give due honor to their father's friends.
Whoever breeds a child that will not help,   645
what has he sown but trouble for himself,
and for his enemies laughter full and free?
Son, do not let your lust mislead your mind,
all for a woman's sake, for well you know
how cold the thing he takes into his arms   650
who has a wicked woman for his wife.
What deeper wound than a loved one who is evil?
Oh spit her forth forever, as your foe.
Let the girl marry somebody in Hades,
Since I have caught her in the open act,   655
the only one in town who disobeyed,
I shall not now proclaim myself a liar,
but kill her. Let her sing her song of Zeus
the guardian of blood kin.
If I allow disorder in my house
I'd surely have to license it abroad.   660
A man who deals in fairness with his own,
he can make manifest justice in the state.
But he who crosses law, or forces it,
or hopes to dictate orders to the rulers,
shall never have a word of praise from me.   665
The man the state has put in place must have
obedient hearing to his least command
when it is right, and even when it's not.
He who accepts this teaching I can trust,
ruler, or ruled, to function in his place,
to stand his ground even in the storm of spears,   670
a comrade to trust in battle at one's side.
There is no greater wrong than disobedience.
This ruins cities, this tears down our homes,
this breaks the battlefront in panic-rout.
If men live decently it is because
obedience saves their very lives for them.   675
So I must guard the men who yield to order,
not let myself be beaten by a woman.

Better, if it must happen, that a man
should overset me.
I won't he called weaker than womankind.   680

CHORUS LEADER

We think—unless our age is cheating us—
that what you say is sensible and right.

HAEMON

Father, the gods have given men good sense,
the highest and best possession that we have.
I couldn't find the words in which to claim   685
that there was error in your late remarks.
Yet someone else might bring some further light.
Because I am your son I must keep watch
on all men's doing where it touches you,
their speech, and most of all, their discontents.
Your presence frightens any common man   690
from saying things you would not care to hear.
But in dark corners I have heard them say
how the whole town is grieving for this girl,
unjustly doomed, if ever woman was,
to die in shame for glorious action done.   695
She would not leave her fallen, slaughtered brother
there, as he lay, unburied, for the birds
and hungry dogs to make an end of him.
Does she not truly deserve a golden prize?
This is the undercover speech in town.   700
        Father, your welfare is my greatest good.
What precious gift in life for any child
outweighs a father's fortune and good fame?
And so a father feels his children's faring.
So, do not have one mind, and one alone   705
that only your opinion can be right.
Whoever thinks that he alone is wise,
his eloquence, his mind, above the rest,
come the unfolding, it shows his emptiness.
A man, though wise, should never be ashamed   710
of learning more, and must not be too rigid.

Have you not seen the trees beside storm torrents—
the ones that bend preserve their limbs and leaves,
while the resistant perish root and branch?
And so the ship that will not slacken sail,   715
the ropes drawn tight, unyielding, overturns.
She ends the voyage with her keel on top.
No, yield your wrath, allow a change of stand.
Young as I am, if I may give advice,
I'd say it would be best if men were born   720
perfect in wisdom, but that failing this
(which often fails) it can be no dishonor
to learn from others when they speak good sense.

CHORUS LEADER

Lord, if your son has spoken to the point
you should take his lesson. He should do the same.   725
Both sides have spoken well.

CREON

At my age I'm to school my mind by his?
This boy instructor is my master, then?

Discussion Questions

1. Why is the burial of Polyneices, the dead brother of Antigone forbidden by Creon?
2. On what ground does Antigone feel justified in defying the state authority?
3. Do you agree with Haemon that a child can disobey parents when their authority does not reflect reasoned opinions?
4. What would you do if you faced a moral dilemma between personal obligation for the family and your citizenry obligation owed to the country?
5. What is an appeal of the ancient Greek tragic drama to the audience of the digital age?

Painting, Metaphor, and the Body

Titian, Bellini, De Kooning, Etc.

Richard Wollheim

A.1

In this lecture I shall consider a final way in which a painting can gain content or meaning. This is *the way of metaphor,* through which a painting gains *metaphorical meaning*. Metaphorical meaning is a case of primary meaning: that is to say, it accrues to a painting through the making of it, but not through what the making of it means to the artist.

When the way of metaphor works, and the painting acquires metaphorical meaning, there is something for which the painting becomes a metaphor or, as I shall barbarously put it, something which the painting 'metaphorizes'. And 'something' here means 'some *thing*'. It is always an object that the painting metaphorizes. In point of fact I further believe that the fundamental cases of pictorial metaphor are those where a corporeal thing is metaphorized: the painting becomes a metaphor for the body, or (at any rate) for some part of the body, or for something assimilated to the body. In some cases the painting metaphorizes both the body and something other than the body, and in other cases the painting doesn't metaphorize the body at all. But to my mind it is only in so far as the painting metaphorizes the body, with the body taken in the extended sense I have just suggested, that it uses the resources of pictorial metaphor to the full.

For this last claim about pictorial metaphor I have no direct argument, only a set of considerations which may sway the mind. However it is perfectly possible to accept in general outline the account that I shall offer of what pictorial metaphor is without accepting my claim about just what it is that is metaphorized in the fundamental cases, or indeed without accepting the claim that some cases of pictorial metaphor are fundamental and others aren't. I hope that those who can go thus far with me will.

In this lecture I shall consider only cases in which what the painting metaphorizes is the body.

2

At the core of pictorial metaphor there is a relation: a relation holding between a painting and some thing for which it is, in virtue of this relation, a metaphor. I call this relation metaphorizing, and I start with the question, What is metaphorizing?

Earlier on in these lectures I tried to explain the relations that lie at the core of the two basic forms of pictorial meaning: representation, and expression. I tried, in other words, to explain representing and expressing. And I employed the same method in each case. I looked for a certain kind of experience which a spectator can have through looking at a marked surface and which in consequence an artist can, when it is appropriate, induce in the spectator by the way he marks the surface. I did so, because in each case my hope was that the painting's capacity to produce that kind of experience could explain the relation: not single-handedly, but it could explain it in large part. The supplementary factor would always be a standard of correctness. For it is only if the experience that the spectator has is the correct one for him to entertain that it shows that the relation holds, and the standard of correctness that adjudicates this in turn goes back to what is broadly the intention of the artist. The fulfilled intention of the artist decides which, out of the experiences that a particular painting is able to produce in a spectator, is the correct one for him to have on looking at it.

So, in the case of representation, I offered to explain what representing is by reference to a kind of experience that a representational painting can produce in a spectator: that of seeing-in. My contention was that what a painting represents can be defined in terms of what a spectator can see in it, provided only that what he sees in it concurs with, and is brought about through, the artist's fulfilled intention. The spectator's experience is a determinant of the painting's representational content if he perceives the picture not only representationally but correctly.

This method of explanation recommended itself to me because it conforms to—and, if it could be carried through, would confirm—the kind of psychological account of pictorial meaning to which these lectures are committed: an account that, forswearing any except a peripheral appeal to rules, or conventions, or codes, or symbol systems, grounds pictorial meaning in psychological factors and their interrelations. Accordingly, why not use this method in the present case to try to explain the metaphoric relation, or the relation at the core of pictorial metaphor?

If we do, what explanation proposes itself?

I suggest the following: In the first place, the characteristic experience in which metaphorizing is grounded is not exclusively visual. It is triggered off by perception, and it remains a way of seeing the picture, but it is largely affective. In this respect, the experience is like that in which expressing is grounded, but it goes further in that direction.

Secondly, this affective response will draw upon emotions, sentiments, phantasies, ordinarily directed on to the object metaphorized: in the profounder cases, if I am right about them, the body. However the requirements of metaphor will not be met unless, as well as recruiting to the perception of the picture emotions, sentiments, phantasies already directed on to what it metaphorizes, the picture also encourages the development of fresh feelings. Profound pictorial metaphor modifies, deepens, intensifies, our attitude to the body.

And, thirdly, the complex experience thus aroused in response to the picture is a response to the picture as a whole, or at least to some large zone of it. It is not a piecemeal response.

Now there have been many critics and theorists of painting over the last hundred years who have recognized or stressed the importance of some sort of global or gestalt response in our perception of pictures. Most of them have done so in order to do justice to the new art of their day. But, sometimes sensitive, sometimes insensitive, their criticism has a common feature that certainly makes it irrelevant to the understanding of pictorial metaphor. For all these critics have presented the global response that they advocate as a preferential response. It is a response that is prior to other modes of perception: specifically, to representational seeing. But, whatever the importance of such a response for painting in general, the kind of experience that grounds metaphor cannot be like this. So far from being preferential, it is last in line. It comes after, and therefore can benefit from, other modes of perception. It capitalizes what they deliver and uses it as the cognitive stock which it draws upon. It does this above all with the proceeds of representational seeing.

Having identified a kind of experience or response, I shall now say that the relation of metaphorizing is exemplified when a picture correctly arouses such a response. Furthermore, what it metaphorizes is given by what the emotions, sentiments, phantasies, which the response mobilizes, are normally directed on to.

3

The question that arises is, Why do I call the kind of meaning that such an experience conveys pictorial metaphor? What is there in common between a painting that causes such an experience and that use of language exemplified when a poet says, 'Juliet is the sun,' or when a great thinker says, 'Religion is the opium of the people'?

If we isolate what, on the best understanding of the matter, are the three major features of linguistic metaphor, we shall see that these features are also exhibited by what I have called pictorial metaphor.

In the first place, linguistic metaphor does not require that the words that effect the metaphor lose their normal sense. In my examples neither 'sun' nor 'opium' means something new, and indeed reflection shows that, if these metaphors are to work, if they are to convey the life-giving quality of Juliet or the stultifying effect of religion, then the sense of the crucial words must not change. What some thinkers have pursued as the metaphorical sense of language is an unwanted fabrication. In just the same way, the representational or the expressive meaning of a metaphorical painting undergoes no change, and, again, reflection will show that, if the painting is to convey its metaphorical meaning, this must be the case.

Secondly, linguistic metaphor does not require that there is a special or pre-existent link between what the words carrying the metaphor pick out and the thing metaphorized. There does not have to be a symbolic link between Juliet and the sun, or between religion and opium. If there were, the metaphor could probably survive it, but it is likely that it would be weakened or made banal by being anticipated in this way. Similarly there doesn't have to be, say, an iconographical link between what the picture represents or what it expresses and what it metaphorizes. Pictorial metaphor too could survive such pre-existent links, though such links would tend to trivialize the metaphor. Certainly the metaphor cannot be grounded in them. There is however an exception to this principle, which is when the links are themselves metaphorical: such links can ground pictorial metaphor. I shall return to this very last point.

These first two features of metaphor, which are exhibited both by linguistic and by pictorial metaphor, reflect the essentially improvisatory character of metaphor. Indeed, given the rule-, or convention-, free nature of pictorial meaning, which is something that I have been stressing in these lectures, pictorial metaphor is doubly improvisatory. It is an improvisation upon what is already improvisatory.

Finally, the aim both of linguistic and of pictorial metaphor is to set what is metaphorized in a new light. Juliet, religion, the body—we see whatever it is afresh. Just what it is about the thing metaphorized that we are enabled to see by the light of the metaphor, or how the object looks new, will vary both in specificity and in amenability to description in language. This last point about the way in which metaphor works, to varying degrees revelatory, to varying degrees ineffable, I shall put by saying that paintings that are metaphorical metaphorize their object *under some conception of that object.*

FIGURE 6.1   William Blake, *The River of Life c. 1805,* watercolour

FIGURE 6.2   Jean-Baptiste-Siméon Chardin, *House of Cards c. 1735*

And now for the big difference between linguistic and pictorial metaphor. Linguistic metaphor illuminates what it metaphorizes by pairing it with something else. Juliet is paired with the sun for the better illumination of Juliet: religion is paired with opium for the better illumination of religion. This is the essential metaphoric strategy, which pictorial metaphor follows to the extent of pairing the object metaphorized with something other than that object. But—and this is the crucial point—in the case of painting this something is the picture itself. It is not—as linguistic metaphor might suggest—something that the picture picks out: even though the picture, at any rate normally, has to pick out something, indeed has to represent something, in order to fit itself to be a metaphor. When the way of metaphor works, what is paired with the object metaphorized is the picture as a whole. It is the picture as a whole that is the first term to the metaphoric relation, and this fully coheres with what we have seen to be the nature of the experience in which pictorial metaphorizing is grounded: that it is a response to the picture as a whole. When, in what is for me the fundamental case, the picture metaphorizes the body, I shall say that the experience that grounds this relation attributes to the picture the global property of *corporeality*. In this lecture I shall address the question, How does this happen? What is the experience of corporeality?

But, first, a distinction which may clear the air.

4

In this lecture I shall be talking about metaphorical paintings, or about paintings that are metaphors. Let me distinguish between paintings that are metaphors and paintings that have

FIGURE 6.3   Thomas Cole, *The Voyage of Life: Childhood 1842*

FIGURE 6.4   Thomas Cole, *The Voyage of Life: Youth* 1842

metaphors as their content, specifically as their textual content. Examples of this latter kind would be: a landscape by William Blake, whose textual content is, Life is a river; a domestic scene by Chardin whose textual content is, Life is a pack of cards; or the famous series of paintings by the American artist Thomas Cole, each of which has as its textual content, Life is a journey.

None of these latter paintings metaphorizes anything. The texts they contain do. The texts metaphorize life, embodied life, and what the paintings do is to represent that which the metaphors pair life with. The paintings represent a bubble, a house of cards, a journey. As we saw in Lecture IV, this representational content does not by itself guarantee that the paintings have the corresponding metaphors as their textual meaning. What is further required is that the paintings should show what the metaphors themselves meant to Blake, to Chardin, to Thomas Cole. In citing these paintings as examples of pictures which, though not themselves metaphorical, have metaphors as their textual content, I am simply assuming that this further requirement is met.

B 1.

I start with two famous paintings, which belong to Titian's first period as an artist with a formed style. Both represent pastoral scenes of great lyricism and considerable mystery. The mystery is there to be experienced, certainly not to be resolved: once we cease to find these paintings mysterious, we no longer understand them. And in both paintings Titian gives full vent to what is the main expressive theme of his whole work: human vitality—human vitality as something tied to the body, and tied in consequence at once to physical sensation and to mortality. The two paintings I have in mind are the *Concert Champêtre* (Louvre, Paris), of around 1510, still believed by some (as it was by Manet) to be by Giorgione, and the exquisite *Three Ages of Man* (collection Duke of Sutherland: on loan to the National Gallery of Scotland, Edinburgh), of about three or four years later.[1]

Both these paintings metaphorize the body in addition to representing it, and the conception under which they metaphorize it corresponds to how Titian at this time thought and felt about it: as the locus of pleasure, beauty, and death. Both paintings have corporeality, and in front of them is a good place to ask how Titian secures this effect. How *Titian* secures it: for the achievement of corporeality is best considered within the work of a particular artist. This is not because there are no common sources of corporeality. There are: but different artists are likely to draw upon these sources in such different ways as to put a common account out of the question.

It is convenient to think of the sources, the broad sources, of corporeality as three in number, and in consequence the answer to any question such as that which I ask of Titian is likely to fall into three parts, not sharply demarcated. Partly corporeality is a matter of how the picture represents what it does, and specifically of how it does this in such a way as to stir thoughts, emotions, phantasies, about the body. Partly corporeality is a matter of how such responses are then transferred to the picture itself. And partly it is a matter of how by other means, or independently of its central representational content, the picture manages to attract to itself feelings directed on to the body: I call this directly inducing corporeality. I list the three sources of corporeality in this order for a good reason. The reason is local, and it is because within the art of Titian the lion's share goes to the first source: to the way the body is represented. So powerful a sense of the body does his art generate—something that is constant under the changing conceptions of the body that his work exhibits—that, once this has been achieved, all that he needs to do is to make certain that nothing gets in the way of this aura of physicality resettling around the painting as a whole. Directly inducing corporeality, or developing it out of non-figurative, let alone non-representational, means, is less of an issue.

How then does Titian represent the body so as to give rise to this powerful sense of human vitality? His central device exploits what I have been calling twofoldness, or the way in which, when we see, say, a human body in a picture, there are two aspects, two distinct but inseparable aspects, of the experience. One aspect involves recognizing something absent, in this case a body: the other is awareness of the marked surface. Correspondingly there are two aspects to Titian's device. Recognitionally we sense that the body that we see is about to move into action: configurationally we become aware of the coloured expanse in which we see the body as something spreading or pushing outwards.[2] And—as is the case with twofoldness itself—we attend to these two effects not sequentially but simultaneously: they are twin aspects of a single, complex experience.

Titian, I have said, connects the represented body with action. That is one half of his particular route to corporeality. But, if we are to do full justice to Titian, action must be understood

FIGURE 6.5   Titian *Concert Champêtre c.* 1510

FIGURE 6.6   Titian *The Three Ages of Man* 1513–14

broadly. It must be taken to include not only behaviour, or something involving the movement of the limbs, but also, as these early pastoral paintings evince, the relaxation of the body, the sudden sagging of the limbs, in which the body also reveals its vitality. Indeed for Titian the distilled essence of action is the gaze: the probing, searching activity of the eye, seeking to gain knowledge, to express adoration, to arouse desire, to catch, to return, to elude, the gaze of the other. After what I found to say in the last lecture about the gaze, I should make clear that with Titian the gaze is not at all a secret weapon. It is, rather, the outpouring of the mind: it is a second, a naïve, voice. From the very earliest painting that we can attribute to Titian's hand, *Jacopo Pesaro presented to St Peter by Pope Alexander VI* (Musée Royal des Beaux-Arts, Antwerp), of 1506 or so, the passionate gaze is the mark of Titian's work. For Titian human vitality, along with its companion, the awareness of death, is concentrated in the soft black orb which glows under the single brushstroke with which Titian characteristically describes the curve of the eyebrow.

FIGURE 6.7   Titian *Jacopo Pesaro presented to St Peter by Pope Alexander VI* probably 1506

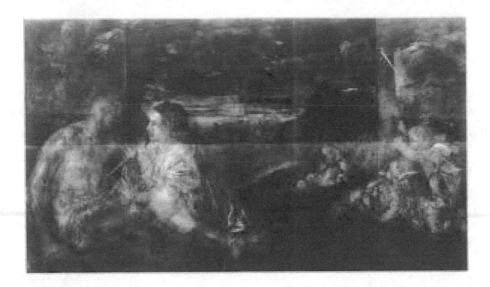

FIGURE 6.8   Titian *The Three Ages of Man*, X-ray of left-hand side

FIGURE 6.9   Titian *The Three Ages of Man*, detail, 1513–14

The pairing of incipient action, concentrated in the gaze, with the other half of Titian's way of securing corporeality, or the effect of spreading configuration, is something that is reiterated across these early paintings. In the *Concert Champêtre* we even become sensitized to the gaze of the seated woman who has her broad back turned to us. In the *Three Ages of Man* Titian elaborates on the effect in a way that is instructive to us. *Three Ages of Man* Titian elaborates on this effect in a way that it is instructive to follow. First, he bends the bodies of the young girl and her lover away from one another, he makes them open up like the pages of a book: thereby he extends the silhouette that they jointly form to its maximum, so as to generate the spreading effect. Then, having done this, like an afterthought—and, if we look at the X-rays of the picture, we can perceive that this is exactly what it was, an afterthought[3]—he twists the girl's head back towards the young man, so that, the full breadth of the silhouette maintained, her gaze and his gaze are free to ferret each other out. Their eyes copulate.

As to the factors that facilitate the transfer of this particular sense of the body, once achieved, outwards to the painting as a whole, we should first note what a mixed bag they are. In defiance of monistic aesthetic theories, they jumble the configurational, the representational, the expressive: they draw alike upon mark, motif, and image. They include the following: First of all, there are the equivalences that Titian establishes between body and nature: for instance, in the *Concert Champêtre* between flesh and stone, between hair and foliage, or in *The Three Ages of Man* between young skin and sky. Secondly, there is the anonymity of the represented figures, which in turn brings them closer to nature. This anonymity is something which Titian inherited from Giorgione, but it obviously had for Titian a singularly liberating significance. It takes us deep into his psychology. We shall find, revealingly enough, anonymity even in some of his portraits. Thirdly, there is the simplification of colour, and in particular the use of near-complementaries,[4] which has a special binding effect. Fourthly, there is the benign neglect of perspective used as a way of regimenting space—note, for instance, the abandonment of foreshortening in the left leg of the seated woman in the *Concert Champêtre*. This retreat from perspective encourages the global response to the picture as a whole: it was Vasari who noted the aptness of Venetian paintings to be taken in within *'una sola occhiata'*, at a glance. Fifthly, there is the production of what asks to be thought of as a paint skin. In the *Concert Champêtre* this is of a uniform graininess, exploiting the coarse weave of the canvas to which Titian inclined: in *The Three Ages of Man,* which is at once a more evolved and a better preserved work, there are many deliberate alternations of texture, so that the visible brushstroke at one moment is there to portray detail, say a leaf in the foreground, and at the next moment suggests mass, such as the swelling foliage of the hedge beyond the near meadow.

Finally, to complete the discussion of corporeality and how it is achieved by Titian, I want to turn to a specific element present in both these paintings and in others of the same period. This element is a residue from the great High Renaissance structures of Leonardo and Raphael, but self-consciously torn out of its context. I refer to the diminutive profiles cut totally in conformity with linear perspective by figures in the middle distance or the background: for example, the silhouette of the shepherd in the Louvre picture, or that of the old man in the Sutherland picture. In a Leonardo or a Raphael these figures, by marking out the space they inhabit, would add to the monumental effect: they would enhance the sense of the world as a great basilica. But here, in these very different pictures, with no orthogonals, with no vanishing point, with no indicated point of origin, in the absence, indeed, of all the obvious signs of a projective system in use, these small delicate cut-outs take on a contrary character: they turn into tiny decorative fragments which have been scattered across the picture. But how, it might be asked, does this aid corporeality?

It does so not immediately, but mediately. One constituent of corporeality, which is an optional aspect, for corporeality does not insist on it, is that a picture endowed with corporeality will get itself thought of—thought of metaphorically, of course—as something which a body also is. It will get itself thought of as a container. This thought can be induced in a number of ways. In connection with de Kooning, I shall talk of a way in which the use of the medium encourages the thought. But one way in which the thought can be induced, and a comparatively straightforward way, is for the picture to display elements that themselves invite being thought of—again metaphorically—as things that can be put away in a container. Elements of the picture assimilate themselves to toys, or to jewels, or to mere odds and ends. Inviting this thought, they then compel the prior thought that the picture within whose four sides they lie is a container. It is, then, by activating this train of thought that the delicate, wispy figures, which Titian strews across his pictures, and which momentarily detach themselves from their environment, contribute, all likelihood to the contrary, to the overall effect of corporeality.

But the most specific, the most active, factor working for the conception of the painting as a container is something else again. It is a factor which the writer who, to my mind, remains the most precise and most percipient critic of early Cinquecento Venetian art identifies as its central topic. Sound, Walter Pater observed, and by sound he included the sound of music, the sound of water, the sound of a novel read aloud, the imagined sound of time passing, is at the core of this kind of painting.[5] Sound penetrates both the *Concert Champêtre* and *The Three Ages of Man*. There are the notes exchanged between the young aristocrat and the peasant, and which the woman who is the third of their party will soon take up: there are the notes which the young girl has played to her naked lover, and which he will take up: there is the sound of water as it falls out of the jug, through the air, back into the cistern.

But how is this so? How does the sound get into these pictures? There is no systematic answer to this question: there is no answer like 'via representation', or 'via expression'. It is rather, as I see it, that the picture gives rise to the thought that the sounds lie around inside it: as we might feel that the notes lie around inside the music box when the tune has stopped, or that the hum lies around inside the fridge. Open up the music box, open up the fridge, open up these paintings, and there we would find the notes. Of course, all these thoughts are metaphorical thoughts, but they are metaphors that record our attempts to capture an impression made upon us. And, once again, these metaphorical thoughts induce the metaphorical thought that they presuppose. The painting is a container: like a body.

Notes

1   For the subject matter of *The Three Ages of Man,* see Erwin Panofsky, *Problems of Titian, Mostly Iconographic* (New York and London, 1969), pp. 94–96. For a discussion of the subject-matter

of the *Concert Champêtre* that, in its complete neglect of artist's intention, is to my way of thinking a model of how pictorial meaning should not be established, see Patricia Egan, 'Poesía and the *Fete Champêtre*', *Art Bulletin*, Vol. XLI, no. 4. December 1959, pp. 303–313. The author concedes the point on the penultimate page of her article. A highly imaginative reinterpretation of the *Concert Champêtre* is put forward in Philipp Fehl. 'The Hidden Genre: A Study of the *Concert Champêtre* in the Louvre', *Journal of Aesthetics and Art Criticism*, Vol. XVI, no.2, December 1957, pp. 153–160. Though the argument is very persuasively presented, the interpretation that it proposes, which is that the two women are nymphs who therefore inhabit a different domain from the young men, requires such a radical shift in our perception of the picture that I feel we need stronger visual evidence than we are provided with before we should accept it. Fehl himself tends to underestimate the perceptual revision that his interpretation calls for. He summarizes his interpretation by saying that the women are 'as *invisible* to the young men as they are visible to us, (his italics). This is correct. But on my view of representation, this requires that, in seeing the women, we should see them as invisible to the men. Precisely what this would involve is obscure. In his article Fehl also applies this interpretation to *The Andrians* (Prado, Madrid) and to the *Pardo Venus* (Louvre, Paris). In his 'The Worship of Bacchus and Venus in Bellini's and Titian's Bacchanals for Alfonso d'Esle', *Studies in the History of Art: National Gallery of Art. Washington,* Vol.6, 1974, pp. 37–95, Fehl extends the interpretation to two further paintings by Titian. These are *The Amores* (Prado, Madrid) and *Bacchus and Ariadne* (National Gallery, London).

2   For pointing out this configurational effect I am deeply indebted to Johannes Wilde, Venetian *Art from Bellini to Titian* (Oxford, 1974): a work whose modesty of presentation conceals a wealth of the most profound pictorial observation.

3   See Giles Robertson. The X-ray examination of Titian's *Three Ages of Man, Burlington Magazine,* Vol. CXIII. No. 825, December 1971, pp. 721–726.

4   On the use of near-complementaries, see Adrian Stokes, *Colourand Form* (London, 1937), reprinted in *The Critical Writings of Adrian Stokes,* ed. Lawrence Gowing (London, 1978), Vol. II. Stokes contends that near-complementaries are more effective than complementaries in securing simultaneous contrast. This is the optical effect whereby one coloured area encourages a neighbouring greyed area to move towards its complementary: for instance, an orange area will induce a neutral area adjacent to it to move towards blue.

5   Walter Pater, *The Renaissance* (2nd edition, London, 1877), pp. 150–154.

Discussion Questions

1. In what sense is metaphorical meaning a primary content of a painting, according to Wollheim?

2. What are the three features that pictorial metaphors share with literary metaphors such as "Juliet is the sun" or "Religion is the opium of the people"?

3. Do you think that Titian's painting *The Three Ages of Man* is a metaphor of human vitality as Wollheim claims? Can you think of any other conspicuous content of the painting as you try to understand and appreciate the work?

4. Have you been struck by a painting (a real painting, not a print or a poster reproduction) during your visit of an art museum? What was it in the painting that captivated you? Can you describe the content of the painting in terms of the pictorial meaning?

5. What are primary ways in which a painting communicates with the viewer? Representational content or emotional expression? What else?

Silences

Triumph of the Aesthetic

Larry Shiner

I n Émile Zola's novel *L'assommoir* (1877), a working-class wedding party decides to celebrate by a visit to the Louvre, thinking the edifying majesty of the art museum accords well with the occasion. Only one of them has been in an art museum before and they are overwhelmed by the finely dressed guards, the sumptuous surroundings, the mirror finish of the parquet floors, the heavy gold frames. When they come on Ruben's painting of a country festival *(The Kermis),* showing drunken, vomiting, urinating peasants, many lewdly grabbing each other, the women "utter little cries; then turn away blushing deeply." The men stare and snicker, "looking closer for obscene details" ([1877] 1965, 92; [1877] 1995, 78). Finally, the wedding party gets lost in the labyrinth of galleries, and they scurry from room to room, numbed by the endless rows of paintings, etchings, drawings, statues, and cases full of figurines. Zola's working-class wedding party whirling through the Louvre strikes us as comic because they lack the rudiments of what we believe necessary to appreciating museum art—some knowledge of art history, some sense of aesthetic distance. They give way to their instinctive sensual or moral reactions and are captivated by eroticism or the riches of gold frames and mirror-finished floors. Yet despite their chatter and scurrying, they at least behave with a certain respect, no singing, shouting, or game playing of the kind that had to be forbidden seventy-five years before.

Learning Aesthetic Behavior

In America, where the great public museums only began to appear in the 1870s, there is evidence that it took more time to teach visitors both proper respect and the beginnings of an aesthetic response. By 1897, however, the director of New York's

Metropolitan Museum could proudly describe the success of vigilance, admonitions, and a few ejections; "You do not see any more persons in the picture galleries blowing their nose with their fingers; no more dogs brought in ... no more spitting tobacco juice on the gallery floors ... no more nurses taking children to some corner to defile the floors ... no more whistling, singing, or calling aloud" (Tomkins 1989, 84–85). But the issue soon became not just middle-class decorum but the proper aesthetic attitude in the "temple of Art," as well. Even art education, always an aim of museums since the eighteenth century, was not enough. In the 1890s, many American art museums, such as those in Boston and Chicago, still exhibited plaster casts of ancient sculptures but finally put them in storage after younger curators and critics argued that only the finest "original" works belonged in the museum. The first aim of an art museum, the assistant director at Boston declared in 1903, is to "maintain a high standard of aesthetic taste" by choosing objects for their "aesthetic quality" and, thereby, afford its visitors "the pleasure derived from a contemplation of the perfect" (Whitehall 1970, 1:183, 201).

Similar behavioral norms were taught theater and concert audiences, although the lessons were aided by a gradual separation of the "legitimate" theaters and concert halls from venues for farce, melodrama, and popular music. In Europe Honoré Daumier caught the passionate reactions of lower-middle-class theater audiences in his "A Literary Discussion in the Second Balcony" (fig. 59). Lawrence Levine has recently traced the gradual separation of fine art theater from popular theater in America by examining the fortunes of Shakespeare in the nineteenth century. For the first two-thirds of the century, Shakespeare's plays were not only the most frequently performed but also drew large and socially varied crowds, many of whom stamped their feet, whistled, shouted, and demanded instant encores. One reason Shakespeare appealed to such a broad audience was the wholesale alteration of his plays that had begun in the eighteenth century, leaving some versions of *Richard III* with one-third fewer lines and *King Lear* with a happy ending in which both Cordelia and Lear live on! Nineteenth-century promoters also interspersed the acts with other entertainments and usually followed the play with a farce to assure an enthusiastic and demonstrative response. Naturally, the upper classes who sat in the orchestra and boxes were not always happy with the their clamorous inferiors in the balconies, especially when pelted with apple cores (Levine 1988).

Class tensions mixed with cultural differences throughout the century, sometimes to tragic effect, as in the Astor Place Riot of 1849. Twenty-two people were killed when the militia fired into a crowd attempting to storm the Astor Theater and break up a performance of *Macbeth* by the snobbish English actor William Charles Macready. Macready's highly publicized insults to America's noisy, plebeian audiences had ignited popular anger, whereas the same kind of gallery crowds gave standing ovations to Macready's American rival, Edwin Forrest, whose stentorian delivery was enormously popular. Yet only a dozen years later, the editor of *Harper's* derided Forrest's "rant, roar, and rigmarole" as good only for wringing tears out of working-class girls but praised the elegant performances of Edwin Booth for eliciting "refined attention rather than eager interest" (Levine 1988, 59). By the second half of the century, separate theaters for "art" performances began to appear in most of the larger American cities. By the 1890s, the theater audience had divided, and Shakespeare was performed uncut in "legitimate" theaters before

FIGURE 7.1   Honoré Daumier, *A Literary Discussion in the Second Balcony* (1864). Courtesy Bibliothèque Nationale, Paris. In Europe as in America the nineteenth-century lower classes took their theater seriously.

FIGURE 7.2   Moritz von Schwind, *An Evening at Baron Spaun's* (1868). Historisches Museum der Stadt Wien, Vienna. Courtesy Erich Lessing/Art Resource, New York. Franz Schubert is at the piano, tenor Johann Michael Vogl is singing.

silent and respectful audiences. Even if the term "aesthetic" was not always used to distinguish the "refined attention" of the art theater from the "eager interest" of popular halls, a kind of aesthetic *behavior* was being inculcated and those unwilling to adopt it either were expelled or went elsewhere.

A similar division occurred in music. As William Weber has shown, there was a veritable "concert explosion" in Europe from 1830 to 1848, although in this case led entirely by the upper classes, who were divided in their tastes. One group was especially involved in salon concerts, often organized by women and held in fine homes. They favored the relatively popular music transcribed from opera or the symphonic repertoire adapted for virtuosos such as Liszt. Here was an art world where women—who played the piano themselves and oversaw their Children's lessons—were allowed to take the lead (fig. 7.2). Another part of the upper classes prided themselves on their knowledge of the classical symphony tradition of Haydn, Mozart, and Beethoven and preferred concert hall performances faithful to the composer's text. This group was dominated by men who tended to regard their kind of music as "serious" art and looked down on the salon concerts and popular soloists. Weber suggests that the gradual merger of these two upper-class groups under the dominance of the male-led classical tendency marked the emergence of the modern "serious" music system in Europe. As a result, a patriarchal upper class controlled the emerging concert institutions in a way that subordinated the role of women and excluded the lower social ranks both programmatically and economically (Weber 1975).[1]

At the same time that this little world of fine art music was drawing into itself, other concerts, aimed at a broader spectrum of the middle and lower classes, were developing out of the eighteenth-century choral societies and promenade concerts, the latter providing an attractive

FIGURE 7.3   Edgar Degas, *Cabaret* (1882); 91¼, × 17 inches, pastel over monotype. Courtesy Corcoran Gallery of Art, Washington, D.C., William A. Clark Collection. (26.72.)

setting where people could drink, smoke, talk, and walk about. Although a few people of the lower ranks might save up to attend a "classical" concert and the upper classes might drop in on choral performances or promenades, the social and cultural divisions were becoming well marked as the century wore on. There were also new kinds of commercial musical institutions that flourished in the rapidly growing urban centers, such as the café concert in Paris (fig. 7.3). Although people commented on the socially mixed audiences who frequented the café concerts in the 1870s and 1880s, these establishments seem to have been predominantly lower-middle-class venues, where singers expressed an idealized version of the life of "the people" in a music that both fascinated and alarmed the cultural elite who also frequented the symphony and opera (Clark 1984). In America, the gradual segregation of higher and lower forms of instrumental music took slightly different forms. The omnipresent community "band" played not only marches and polkas but also excerpts from operas and symphonic selections from Haydn. As late as 1873, a Boston critic lamented the absence of a permanent symphony in his city to keep alive "acquaintance with the great unquestioned masterworks" (Levine 1988, 120). The symphony orchestras that were founded in city after city across America in the latter half of the nineteenth century were in fact dedicated to becoming just such "museums of musical works."

If the promenade concert in Europe or popular band music in America mixed genres and allowed freer behavior in a relaxed setting, the concerts of the cultured classes were clearly Art rituals in which a special attitude and silent decorum was expected. Yet even the nineteenth-century upper-class audience had to be "trained in the art of listening" (Gay 1995, 19). In 1803, Goethe, who oversaw the court theater in Weimar, demanded that shouting or hissing stop and that audiences limit themselves to applause at the end of the performance.[2] Complaints about talking and moving about during concerts continued throughout the century, but critics, symphony boards, and conductors kept after the audiences. The American conductor Theodore Thomas was famous for staring down talkers and even stopping the orchestra and raising his hands for silence. Here again, the campaign to quiet audiences was not simply about decorum but about the proper response to fine art. As the music critic Edward Baxter Perry put it, audiences must rise above "mere sensuous pleasure or superficial enjoyment, to a higher ... spiritual aesthetic gratification" (Levine 1988, 134).

In the realm of literature, questions of public behavior did not arise in the same way as music, although the development of "legitimate" theaters in which Shakespeare's plays were reverently treated as sacred texts offers one parallel. The literary equivalent of the legitimate theater, the concert hall, or the art museum eventually became the college or university literature course and literature anthology. What needed to be "silenced" in the reading of literary works of art was not physical sound or bodily restlessness but the intrusive noise of thrill or amusement or political and moral ideas. People had to learn to attend to the purely aesthetic qualities of the literary work and not simply consume it the way they did popular genres.

Although the ideas and institutions of art, artist, and aesthetic were largely established by the 1830s, it took the rest of the century to separate completely fine art and popular art institutions and to teach the upwardly mobile middle classes the appropriate aesthetic behaviors. What Jacques Attali has said of the evolution of music in the eighteenth and early nineteenth

FIGURE 7.4   Eugène Laini, *First Hearing of Beethoven's Seventh Symphony* (1840). Courtesy Musée de la Musique, Conservatoire National Supérieur de Musique et de Danse de Paris. Photograph by J.-M. Angles.

centuries could be applied to all the fine arts: "When the concert hall performance replaced the popular festival and the private concert at court ... the attitude toward music changed profoundly: in ritual it was one element in the totality of life; in the concerts of the nobility or popular festivals it was still part of a mode of sociality... in the concerts of the bourgeoisie ... the silence greeting the musicians was what created music and gave it an autonomous existence" (Attali 1985, 46) (fig. 7.4).

The Rise of the Aesthetic and the Decline of Beauty

If it took a long effort to inculcate a behavior of silent and reverent attention, it also took a long time for the term "aesthetic" to be regularly used for it outside of Germany where it had originated.[3] But more important than the term, was the issue of whether there was, in fact, a special "aesthetic" faculty and what its characteristics were. The general belief in a distinct aesthetic faculty seems to have been widely accepted by the 1850s and even gave rise to a psychological "science" of aesthetics, which has continued its fitful course into our own day. One branch of it was carried on in an empirical vein by Hermann Helmholz's studies of the neurological basis of pleasure in music and Gustav Fechner's research on perceptual preferences in the visual domain. Many of those who pursued these investigations clearly believed they were on the track of something wired into the human brain. Herbert Spencer described a distinct aesthetic experience at the end of his *Principles of Psychology* (1872) and Grant Allen analyzed the differentia of the "aesthetic feelings" from a Darwinian perspective, defining its principle as "Maximum of Stimulation with the Minimum of Fatigue or Waste" (Allen 1877, 39; Spencer [1872] 1881, 2:623–48).

If we turn from the general idea that there is a distinctive aesthetic mode of experience to nineteenth-century beliefs about the *characteristics* of the aesthetic, we find a wide range of views. Some writers stressed sensory or emotional pleasure, while others made central such qualities as imagination, intuition, empathy, or intellectual insight. Although the term "disinterestedness" has never been part of everyday talk about the fine arts, the general idea of an unprejudiced, contemplative attitude toward art continued to make its way among both the public and those who wrote about art. Many nineteenth-century writers who used "disinterestedness" intended the weaker sense of merely excluding crassly utilitarian or selfish interests. Others followed the stronger Kantian or Schillerian notion of a contemplative attitude that sets aside any direct theoretical or moral interests. Naturally, both the moderate and strong versions of disinterestedness admitted degrees of exclusion. Victor Cousin and Théodore Jouffroy developed a French version of Schillers position, arguing that even though Art indirectly inculcates morality and puts us in touch with the absolute, "it does not try to do so, it does not pose that as its aim.... There must be religion for religion, morality for morality, as art for art"' (Bénichou 1973, 258). Of course, there were others who denied even Matthew Arnold's belief in a "subtle and indirect effect" on morals (1962, 270). By 1868 Algernon Swinburne, paraphrasing Scripture, could declare: "Art for Art's sake first of all, and afterward the rest shall be added to her... but from the man who falls to artistic work with a moral purpose shall be taken away even that which he has" (Warner and Hough 1983, 237). By the end of the century small groups of intellectuals and artists had transformed the idea of the aesthetic from the notion of a disinterested faculty for experiencing fine art into an ideal of existence. In a way, the "aestheticization" of life proposed by many of the aestheticists, such as Oscar Wilde, was simply an extension of the superiority of the artist's sensibility into every sphere—although this rejection of mundane instrumentality could take many forms, from the languorous sensuality of Pater to the Promethean overflow of Nietzsche.

We cannot leave the topic of the nature of aesthetic experience without noting one of the most striking differences between nineteenth- and twentieth-century discussions: the near disappearance of beauty as a central concept of aesthetics since the 1950s. The roots of beauty's decline go back to the end of the eighteenth century and the emergence of the idea of the aesthetic itself. As we have seen, eighteenth-century theorists of taste not only were interested in beauty but developed concepts of the sublime, the picturesque, and the novel as well. Beauty, once the sole epithet for highest attainment in the arts, now had several rivals, and one of them, the sublime, was believed by many writers of the eighteenth and nineteenth centuries to be a deeper and more powerful experience. Various nineteenth-century artists and critics added still other values and experiences, such as the grotesque (Hugo), the strange (Baudelaire), the real (Flaubert), and the true (Zola), which they sometimes took to be more forceful than beauty. But there were also problems inherent in the concept of beauty itself. On the one hand, it was too closely associated with academicism and traditional criteria of ideal imitation, harmony, proportion, and unity. On the other hand, it was too mixed up with everyday notions of prettiness and praise—a beautiful horse, a beautiful shot, a beautiful investment. Although Schiller spoke of beauty along with fine art as humanity's salvation in the *Aesthetic Letters* of 1793, a few years later he was writing to Goethe that "beauty" had become so problematic that it should perhaps be "dismissed from circulation" (Beardsley 1975, 228). In England, Richard Payne Knight lamented that "the word Beauty is ... applied indiscriminately to almost anything that is pleasing" (1808, 9). Nevertheless, most nineteenth- and early twentieth-century critics and philosophers from Hegel to George Santayana continued to use "beauty" as the overarching term for the highest aesthetic value, and aesthetics itself was often defined simply as the theory of beauty. The history and prestige of "beauty" was such that, like "Art," it remained the name for whatever writers found most precious and transcendent in felt experience. Not until the full implications of modernism and the early twentieth-century anti-art movements had made themselves felt was "beauty" relegated to a minor role in critical and philosophical discourse on the arts.

The Problem of Art and Society

When historians of aesthetics or literary theory come to the nineteenth century, they often reserve a section of their works for the problem of "art and society." This issue is typically described in terms of a battle between those who believed in "art for art's sake" (Gautier, Baudelaire, Whistler, Wilde) and those who believed in the "social responsibility of art" (Courbet, Proudhon, Ruskin, Tolstoy). Some historians have found it necessary to explain why it was that a "theme that had not been given such serious attention between Plato and Schiller" should suddenly become so urgent (Beardsley 1975, 299). The reader who has followed my argument up to this point will have no difficulty understanding one reason why the art and society problem in this broad sense did not receive "serious attention" up to Schiller. It did not because it could not. No one between Plato and Schiller wrestled with the problem of Art and society in this generalized form because they had no concept of Art as a distinct realm or social subsystem whose relation to society needed to be conceptualized. Only *after* fine art was constructed as a set of canonical disciplines and specialized institutions that were then reified as an autonomous domain could one ask what function the realm of Art should play within the larger society.

During the first half of the nineteenth century, there was only occasional talk of "Art for Art's sake" (Gautier), whereas almost everyone still believed that serious works of art should embody a significant moral content, even if some people thought of artworks as having only an indirect moral effect. The full implications of the idea of art as an autonomous realm did not become apparent until near the end of the century. Even so, we can trace the development of a tendency to avoid direct engagement with political and moral issues. This retreat appeared in different countries at different times and was often related to the violent class conflicts of the period. Although there were always writers, painters, and composers who spoke to moral and political questions, the deeper problem was that the relative autonomy of the fine art institutions tended to neutralize social and political content by confining art works within the "world" of art.

The turn from social and political concerns seems to have occurred in the Germanies earlier than elsewhere. Although Schiller and Goethe never completely abandoned the hope that art might improve society, by the late 1790s, both had given up the eighteenth-century view of art as a means of public enlightenment. Schiller could even write in 1803 that Art should "totally shut itself off from the real world" (Berghahn 1988, 96). Many saw art as fundamentally alien to a society propelled by commerce and industry. Moreover, following the collapse of the Napoleonic empire, the various absolute monarchies of Central and Eastern Europe vigilantly exiled or imprisoned most social and political dissenters, including those who championed a politically engaged art, such as Heine. This made it easier for the idea of a completely autonomous art to gain early acceptance. The rest of society might be dominated by the police power and by middle-class materialism, but Art could be a refuge where the human spirit might roam freely (Schulte-Sasse 1988).

In France, in contrast, many romantic poets, painters, and composers remained politically engaged (whether as royalists or republicans) and saw art as a social instrument right up through the Revolution of 1848, when the poet Alphonse de Lamartine's role as head of the failed provisional government symbolized Art's failure in politics. The collapse of the idealism of 1848 and the political repression under Napoleon III blunted many artists' political involvement (with brilliant exceptions, such as Victor Hugo and Gustave Courbet) and led them to a preoccupation with issues within the world of art. Another reason for the decline of political concern was the concurrent growth of the art world itself. After 1848 there was a steady expansion of specialized art institutions, such as the dealer-critic-curator-collector complex for painting and similar support complexes for music and literature. Now success as a writer, composer, or painter meant recognition by one of these art, music, or literary worlds, which were increasingly apolitical as a locus of upper-middle-class leisure activity. Although the deep cleavages in French society (e.g., the Dreyfus Affair) could still draw artists and writers such as Zola into its conflicts as individuals, the worlds of art, music, and literature had taken on a life of their own.

In Britain, as in France, many of the early romantics expressed their social and political engagement through their work, and later, the Victorians, led by Carlyle, Ruskin, and George Eliot, never doubted the high moral and social purpose of Art in reforming and beautifying a crassly utilitarian and materialistic society. One can even find a strain of "aesthetic democracy" in people associated with the aestheticst movement like Walter Pater and Oscar Wilde (Dowling 1996). But once the modern discourse of fine art, artist, and aesthetic was firmly established in Britain around mid-century, the inherent tension between Art as a distinct institution and its role as moral or social educator began to be increasingly acknowledged. The subsequent emergence of a belief in the absolute autonomy of art in some circles went hand in hand with the rise in status of the artist and the growth and privatization of the various art worlds. Late in the century when aestheticists such as Wilde or formalist critics such as Roger Fry attacked Victorian moralism in art, they often argued that artworks should be seen strictly in terms of their relation to the art world.

To follow out the arguments between the proponents of Art for Art's sake and those who believed in the social responsibility of art would take us beyond our main subject and into the details of the history of aesthetics and art or literary theory. What is relevant to our theme is that both sides in these debates were often prisoners of the same regulative polarities of art. The declarations of a Gautier, Wilde, or Bell that Art has nothing to do with morality, politics, or "worldly" life but exists only for itself are a sort of reverse image of the declarations of a Proudhon, Tolstoy, and some marxists that Art exists primarily to serve humanity, morality, or the revolution. The extreme expressions of both positions assumed that Art is in fact an independent realm that has an external relation to the rest of society. For the one side, Art became a spiritual world of its own into which the aesthetically sensitive might retreat from a sordid, materialistic society; for the other Art was seen as a powerful instrument of communication for changing that society. Few nineteenth-century writers attacked the problem at its root: the regulative polarities of the modern system of art. Eventually, artists and critics who shared John Ruskin's or George Eliot's belief in a more intimate connection between works of art and the social good would have to challenge the underlying polarities of the fine art system.

Notes

1   As Weber (1975) shows, ticket prices were set at a level effectively excluding most of the lower soical ranks, and innovations such as reserved seats further limited social range. As with most general trends, there were variations and exceptions, opra in Italy retained, and retains to this day, broader audience than in northern Europe and America.

2   Peter Gay mentions a middle-class cultural society in Frankfurt that adopted the following guidelines in 1808: "During literary or musical performances everyone is asked to refrain from speaking.... Signs of disapproval are not to be expected.... Dogs are not tolerated" (1995, 18–19).

3   Most writers in the first half of the century continued to use the term "taste" despite the disadvantages Wordsworth noted in his preface to the *Lyrical Ballads* of 1802, e.g., that the word "taste" seems to reduce the experience of fine art to the same level as rope dancing or sherry. Coleridge still regretted in 1821 that there was not "a more familiar word than aesthetics for works of taste and criticism" (Williams 1976, 21). And the *Encyclopedia of Architecture* in 1842 could complain that "there has lately grown into use in the arts a silly pedantic term under the name of Aesthetics" (Steegman 1970, 18). In France, the term "aesthetic" played little role in Victor Cousin's influential lecture course *Du vrai, du beau, du bien* (the true, the beautiful and the good) of 1818, but in 1826 Théodore Jouffroy called his lecture series *Cours d'esthétique* (Jouffroy 1883). The Academic Française finally accepted the term in 1838, and Comte and Baudelaire both used it in the 1850s (Comte [1851] 1968; Baudelaire [1859] 1986).

Discussion Questions

1. What are the efforts that art institutions (museums, theatres, concerts) in the early nineteenth century made to teach the audience proper aesthetic behaviors?
2. What is the meaning of "disinterestedness" when it is used to refer to appropriate aesthetic attitude?
3. How is beauty different from the sublime? Can you think of an artwork that evokes beauty but not sublime? Or artwork that evokes the sublime but not beauty? Which is more valuable in terms of aesthetic value?
4. Do we expect art to raise a social consciousness and manifest a certain degree of social responsibility? If an artwork makes no comment on social issues, do we consider it inferior to those that bear social responsibility?
5. What is your response to the statement that "art has nothing to do with morality, politics, or worldly life but exists only for itself"? Is art intrinsically valuable without reference to the social context where it is created?

A First Chapter

Alice Kaplan

Camus disliked Oran, Francine Faure's home town, and yet it was in this dull, enervating place, in the first months of 1940, that *The Stranger* began to take shape.[1]

The port of Algiers accommodated entire worlds—a dance hall, a swimming pool, fish restaurants, warehouses transformed into theater space. In Oran, located on the same north coast of Algeria, looking out at the same Mediterranean Sea, 250 miles to the west, there was no seaside promenade at all, only a commercial port at the bottom of a steep seawall, inaccessible to walkers in the city. There had once been a city beach, at the old place Sainte Thérèse, but it was gobbled up by the port in 1936, a victim of the city's commercial soul. In Algiers, Camus could *se taper un bain* anytime he wanted (he liked the local expression, which means something like "take a dip"), but in Oran he had to travel by bus, five kilometers out of the city, to Mers-el-Kébir, Bouisseville, or Trouville, or on his good days, get on his bike. Once he got there, his sour attitude towards Oran fell by the wayside, and he opened his heart to the sea: "On these beaches in the province of Oran each summer morning feels like the world's first. Each dusk feels like the last, a solemn death proclaimed at sunset by a final light that deepens every shade. The sea is aquamarine, the road the color of dried blood, the beach yellow."[2]

Oran was reputedly the most European of any Algerian city. Unlike in Algiers, where the Casbah defined the center of the city, the "native" population of Oran was isolated in a district in the heights known as the *village nègre*. In 1936, 76 percent of the Oran population was European (a figure that included Jews), while only 14 percent was Muslim—in dramatic contrast with the country as a whole which was 86 percent "native" and 14 percent European.[3] Francine lived on the rue d'Arzew, Oran's equivalent of the commercial rue de Rivoli in the center of Paris—several blocks of shops and wide sidewalks under connecting stone arches. Her grandfather had developed the stretch

Alice Kaplan, "A First Chapter," *Looking for the Stranger: Albert Camus and the Life of a Literary Classic*, pp. 63-70, 225-226, 265-269. Copyright © 2016 by University of Chicago Press. Reprinted with permission.

of commercial properties under the arcades, though the family fortune was a thing of the past. Francine's father had died in the same Battle of the Marne where Lucien Camus had perished. Her widowed mother had gone back to work, rising in the ranks of the civil service at the post office. Francine, whose great love was the piano, had a job teaching math at Oran's lycée for girls. Her sister Christiane, as domineering as Francine was delicate and shy, was a litertature professor, a product of the prestigious École Normale Supérieure in Paris. Camus felt scrutinized by this family of disciplined, talented women. Christiane was not convinced that her sister had found a suitable mate in the unemployed, ailing journalist from Algiers. She told Francine he looked like a monkey. "The monkey is the closest mammal to man," Francine is supposed to have replied—and when she reported her comeback to Camus, his affection for her deepened.[4]

In the winter of 1940, Camus was getting his mail at the Faure apartment. He complained in letters to friends that he was suffocating. To distract himself, he continued working on his satirical essay, "The Minotaur, or Stopping at Oran." He began with the idea that Oran turned away from the sea, like a snail curving inward on itself. The town was a labyrinth and the Minotaur within was boredom. The downtown place d'Armes was decorated with bronze statues of lions on squat legs: urban legend had it that they urinated on the square by night. The boxy "Maison du Colon," built to celebrate a hundred years of colonization, combined the worst of Byzantine, Egyptian, and German grandiosity. Camus's Oran was a place where the worst taste of Europe and the Orient met, a capital of dust and stones.[5]

In early 1940, Camus went back and forth between Oran and Algiers, where a young woman named Yvonne Ducailar made him wonder if he was ready to marry Francine. He accumulated notes on future characters for his novel: "a old man and his dog, eight years of hatred" was the germ of his story about Meursault's neighbor Salamano and his mangy pet. He imagined another character who couldn't resist adding "I'd even say" to every sentence: "He was charming, I'd even say pleasant." He gave the tic to Raymond's friend Masson.[6] In a time of hesitation in all other realms, conceiving the first pages of *The Stranger* was an amusement and an unexpected anchor. His work-in-progress diaries included notes on the "burning blue beach" and two people playing in the water. That image stayed with him, but it wasn't his opening. Instead he started *The Stranger* with the paragraph he had jotted down back in August 1938: "Today, Maman died. Or perhaps yesterday, I don't know. I received a telegram from the home: 'Mother deceased. Funeral tomorrow. Our best regards.' That means nothing. It might have been yesterday."[7]

From the notebooks to the published novel, he altered not a single word of these confounding first sentences. He knew this was his beginning, and he stuck with it.

That first paragraph dictated the whole movement of chapter 1, and with it the temperament of his central character, Meursault. Camus took Meursault to the old people's home at Marengo, using his memories of the day he accompanied his brother Lucien to a funeral there. The director of the funeral home is the first person in the novel to utter the narrator's family name: "Madame Meursault came to us three years ago."

In the only surviving manuscript of the novel, housed today in the Camus archives in Aix-en-Provence, Camus still spells his narrator's last name "Mersault," identical to the hero of *A Happy Death*. Later, he would differentiate him from the main character of *A Happy Death*, by adding the "u" to Meursault's name. When you pronounce "Mersault" without the "u," it sounds ethnically Spanish, like "Merso"—a name that could have belonged to heavily Spanish ethnic Europeans who lived in Oran, or to someone who was kin to Camus's mother, Catherine Sintès. Where did the "u" come from? Some Camus experts claim he thought of the name change at a dinner party where he was served the delicious and expensive white Burgundy wine, Meursault. Whether or not the story about the Paris dinner party is true, there is something more expected about the way *Meur*-sault sounds to a French ear than *Mer*-sault, and the coincidence might have pleased Camus, since the extra "u"—signifying *meur* (death)—served his novelistic purposes in every other way. Which may be why, late in his process, Mersault/Merso, a Spanish/Algerian sounding name, became quintessentially French: Meursault.

Openings set the tone, and *The Stranger* begins with an unsettling mix of the present, the past, and the future ("Today, Maman died.... I'll take the bus at two").[8] The narrator doesn't know, or seem to care, whether his mother died today or yesterday. After the opening paragraph, he recounts, in a flat, factual voice, how he took the bus downtown, ate at Céleste's, almost missed the bus to Marengo, arrived at the home, met with the director, attended the wake, and marched in the funeral procession under a blazing sun. While he sits with his mother's casket, he decides that the presence of her corpse means nothing to the old people around him. Then he adds, "But I believe now that it was a false impression." Where is he when he corrects himself? Camus does not explain when and where Meursault is when he tells his story. In one page, he solved the problem that made *A Happy Death* impossible to revise: he has endowed his narrative with momentum, with a mystery that needs to be resolved.

To position Meursault in time, Camus used one of the features that makes James M. Cain's *The Postman Always Rings Twice* so unsettling. The reader of Cain's novel will eventually discover that Frank Chambers is telling his story from his prison cell on death row—or he may be telling it after his own death, like one of those Hollywood movies narrated by a dead man who never explains how he can have a voice in the first place. That became Camus's plan for Meursault, and part of the magic of the first pages of *The Stranger* is that the story is told both in the moment, like a diary, and from a mysterious future beyond the grave. During the funeral, Meursault speaks in the present tense about the weather as if he were in the moment: "But today, with the sun bearing down, making the whole landscape shimmer with heat, it was inhuman and oppressive." He also recollects that day, or tries to recollect, as if it were long past: "After that, everything seemed to happen so fast, so deliberately, so naturally that I don't remember any of it anymore." Some sentences in the book suggest that the story is part of a diary he might have kept at the end of his life: "Several other images from that day have stuck in my mind."

Cain's Frank Chambers is a man with no real interior, recounting the most shocking events in a flat, neutral tone. As Camus adapted the flat American voice to his own story of a wake and a funeral in Marengo, he enabled Meursault to zero in on his surroundings more precisely than Frank Chambers had done. Meursault watches the world outside himself with painful clarity: he sees two hornets buzzing on the glass roof of the mortuary; he notices that the men's eyes were mere slivers of light in the middle of a nest of wrinkles; he observes that old women have huge stomachs.

The Postman Always Rings Twice was one inspiration for Meursault's voice. But Meursault evolved from something deeper—the conditions of Camus's own life. During his entire childhood and adolescence, until he moved to Uncle Gustave's, Albert Camus lived with a mother whose vocabulary amounted to 400 words and who had little language to give him beyond her gestures. Since his first, most intimate attempts at communication were defined by the absence of verbal understanding, the physical world became essential. To create Meursault, Camus drew on memories of his own attempts to live with a deaf mother and uncle. A concrete world, where objects come first, concepts last, and each sense is given its due. On the bus to Marengo, Meursault takes in "the bumpy ride, the smell of gasoline, and the glare of the sky and the road." In the old people's home in Marengo, Meursault sits with the casket in a whitewashed room and observes: "The furniture consisted of some chairs and some cross-shaped sawhorses. Two of them, in the middle of the room, were supporting a closed casket. All you could see were some shiny screws, not screwed down all the way, standing out against the walnut-stained planks."

Rather than making the coffin the center of the comparison and writing that "the casket was resting on two sawhorses," Camus gives the sawhorses a strange kind of agency in supporting the coffin ("two of them ... were supporting a closed casket"). When the screws on the casket are tightened, Meursault notices.[9]

Camus lent Meursault's mother some of his own deaf mother's traits: "When she was at home with me," Meursault recalls, "Maman used to spend her time following me with her eyes, not saying a lot." In his debut collection of essays, *The Wrong Side and the Right Side*, Camus evoked a child's acute awareness of his deaf mother, and in his work-in-progress notebooks, he'd described a son whose bizarre feeling for his mother was his entire sensibility. He believed that writers have a very few things they want to express, that they end up writing the same book over and over again. But *how* they write that book is different every time. Meursault contains both Camus's mother—walled off from the world—and the son to that mother, hyperattentive to what he hears, as though he could compensate for her deafness by hearing for her.

Meursault often makes comments about people's voices and the way they speak. He notices that the nurse "had a peculiar voice that didn't match her face, a melodious, trembling voice." And while he is attuned to objects and to his senses, he is closed off from other people, reluctant to engage. On the bus to Marengo, he dozes off and wakes up slumped against a soldier who smiles at him and asks him if he's been traveling long: "I said 'Yes,'" Meursault reports, "just so I wouldn't have to say anything else."

Through the relentless gaze of his narrator, Camus orchestrates the funeral procession with strict precision. Meursault sees the people around him the same way he sees nature, as pure matter. And yet those people have their own subjectivity, emotions he observes without sharing them. Thomas Pérez, his mother's fiancé, appears, disappears, and reappears because he knows the shortcut to take on the blistering hot day; he has taken that path many times on promenades with Meursault's mother. Meursault's view of Pérez is syncopated, interrupted by the landscape and the funeral march itself. At each glance, a different piece of Pérez comes to the fore: the soft felt hat with the wide brim that he puts on and takes off when the casket is near; his pants corkscrewed around his ankles; his thick red ears sticking out through his wispy hair, his slight limp.

Then Camus goes a step further. He saves the most radical description of Pérez and marks it as a memory from the past: "Several other images from that day have stuck in my mind: for instance, Pérez's face when he caught up with us for the last time, just outside the village. Big tears of frustration and exhaustion were streaming down his cheeks. But because of all the wrinkles, they weren't dripping off. They spread out and ran together again, leaving a watery film over his ruined face." The image of Pérez's frustration on the wrinkled varnished surface of his face (the French is "a varnish of water") is born of Camus's "sensibility of the absurd."

In the winter of 1940, Camus's future was uncertain, but that first chapter was a promissory note: he knew that all he needed to keep going was a place to write, and time. He had found in Meursault an agent to transform his earliest perceptions of the world and to make good on the challenge he had set himself: "The true work of art is the one that says the least."[10] With this discovery that he didn't have to be ornate to be a writer, that he could say "I" without confessing, he had what he needed to continue with the rest of the novel.

Being laconic did not mean giving up on lyricism. It meant refusing to lend to the world a meaning it didn't have, and not reassuring with false connections. The last sentence of the first chapter Camus wrote is nearly a half-page long, an extended musical performance of the absurd, juxtaposing flowers, earth, bodies, voices, and sliding without warning into Meursault's fatigue and relief as he leaves Marengo and returns to Algiers: "Then there was the church and the villagers on the sidewalks, the red geraniums on the graves in the cemetery, Pérez fainting (he crumpled like a rag doll), the blood-red earth spilling over Maman's casket, the white flesh of the roots mixed in with it, more people, voices, the village, waiting in front of a café, the incessant drone of the motor, and my joy when the bus entered the nest of lights that was Algiers and I knew I was going to go to bed and sleep for twelve hours."

Camus found his rhythm. When he was interviewed by a French professor about what made *The Stranger* work, he remembered how it happened: "once I discovered the trick, all I had to do was write."[11]

Notes

1 Yosei Matsumoto addresses this issue in detail in "Le Processus d'élaboration de L'Étranger" (the process of creating L'Étranger), *Études camusiennes: Société japonaise des Études camusiennes* 12 (2015): 72–86.

2 "Le Minotaure ou la Halte d'Oran," *Œuvres complètes*, ed. Raymond Gay-Crosier, vol. 3, 1949–1956 (Paris: Gallimard, Bibliothèque de la Pléiade, 2008), 582–83; in English, "The Minotaur, or Stopping in Oran," *Lyrical and Critical Essays*, trans. Ellen Conroy Kennedy (New York: Vintage, 1970), 129, edited.

3 The European or non-Muslim figure included, along with the French, Jews—French citizens as of 1870—and many people of Spanish heritage. Kamel Kateb, *Européens, "indigènes" et juifs*

en Algérie, 1830–1962 (Paris: Presses Universitaires de France, 2001), 286. See David Carroll's brilliant analysis of René Lespès colonialist demographics in *Camus the Algerian: Colonialism, Terrorism, Justice*, (New York: Columbia University Press, 2007), 45–50.

4   Olivier Todd, *Albert Camus: Une vie* (Paris: Gallimard, 1999), 305.

5   "Le Minotaure ou la Halte d'Oran," *Œuvres complètes* 3:567–85; *Lyrical and Critical Essays*, trans. Kennedy, 109–33: "The streets of Oran are reserved for dust, pebbles and heat" and "All the bad taste of Europe and the Orient meets in Oran."

6   Albert Camus, *Carnets 1935–1948*, *Œuvres complètes*, ed. Jacqueline Lévi-Valensi, vol. 2, 1944–1948 (Paris: Gallimard, Bibliothèque de la Pléiade, 2006), 905; in English, *Notebooks: 1935–1942*, trans. Philip Thody (New York: Knopf, 1963, rpt. New York: Rowman & Littlefield, 2010), 168, edited.

7   *L'Étranger, Œuvres complètes*, ed. Jacqueline Lévi-Valensi, vol. 1, 1931–1944 (Paris: Gallimard, Bibliothèque de la Pléiade, 2006), 141. *The Stranger*, trans. Matthew Ward (New York: Knopf, 1988), 3, edited.

8   Ryan Bloom argues convincingly that the best translation of the first line of *The Stranger* should begin with the word "today"—as does the French sentence, which emphasizes the fact that Meursault lives in the present. Matthew Ward, whose excellent translation I use in all other instances, begins with "Maman died today." See "Lost in Translation: What the First Line of 'The Stranger' Should Be," *New Yorker*, May 11, 2011; http://www.newyorker .com/books/page-turner/lost-in-translation-what-the-first-line-of-the-stranger-should-be (accessed September 1, 2015).

9   Jean Dagron, a physician specializing in deaf culture, describes the connection between Camus's object-oriented writing and the verbal style of his deaf mother and uncle. Dagron compares the wall between Meursault and the rest of the world to the perceptions of the nonhearing. See Jean Dagron, *Albert Camus, l'empreinte du silence* (Marseille: Éditions du Crilence, 2013).

10   Camus, Carnets, *Œuvres complètes* 2:862; in English, *Notebooks*, trans. Thody, 103.

11   Alfred Noyer-Weidner, referring to a 1959 conversation with Camus, in his article "Structure et Sens de 'L'Étranger," *Albert Camus 1980*, ed. Raymond Gay-Crosier (Gainesville: University Press of Florida), 72.

Bibliography

Albert Camus–Jean Grenier, Correspondance 1932–1960. Ed. Marguerite Dobrenn. Paris: Gallimard, 1981. Available in English as *Albert Camus and Jean Grenier Correspondence, 1932–1960*. Trans. Jan F. Rigaud. Lincoln: University of Nebraska Press, 2003.

Alger-Républicain (Algiers). Bibliothèque nationale de France (BNF), Paris. This large paper, founded in 1938, became the smaller evening paper *Le Soir Républicain* (Algiers) in 1939, when *Alger-Républicain* was shut down. Camus worked for these papers as an editorialist, literary critic, and investigative reporter from 1938 to 1940. Both are archived at the Bibliothèque Nationale de France.

Cahiers Albert Camus 3: Fragments d'un combat 1938–1940, Alger-Républicain, Le Soir Républicain. Ed. Jacqueline Lévi-Valensi and André Abbou. Paris: Gallimard, 1978.

Œuvres complètes. Ed. Jacqueline Lévi-Valensi (vols. 1 and 2) and Raymond Gay-Crosier (vols. 3 and 4). Paris: Gallimard, Bibliothèque de la Pléiade, 2006–2008. The definitive scholarly edition in four volumes, known as The Pléiade, assembled by leading Camus scholars working with original manuscripts. An earlier two-volume Gallimard Pléiade edition compiled by Roger Quilliot shortly after Camus's death, *Théâtre, récits, nouvelles* (1962) and *Essais* (1965), is still valuable for its editor's notes. Whereas Quilliot's Pléaide is organized by genre, the series edited under the direction of Jacqueline Lévi-Valensi looks at the work in chronological order, and includes texts that weren't yet published in the 1960s, such as Camus's notebooks and the posthumous novels *A Happy Death* and *The First Man.*

Lottman, Herbert. *Albert Camus.* Corte Madera, California: Gingko Press, 1997. Still unsurpassed for its chronology and for its interviews with so many of Camus's close friends and colleagues, this American-style, fact-based biography was first published in 1979 by an expatriate journalist at *Publishers Weekly.*

Lyrical and Critical Essays. Ed. Philip Thody, trans. Ellen Conroy Kennedy. New York: Vintage, 1970. Includes "The Wrong Side and the Right Side" (1937); "Nuptials" (1939); "The Minotaur, or Stopping in Oran" (1954); "On Jean-Paul Sartre's La Nausée" (1938); "Intelligence and the Scaffold" (1943); "No, I am not an existentialist" (1945).

The Myth of Sisyphus and Other Essays. Trans. Justin O'Brien, New York: Vintage, 1991.

Notebooks, 1935–1942. Trans. Philip Thody. New York: Knopf, 1963, rpt. New York: Rowman & Littlefield, 2010

Séry, Macha. *Camus à 20 ans: premiers combats.* Lalaune: Au Diable Vauvert, 2011. A precise and gripping political and cultural mapping of Camus's young adulthood by one of France's best literary journalists.

Todd, Olivier. *Albert Camus: Une vie.* Paris: Gallimard, 1999. Especially strong on Camus's correspondence, citing letters not otherwise available, and with a deep understanding of the Parisian literary world by one of its insiders. An emphasis on the writer's romantic life. A French-style biography, writerly and interpretive. Note that the English translation by Benjamin Ivry, *Albert Camus: A Life* (New York: Knopf, 1997) is substantially abridged.

Discussion Questions

1. *The Stranger* begins with an unsettling mix of the present, past, and the future ("Today, Maman died ... I'll take the bus at two"), which Kaplan interprets as the narrator's apathy regarding his mother's death. What is your interpretation of this opening line?

2. Camus grew up with a deaf mother with little or minimal verbal communication. This made Camus be in touch with physical reality more intimately than human experiences mediated through language. What is it like to imagine Camus recounting his mother's death, taking into account the unusual mode of communication he grew up with?

3. According to Kaplan, *The Stranger* is told from two temporal points present and future. What is the literary effect of such dual temporal points of view in regard to the protagonist's psychological world?

4. What is your reaction to such a "flat" recount of the death of one's own mother? Can you relate the kind of human experience portrayed by the narrator (Meursault the protagonist) to your own experience?

5. Kaplan understands Camus' intent to say the least and be laconic as refusal to lend to the world a meaning it didn't have. Isn't storytelling a process in which new meanings are created in a narrative world of characters in events? Appraise Kaplan's critic of Camus.

UNIT III
MAKING SENSE OF SCIENCE

In the ninth chapter, Peter Bowler and Iwan Morus examine the characteristics of modern science in the era of Scientific Revolution, focusing on the mechanical mode of the explanation and experimental method of knowledge. In the tenth chapter, Charles Darwin presents significant evidence that suggests that humans have evolved from lower animals, such as similarities in bodily structure and embryonic development among mammals. In the eleventh chapter, Paul Halpern presents an intriguing story on the partnership and rivalry between the two leading quantum theorists—Einstein holding firmly a deterministic view and Schrödinger reserving the unpredictable nature of the universe. In the twelfth chapter, Anne Ross et al. discuss a distinct mode of thinking and theorizing in an indigenous scientific community that essentially involves the historical narrative and human-nonhuman animal interaction.

Magic and Mechanism

Peter J. Bowler and Iwan Rhys Morus

What kind of world did the new systems of natural philosophy that emerged around this period describe? One common feature of the various new natural philosophical systems that were offered up during the sixteenth and seventeenth centuries is that they were quite self-consciously novel. Authors offered up books with titles like *Novum organum* (Francis Bacon), *Due nuove scienze* (Galileo), or *Phonurgia nova* (Athanasius Kircher). There was no mistaking these authors' ambitions. They wanted to set the study of the natural world on a completely new footing. It is difficult for the historian to generalize too freely when trying to find ways of characterizing these new systems of natural philosophy. We now know that in their specifics, at least, these attempts at creating a new science varied a great deal. There was a great deal of disagreement over what the New Science would look like, what the most secure way of proceeding might be, and what the results of the investigation might deliver. At least some of the avenues that the Scientific Revolution's protagonists followed in their search for knowledge appear distinctly unpromising from a modern perspective. Others fit more comfortably into our conceptions of what science should be like. It is important to remember, however, that these early modern natural philosophers had very different conceptions of the world from ours—and very different views of what science should be able to deliver (Lindberg and Westman 1990).

Magic seemed, to some natural philosophers at least, to be a promising way of investigating nature. Sixteenth- and seventeenth-century magicians traced their traditions back to the mythological figure of Hermes Trismegistus. Magic was regarded as a search for the hidden, "occult" qualities of natural objects and phenomena. Understanding these occult qualities would provide a way of comprehending the hidden operations of nature and the relationships between different kinds of natural objects (Yates 1964). Particular objects—such as magnets, for example—could clearly be seen to influence other objects without apparent contact. Astrology seemed to many a promising avenue of occult enquiry as well. Trying to understand the ways in which the movements of the stars and planets influenced the unfolding of earthly events was a way of coming to grips with the hidden operations of the universe. Similarly, alchemy appeared to offer a way of understanding the ways in which different substances influenced each other and what their essential qualities might be. There was a flourishing tradition of natural magic in the sixteenth and seventeenth centuries as well. Natural magicians like the Elizabethan courtier and mathematician John Dee or the Jesuit scholar and polymath Athenasius Kircher could produce spectacular phenomena at will. Kircher, for example, was famed for his invention of the magic lantern and a clock driven by a sunflower seed that followed the course of the sun from sunrise to sunset just like a sunflower blossom, demonstrating the sun's occult influence over natural objects.

Less controversial—to modern sensibilities at least—than magic as a tool for understanding nature was the mechanical philosophy. This was the view that the best way of understanding the cosmos was to regard it as a huge machine and that the task of natural philosophy was to understand the principles by which the machine operated. In some ways, at least, the mechanical philosophy was the antithesis of the magical tradition since it denied the very existence of the occult qualities that magic tried to investigate. Clockwork was the dominant metaphor of the mechanical philosophy. All the parts of a clock worked in harmony together to produce the final motion. This was how some natural philosophers visualized the workings of the universe, too—all the parts worked in unison to produce the movements of the earth and the planets. The clockwork metaphor had the major advantage of implying the existence of a celestial clockmaker as well: if the universe were a piece of a complex mechanism like a clock, then just as clocks had clockmakers, the universe must have had a creator too. Mechanical philosophy did not apply only to large-scale phenomena like the movements of the planets, though. Mechanical philosophers devoted their ingenuity to finding out mechanisms for all the phenomena of nature. They aimed to banish occult qualities completely from natural philosophy by showing that even the most mysterious forces could be reduced to the operations of simple mechanical principles.

The doyen of the mechanical philosophy in the early seventeenth century was undoubtedly the French natural philosopher and mathematician René Descartes. A Jesuit-trained scholar and former mercenary soldier during the Thirty Years' War, Descartes had famously resolved to reduce all human knowledge to first principles, eventually producing what is probably the most recognizable philosophical dictum in modern history—*cogito ergo sum*. Descartes laid out his plans for a new and ambitious philosophy of nature in his *Discourse on Method* (1637). The picture of the universe he produced was unambiguously mechanical. Descartes conceived of the universe as a plenum, that is to say, full of matter. There was no room for a vacuum in Descartes's cosmology. Since the universe was full of matter, if one part of it moved, then other parts of it had to move as well. The simplest means of achieving this was movement in a circle—hence the circular motion of the planets around the sun. For Descartes, therefore, the universe was made up of an indefinite number of vortices, each swirling around a sun or a star and carrying the planets around with them. The planets were held in stable orbits by the constant pressure of subtle matter continually swirling outward from the central sun. Descartes could even use his theory of vortices to explain the motion of the tides—one of the most intractable problems of seventeenth-century practical mathematics.

Like other mechanical philosophers, Descartes's theories accounted for more than large-scale phenomena such as the motions of the planets and the movements of the tides. Everything in Descartes's universe was made up of particles of matter. Light, for example, consisted in a stream of subtle particles flowing outward from the sun. He also tried to account for the phenomenon of magnetism on mechanical, corpuscularian principles (fig. 9.1). Magnetism was one of natural magicians' favorite examples of evidence for the existence of occult qualities. Even William Gilbert, author of *De magnete*—the first comprehensive account of magnetism published in 1600—had compared the actions of the magnet to those of the soul. According to Descartes, magnetism was the result of a stream of corpuscles (or particles) flowing out from the magnetic body. These corpuscles were shaped as either left-handed or right-handed screws, so that depending on their shapes they could cause objects they passed through to move either toward or away from the magnet. Descartes's mechanical philosophy even extended to animals and people. Descartes famously described all animals as no more than complex machines. He took the same view of human bodies as well, except that humans were possessed of an animating soul that controlled their bodies through the medium of the pineal gland. Descartes was convinced that proper management of the body's mechanism through proper diet could lead to the indefinite extension of human life (see chap. 19, "Science and Medicine").

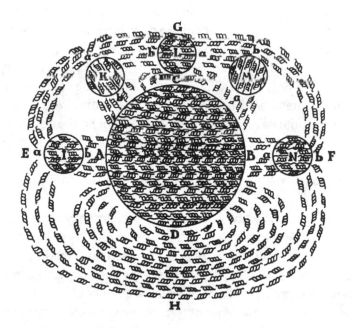

FIGURE 9.1   Descartes's model of the mechanical origins of magnetism. The magnetic body emanates a stream of magnetic particles, shaped like little screws. When those screwlike particles pass through other bodies, they cause them to move either toward or away from the magnetic body, depending on whether the screws are right- or left-handed.

The Anglo-Irish natural philosopher Robert Boyle shared with Descartes the view that all natural phenomena could be accounted for by the mechanical action of minute particles or corpuscles of matter. Boyle held that at the original creation of the universe, the uniform, homogenous matter of which it originally consisted was divided into a whole array of differently shaped and textured moving corpuscles. It was the different sizes, shapes, and textures of these particles of matter, along with the different ways in which they moved, that explained the various visible and tangible properties of matter. Boyle differed from Descartes in being rather more cautious in specifying just what the various shapes and sizes of these invisible particles might actually be. Where Descartes was prepared to specify the precise shapes of the particles causing magnetism, for example, Boyle was satisfied to leave such matters open. What mattered as far as he was concerned was simply that these kinds of mechanical explanations of natural phenomena, in terms of the behavior and form of material corpuscles, were accepted as the most plausible ones available. While Boyle accepted that in general the best explanation of the color or texture of an object, for example, would be in terms of the kinds of particles from which it was made, he also accepted that the issue of just what those particles were like remained a matter for speculation.

The caution with which Boyle approached the issue of providing specific rather than general mechanical explanations of the phenomena is clear in his accounts of his famous air-pump experiments—of which more later in this chapter. During the late 1650s and early 1660s Boyle carried out a number of experiments with a new item of philosophical apparatus—the air pump—designed to investigate the properties of the air. On the basis of these experiments, Boyle argued that the air was made up of springlike particles. It was as a result of this springlike character of the particles from which it was made up that air could resist any force exerted on it and could expand when those forces were removed. In his *New Experiments Physico-Mechanical Touching the Spring of the Air* (1660), Boyle argued that while he could be effectively certain of the truth of the phenomena produced in his air pump—in other words, air did indeed act as he had described it—he could have no such certainty concerning the details of a causal explanation of those phenomena. As a mechanical philosopher he could be sure that the causes of the phenomenon were mechanical in nature but any account of the detailed mechanism could be, at best, only probable. Particles of air might be just like steel springs but, conversely, they might not.

Despite this kind of circumspection, the mechanical philosophy certainly seemed to many of its adherents to be the best way of formulating causal accounts of natural phenomena. The English natural philosopher Robert Hooke, once Boyle's assistant experimenter, even suggested that in due course it might be possible actually to see the basic particles of matter through the medium of the recently invented microscope. Even in the absence of such direct sensory evidence of the existence of these "small Machines of Nature," most natural philosophers were willing to concede that hypothesizing their existence was the best way of proceeding in constructing philosophically respectable accounts of nature. It was certainly a better alternative than falling back on the assumption of occult qualities inherent in different kinds of matter. When Evangelista Torricelli carried out experiments with pumps and liquids in 1644 it was with the aim of showing that the phenomena could be explained mechanically without having to fall back on the notion that "nature abhors a vacuum." Blaise Pascal had the same kind of end in view when he repeated the experiments in 1648 on the slopes of Puy de Dôme in France. One advantage many pointed to in adopting mechanical explanations was that it did away with the temptation of endowing matter with animistic qualities. As the French priest Marin Mersenne argued, making matter active could lead to the dangerous possibility of breaking down the distinction between God and nature. It was far better to follow the mechanists and accept that matter was essentially passive and only differed in the size and shape of its particles.

As we have already seen with Descartes's example, these kinds of mechanistic arguments applied to animal and human bodies as much as they more conventionally did to the inanimate world. The English physician William Harvey's description of the circulation of the blood was widely hailed by contemporaries as a classic example of the mechanical philosophy applied to animated bodies, though Harvey himself was dubious of the mechanical philosophy's merits. His *De motu cordis et sanguinis* (1628) argued that blood circulated through the body, passing through the heart and lungs into the arteries and through them to the extremities of the body before returning through the veins to the heart. Following what they regarded as Harvey's example, self-proclaimed iatromechanists (from the Greek *iatro,* meaning doctor) such as Giovanni Borelli argued that understanding the human body as a complex machine was the key to improving medicine. Hermann Boerhaave argued that all the anatomical components that made up the body could be seen to have their equivalents in various kinds of machinery: "We find some of them resembling *Pillars, Props, Crossbeams, Fences, Coverings;* some like *Axes, Wedges Leavers* and *Pullies;* others like *Cords, Presses,* or *Bellowes;* others again like *Sieves, Strainers, Pipes, Conduits,* and *Receivers;* and the Faculty of performing various motions by these Instruments, is called their Functions; which are all performed by Mechanical Laws, and by them only are intelligible." For Boerhaave, the human body was just like a complex hydraulic machine (see chap. 19, "Science and Medicine").

Proponents of the mechanical philosophy often ranged themselves quite explicitly in opposition to practitioners of magic and those who argued for the existence of occult qualities in nature. To many, it seemed that simply explaining some feature of nature in terms of the inherent qualities of matter was no explanation at all. This was what dramatist Jean-Baptiste Molière lampooned with his description of natural philosophers explaining the sleep-inducing capacities of opium by reference to its possession of "dormative qualities." Recent historians have been rather more careful than their mechanically minded contemporaries in dismissing magical practitioners completely out of hand. Most historians of the Scientific Revolution accept that magic had an important role to play in the intellectual debates of the period. Magicians and mechanical philosophers do appear to have shared a concern to elucidate the properties of matter by examining its hidden qualities, whether those qualities were regarded as being innate or not. They also shared the stance of self-conscious novelty. Most natural philosophers during this period shared a perception that they were engaged in a fundamentally novel project, however they might then characterize the details of the project itself.

New Ways of Knowing

When celebrating the novelty of the New Science, its practitioners had more in mind than just what they were finding out about the nature of the universe. Just as important in their view was the question of how that new knowledge had been acquired. Almost all were united in agreeing that the big difference between their brand of knowledge as compared to previous varieties was that it was based on experience rather than authority. The "Schoolmen"—as previous generations of scholars were dismissed—were held to have based their claims to knowledge simply on the authority of ancient texts, primarily Aristotle and his medieval interpreters. Promoters of the New Science, in contrast, claimed that their knowledge was based on actual experience of the world. We have already noted the extent to which seventeenth-century natural philosophers emphasized the novelty of their science. This is what they mainly had in mind with such claims. Their science was new because it was based on an entirely different set of assumptions about how we might best go about acquiring knowledge in the first place. Where previous generations of scholars had searched for knowledge in the books of Aristotle, the new generation prided themselves on their realization that the best approach to knowledge was to read it in the "book of nature."

Increasingly, also, many natural philosophers argued that the language in which the book of nature was written was the language of mathematics. This represented a major shift in the epistemological—and social—status of mathematics. As we have already seen, mathematics had traditionally been regarded as epistemologically inferior to natural philosophy. Natural philosophy was taken to deal with the real nature of things—their essences. Mathematics, in contrast, simply dealt with accidental qualities like numbers. Mathematics was certainly regarded as providing certainty of a particular kind, but natural philosophers argued that what it provided was a very limited kind of certainty. Conclusions derived by means of mathematical reasoning were true only insofar as the premises from which the argument started were taken to be true—and establishing the truth of such premises was held to be beyond the scope of mathematical reasoning. Along with these differences in epistemological status came differences in social status. Mathematics did not occupy as exalted a position in the university curriculum as did natural philosophy. Professors of mathematics, as Galileo, for one, was well aware, earned less than their philosophical counterparts. It was also widely regarded as a far more practical endeavor than natural philosophy.

Mathematics not only embraced those aspects that might now be characterized as "pure" reasoning, such as geometry, for example; it also embraced more practical activities, such as arithmetic. Some commentators argued that mathematics was not, properly speaking, an academic activity at all—it was something that mechanics did, "the business of *Traders, Merchants, Seamen, Carpenters, Surveyors of Lands,* or the like." This is an extreme example, but it does, nevertheless, highlight the sense in which mathematics was considered by some, at least, to be a socially inferior epistemological practice. Practical mathematics was an activity built around the manipulation of different kinds of mathematical instruments, such as sextants, quadrants, or calculating devices like the slide rule (fig. 9.2). During an age that saw increasing

FIGURE 9.2 The frontispiece of Jonas Moore, *A New System of Mathematicks* (1681). The range of mathematical instruments illustrated here suggests how important practical mathematics was becoming during the seventeenth century.

maritime travel and exploration as well as the start of the drive toward land enclosures and accurate mapmaking, practical mathematics was, however, undeniably useful. Gentleman landowners (and gentleman adventurers) increasingly found themselves in need of the skills of practical mathematicians and even started acquiring a certain level of mathematical proficiency themselves (see chap. 17, "Science and Technology"). All of this certainly resulted in a raising of mathematicians' cultural visibility, particularly around the princely courts and aristocratic households toward which the intellectual center of gravity was decisively shifting, away from the Aristotelian-dominated universities.

It was this kind of shift, as we saw earlier, that Galileo took advantage of in his move from professor of mathematics at Padua to philosopher at the Medici court in Florence. In the same way that he did with his astronomy, part of Galileo's strategy in making the move was to insist on the philosophical status of mathematics. As he and others increasingly argued, the book of nature was written in the language of mathematics. Galileo argued that natural philosophy should be expressed in terms of mathematics because nature was mathematical in its structure. The main aim of natural philosophy, therefore, should be to produce mathematically expressed laws of nature, such as Galileo's own mathematical law of falling bodies, according to which all bodies fell to earth at the same rate regardless of their weight. There was even an ancient pedigree for this claim, to match the Aristotelian pedigree of the Schoolmen. Mathematicians turned to the authority of Plato and Pythagoras to establish the mathematical nature of the natural world. This is what Kepler, for example, did with his early argument that the distances between the planets' orbits were defined by the series of five Platonic solids—cube, tetrahedron, dodecahedron, octahedron, and icosahedron.

Just what the status of mathematical descriptions of the natural world was remained the subject of dispute, however. It did not escape critics' attention, for example, that Galileo's law of falling bodies did not hold true in the real world, but only in a mathematically idealized one. To overcome this, Galileo had to argue that it was actually his idealized, frictionless mathematical model rather than messy reality, that somehow properly captured the essence of the phenomena. Natural philosophers worried about just what kind of epistemological status—what degree of certainty—should be accorded to the results of mathematical arguments concerning the operations of the natural world. Just what was the nature of the fit between the mechanical universe made up of particles in motion and mathematical descriptions of it? How could the integrity of that match be guaranteed? Even a mechanical philosopher like Robert Boyle, who was in principle happy to proclaim that the book of nature was "written in mathematical letters," was in practice far more circumspect about writing his own natural philosophy in mathematical language. One of Boyle's problems with mathematics was that, like many of his contemporaries, he was convinced that to sustain its authority—to appeal to as many people's commonly accepted experience of the world as possible—natural philosophy had to be accessible. The problem with mathematics was that it was not.

Boyle, like many others, was keen to emphasize that the New Science was empirical science. Rather than depending on the authority of the ancients, he and his philosophical contemporaries aimed to base their science on the authority of their own senses. Experience was to be the key to constructing new theories about the natural world. This seems relatively unproblematic from a straightforward modern perspective. This appearance is itself a testimony to the success of early modern natural philosophers in establishing this view of the proper basis for inquiry into the workings of nature. Seventeenth-century commentators themselves, however, were acutely aware of the philosophical problems to be encountered in translating everyday experience into secure knowledge. They knew that reasoning from individual experiences to universal generalizations was fraught with difficulty. They knew that ways were needed of judging which kinds of experiences were to be regarded as trustworthy and which not. This was a period when the horizons of human experience in the Western world were expanding massively, as travelers and explorers brought back tales of strange encounters in distant lands as well as exotic specimens of plants and animals. On the one hand, these novel sources of information seemed to justify skepticism concerning the reliability of ancient authority. On the other hand, as contemporaries were uncomfortably aware, they also raised questions concerning just what kinds of experiences should be considered as legitimate sources of knowledge and what sources of evidence could be trusted.

One of the foremost philosophical advocates of empirical knowledge was the English courtier and lawyer Francis Bacon. According to Bacon, there could be no question that well-attested experience rather than ancient authority was the only credible foundation for real knowledge. But, Bacon argued, to be useful experience had to be properly policed. Drawing explicitly on his legal experiences and his background as a state inquisitor, he insisted that experience had to be organized to be useful. "Just as if some kingdom or state were to direct its counsels and affairs not by letters and reports from ambassadors and trustworthy messengers, but by the gossip in the streets," he scoffed, "such exactly is the system of management introduced into philosophy with relation to experience." Bacon's solution was to make the business of empirical fact-finding into a collective, highly regulated system. In his *New Atlantis*, Bacon advocated the institution of Solomon's House—an establishment dedicated to the collaborative, disciplined acquisition of empirical knowledge. Bacon envisaged a hierarchy of researchers, ranging from humble fact gatherers at the bottom to philosophers on top, all engaged in the systematic production of empirical knowledge. Solomon's House was never built, although Bacon's vision certainly played a role in the seventeenth-century establishment of such collaborative scientific institutions as the Royal Society of London or the Paris Academy of Sciences (see chap. 14, "The Organization of Science"). His sense that distilling knowledge from experience required disciplined method and that not just any (or anybody's) experiences could be considered as a reliable basis for knowledge was widely shared, however (Martin 1992).

Disciplined and carefully regulated experience lay at the heart of Robert Boyle's experimental project, as exemplified in his air-pump experiments. Boyle's experiments were widely regarded—in England, at least—as exemplars of proper experimental practice. Boyle used his experiments to establish a number of claims about the constitution and nature of air (see chap. 3, "The Chemical Revolution"). He was well aware, however, that there was nothing straightforward about the procedure. Everything that took place inside the air pump was artificial, for example. It was not self-evident that the way the air behaved under such circumstances accurately reflected its natural behavior. Even given a general acceptance of a homology between what happened inside the air pump and what happened in nature, Boyle still had to work hard to convince his skeptical audience of the validity of his claims. He produced minutely detailed reports of just what he had seen during the course of the experiments. He carried out experiments in public, before witnesses. All of this was essential if he was to persuade others that his testimony about his experiences with the air pump was to be accepted as reliable. This was one reason that he and others like him felt that establishing scientific societies such as the Royal Society was so important. Even so, Boyle remained circumspect about what might be inferred from his experiments. As we have seen, while he regarded his reports about the behavior of the air as having the status of truth, any inferences from that behavior to the real constitution of the air remained hypothetical (Shapin and Schaffer 1985).

As we have suggested, seventeenth-century practitioners' acute awareness of the need to demonstrate the validity of experience was one factor in the rise of scientific societies. Most philosophical commentators agreed that the key to reliable empirical information lay in the trustworthiness of the witnesses. This was why Boyle and many other made experiments in public. The more witnesses—and the higher those witnesses' social status—the more reliable the results of the experiment. In the absence of witnesses, experimenters made every effort to produce sufficiently detailed and technical reports of their experiences that others would be convinced of their veracity. There was also a new vogue for cabinets of curiosities (Findlen 1994). Natural philosophers and their patrons collected and displayed natural (and artificial) curiosities of all kinds as a way of demonstrating the variety of nature—and their own prestige, of course (see chap. 16, "Popular Science"). Many empiricist natural philosophers concurred with Francis Bacon in his conviction that making new knowledge was an essentially collaborative enterprise. This provided one reason why it mattered that they should be able to trust each others' observations, which was, in turn, a reason why experimenters should be gentlemen, too, as opposed to artisans, tradesmen, women, or even foreigners. Gentlemen were conventionally regarded as more trustworthy because they were meant to be economically independent and therefore free from external influence. Many of them also agreed with Bacon that natural philosophy should be a civic matter as it was something that had an important role to play for the good of the commonwealth—another reason why it might be best carried out by gentlemen. Among other things, this suggested that one role for the new experimental natural philosophy should be to produce useful knowledge as well (Shapin 1994).

As we said earlier, this concern with the openness of natural philosophical knowledge was one of the reasons underlying Robert Boyle's and others' suspicions concerning the place of mathematics in the new mechanical philosophy. The key to making the New Science reliable, as far as they were concerned, was to make it as accessible as possible. New knowledge could be passed around, tested, and attested to and thereby slowly build up into a new consensus. It would become part of the common and universal stock of experience. The insistence that the book of nature was written in the language of mathematics was something of an impediment in this respect. Mathematics was far from being an accessible and commonly understood language in the seventeenth century. On the contrary, it was a highly technical practice that only a very few experts had fully mastered. Despite such concerns, however, few if any enthusiasts for the New Science would deny that mathematics was the language of nature. It was certainly increasingly held up as an exemplar of clear reasoning. Models of good ways of reasoning were just what seventeenth-century natural philosophers were looking for, after all. They wanted to be sure that their way of knowing, as well as their knowledge itself, was built on a secure foundation.

Let Newton Be!

Many of his contemporaries and immediate disciples regarded Sir Isaac Newton as having put the finishing touches on the Scientific Revolution. As the poet Alexander Pope rhapsodized:

> Nature, and Nature's Laws lay hid in Night.
> God said, *Let Newton be!* And all was *Light*.

Newton had succeeded in bringing together the disparate and fragmentary elements of the New Science and had forged them into a coherent whole. In many ways, he was the epitome of the natural philosopher as well: acerbic, difficult, and solitary. He was the archetype of the scientific genius for succeeding generations. Born the son of a prosperous Lincolnshire yeoman on Christmas Day 1642 (or 4 January 1643, as far as the rest of Europe was concerned, having already adopted the Gregorian calendar), Newton studied at the local grammar school before entering Trinity College Cambridge. It was as a fellow of Trinity that Newton produced the two books on which his claim to fame rested: the *Principia,* published in 1687, and the *Opticks,* eventually published in 1704 after Newton's elevation to the presidency of the Royal Society and, not coincidentally, following the death of his archnemesis Robert Hooke. By the time of his own death in 1727, he had transformed himself from a reclusive scholar into a powerful and influential public figure, gathering around himself a coterie of self-confessed Newtonians committed to his vision of what natural philosophy should be and how it should be practiced.

It is worth pausing a moment over the title page of Newton's great mathematical work. The *Principia*'s full title was the *Philosophiae naturalis principia mathematica,* or the *Mathematical Principles of Natural Philosophy.* It heralded an ambitious project. Newton was certainly committing himself to the view that mathematics was the language of nature and that the task of natural philosophy was to uncover the hidden mathematical laws that governed the universe's operations (Cunningham 1991). He was also making it clear to his readers that he knew what those mathematical laws were. In effect, the title page of Newton's *Principia* announced to the world that he had uncovered the secrets of the universe. For such an ambitious book, the *Principia* had relatively obscure origins. According to anecdote, the book began as a response to a question from the astronomer Edmund Halley (discoverer of the eponymous comet), who at a meeting with Newton in 1684 had asked him if he could work out what kind of path an object (such as a planet) would follow under the influence of a force that varied as the inverse square of the distance from the center. Newton replied that he had calculated that such a path would be an ellipse—just like the orbits of the planets around the sun—but that he had mislaid the proof. Halley shrugged his shoulders knowingly and returned to London. Newton sat down to recover the proof. The result a few years later was the *Principia.*

Newton started off the *Principia* with a series of definitions of the physical properties of natural bodies—things like mass, momentum, inertia, and force—that he would deal with in the rest of the book. He then followed with a statement of his three fundamental laws of motion: that a body will rigidly maintain its state of uniform motion in a straight line, or its state of rest, unless it is acted on by an impressed force; that any change in the motion of a body is proportional to the motive force impressed; and that for every action there is an equal and opposite reaction. In the following three books of the *Principia,* Newton put these propositions to work. In book 1 he studied the motion of bodies under the actions of different kinds of forces, showing among other things that if a body follows an elliptical path, then the force acting on it must vary as the inverse square of distance from the center. In book 2 he studied the motions of bodies in various resisting media. In book 3, the "System of the World" he applied the general theory he had developed in book 1 specifically to the motions of heavenly bodies, establishing his universal law of gravitation along the way. Having established that the force acting to maintain the moon in its orbit was the same as that causing the acceleration of falling bodies at the earth's surface, he argued that "the economy of nature requires us to make gravity responsible for the orbital force acting on each of the planets." It was—and was widely recognized as—a veritable tour de force.

Newton's *Opticks* was in many ways a very different book. Despite (or perhaps because of) its comparative accessibility compared with the highly technical mathematics of the *Principia,* it was also considerably more controversial. The *Opticks* was set out as an exposition of the theory of colors that Newton had first developed several decades previously in his "New Theory about Light and Colours" published in the Royal Society's *Philosophical Transactions* in 1672. In that paper, Newton had attacked the prevailing idea that colors were the result of modifications of white light and suggested instead that white light was itself the result of the combination of different colors of light. He used his famous prism experiments in which glass prisms were used first to turn white light into separate colors and then to recombine those colors into white light. It is important to be clear just what status Newton accorded to this experiment. As far as he was concerned the experiment proved his theory of colors—it was an *experimentum crucis,* a crucial experiment that established his theory beyond reasonable doubt. This was why Newton reacted so furiously to Robert Hooke's suggestion that the experiment could in fact be interpreted differently. As far as he was concerned this was not just an attack on his interpretation of the experiment, it was an attack on his personal integrity.

There was far more to Newton's *Opticks* than just his theory of colors. He used the book and its succeeding editions to outline his vision of the future course of natural philosophy. In particular, he introduced a number of Queries that included his view on any number of natural philosophical issues such as the nature of light, the causes of newly discovered electrical and magnetic phenomena, and the possible existence of a universal ether filling all space. The first edition of the book contained sixteen of these Queries, a number that had swelled to thirty-one by the final edition. These Queries—as the name suggests—were frankly speculative in nature, despite the famous motto, *hypotheses non fingo* (I do not feign hypotheses), that he added to the 1713 edition of the *Principia.* He asked, for example, "Are not the rays of light very small particles emitted from shining substances?" The thirty-first query was seemingly the most speculative of all. "Is not infinite Space the Sensorium of a Being incorporeal, living, and intelligent," Newton asked, "who sees the things themselves intimately, and thoroughly perceives them, and comprehends them wholly by their immediate presence to himself?" These were dangerous questions to raise. They are also an indication of the degree to which Newton placed his version of the mechanical philosophy in a thoroughly theological perspective.

While developing the work that led to the *Principia*, Newton was also working on another line of inquiry that he considered at least as important. He was trawling through ancient scriptural texts in an effort to recover a pristine and uncorrupted sacred history of creation. Newton was in fact an Arian—a heretic who denied the validity of the Trinity, the central belief of orthodox Catholicism and Protestantism. Newton held that the early Church had deliberately falsified and obscured the meanings of original biblical writings in order to mystify and confuse its followers. In his view, the ancients had known the truth about the mathematical structure of the universe, but the early Church fathers had deliberately conspired to obscure those truths. His scriptural researches were a systematic effort to recover the original meanings of biblical texts and hence to recover the lost wisdom of the ancients. That is just what he regarded his natural philosophy as doing as well. It was a process of rediscovery rather than discovery. Newton was sure that not only Plato and Pythagoras but Moses and the mythological Hermes Trismegistus as well had known about the Copernican system of the universe and the universal law of gravitation. All he was doing was rescuing that knowledge from the obscurity into which the early Church had condemned it.

Alchemy was another line of inquiry that Newton pursued in his efforts to recover lost knowledge. Newton delved enthusiastically into alchemical texts, producing copious notes and commentaries. He also carried out his own alchemical researches in his laboratory at Trinity College. Writings and experiments like this provided another possible avenue through which he might be able to rediscover what ancient philosophers had known about the nature and structure of the world. Newton regarded the arcane language and symbolism in which alchemical texts were presented as deliberate attempts to keep secret knowledge hidden from the eyes of the vulgar. In reading alchemical texts and attempting to reproduce the experimental procedures they described he was engaged in just the same kind of recovery exercise as he was when trying to wrest sense out of ancient scriptural writings or, for that matter, when producing the *Principia*. Unlike many other enthusiasts for the mechanical philosophy, Newton was also more sympathetic toward the idea of occult qualities in nature. Unlike many other mechanists, he was willing to leave open the question of the physical cause of gravity. He also suggested the possibility that matter might be endowed with "active powers." The German mathematician and philosopher Gottfried Wilhelm Leibniz explicitly accused Newton of reintroducing occult principles into natural philosophy on just these grounds.

It was partly in order to defend himself against such attacks that Newton surrounded himself with disciples. His defense against Leibniz—and his claim that Leibniz had stolen the idea of calculus from him—was undertaken by the young Anglican (and like Newton, secret Arian) clergyman Samuel Clarke. Despite charges such as those leveled by Leibniz, however, Newton's reputation in the early years of the eighteenth century could hardly have been higher. In England, he was regarded as the greatest flowering of English natural philosophy. On the Continent, particularly in France, he was regarded as the harbinger of enlightened rationality. The French writer Voltaire was a particular fan. According to Voltaire, a genius like Newton was born only once in a thousand years. Even Voltaire had to admit, however, that few of his disciples had read Newton, particularly the difficult *Principia*. As he reported back to France, few in London had read the great man "because one must be very learned to understand him." One friend of Voltaire's who clearly had read the *Principia* was Emilie du Châtelet, who wrote the first French translation and helped her lover Voltaire with the mathematical sections of his *Eléments de la philosophie de Newton* (1738). Even while paying lip service to the mathematical bravura of the *Principia*, most of Newton's self-proclaimed eighteenth-century followers were more likely [to] have derived their inspiration from the *Opticks* and its speculative Queries. Experimenters and instrument makers such as Francis Hauksbee or John Desaguliers saw themselves as devising experimental apparatus and techniques that could be used to demonstrate Newton's speculations concerning active powers with spectacular displays of electric or magnetic powers.

Newton's eighteenth-century legacy was in many ways all things to all men. Historians have struggled to define a coherent natural philosophy shared by all those who described themselves as Newton's followers. One strategy has been to divide them into two camps—those who took their Newton from the pages of the *Opticks* and those who imbibed him from the *Principia* instead. Those who read the *Opticks* followed Newton's experimental line of inquiry, studying the phenomena of electricity, heat, magnetism, or light—the active powers that Newton had identified. The *Principia*'s readers devoted themselves to expanding and refining Newton's mathematical treatment and applying it to new problems. There is something rather unsatisfying about this picture, implying, as it does, that the authors of the *Opticks* and the *Principia* had quite different and even unrelated concerns. It might be more promising to recognize that there simply was no coherent "Newtonian" tradition. Different eighteenth-century practitioners borrowed some parts of what they took to be Newton's approach and discarded others. They were all certainly keen to associate themselves with his name, if for no other reason than the tremendous authority it had acquired. Those, like Voltaire, who knew of his unpublished biblical researches found them an embarrassment. Newton had become an icon of the eighteenth-century Enlightenment and its cult of rationality.

Conclusions

And so to return to the question with which we began this chapter, was there really a scientific revolution? It is worth reminding ourselves of just what is involved in the claim that the radical changes that took place in our culture's way of viewing the universe during the seventeenth century or thereabouts constituted no less than a scientific revolution. To begin with, historians have traditionally regarded this a unique event. There may have been several scientific revolutions but only one Scientific Revolution. In other words, the original claim is that the events that took place around the seventeenth century were sufficiently momentous and unprecedented to be considered revolutionary, that this was a unique set of events without parallel elsewhere in history, and that something decisively recognizable as modern science emerged as a result. Until comparatively recently this interpretation would scarcely have appeared worth challenging. All of its elements, after all, appeared to be self-evident. It is a view that would have been shared to some degree or another by historians of science from the eighteenth century until the present day. It is nevertheless worth asking ourselves, in view of the brief sketch presented here, whether the traditional picture really stands up to rigorous scrutiny.

In many ways, it is clear that the traditional account of the Scientific Revolution simply does not add up. Indeed, it fails in all three of its basic assumptions. Historians now typically agree that cataclysmic as the intellectual changes of the Scientific Revolution might arguably be, they are not unique in history. Other changes in worldview have been just as momentous. The term "revolution" itself has been exposed as problematic. Historians have exposed clear continuities between early modern approaches to understanding the natural world and earlier perspectives. There does not seem to be a particular point or event in history to which we can point and say that the Scientific Revolution started there. If this was a revolution, then it was one without a clearly defined beginning and with no decisive ending either. Finally, it is now clear that whatever emerged from the Scientific Revolution, it was not modern science. Certainly there are aspects of Newton's work, for example, that look recognizably modern. This is hardly surprising. At the same time, there are aspects of his work—like his fascination with sacred histories—that seem irrecoverably alien. It simply will not do to bracket off that portion of his work and proclaim the sanitized remainder as the origin of modern science if for no other reason than it would do a gross injustice to Newton's own perception of the enterprise in which he was engaged.

At the same time, despite all this, as we suggested at the beginning of this chapter, many of the protagonists who participated in the Scientific Revolution unquestionably appear to have been convinced in their own minds that something momentous was going on. They demonstrate a rare degree of unanimity (a very rare degree for the period in question) not only that something significant was going on in terms of their understanding of the universe but also regarding just what that something was. On the whole, protagonists agreed that what was special about their approach to knowledge was that it was based on the interrogation of experience rather than authority. Instead of consulting Aristotle they were consulting their own senses. It is a moot point whether this perception was accurate. Modern historians of medieval philosophy take a rather less jaundiced view of its practices than did those who were, after all, explicitly rejecting it. It is nevertheless how they presented their activities. In this light, at least, if we want to take historical participants' own views of what they did at all seriously, then we have to accord some degree of validity to the idea of the Scientific Revolution. It is also true that what they had to say about their activities in this respect does strike a chord with modern perceptions of science. We rather like to think that modern science is based on experience rather than authority as well.

The best answer to our question, in the end, is probably to conclude that it is simply the wrong question to ask. Whether the Scientific Revolution is a useful historical category is largely a matter of perspective. At the very least, such categorizations should be taken with a fairly healthy pinch of salt. They certainly should not be allowed to cloud historical judgment. Categories like the Scientific Revolution are useful, after all, only insofar as they help us understand past science and its place in culture. When defending the category becomes an end in itself, then it is probably time to let it go. What matters about our historical study of the period in question is that we try to understand what happened then and what the various protagonists were trying to achieve on their own terms. Fitting it into a picture that leads from them to us is an important but secondary concern. If we go at it from the other direction—actively looking for precursors of modern science rather than appreciating the full picture—we will almost certainly end up getting hold of the wrong end of the stick.

References and Further Reading

Bennett, J. A. 1986. "The Mechanics' Philosophy and the Mechanical Philosophy." *History of Science* 24:1–28.

Biagioli, Mario. 1993. *Galileo Courtier: The Practice of Science in the Culture of Absolutism.* Chicago: University of Chicago Press.

Burtt, Edwin. 1924. *The Metaphysical Foundations of Modern Physical Science.* New York: Humanities Press.

Butterfield, Herbert. 1949. *The Origins of Modern Science, 1300–1800.* London: G. Bell.

Cunningham, Andrew. 1991. "How the *Principia* Got Its Name; or, Taking Natural Philosophy Seriously." *History of Science* 29:377–92.

Dear, Peter. 1995. *Discipline and Experience: The Mathematical Way in the Scientific Revolution.* Chicago: University of Chicago Press.

Fauvel, John, Raymond Flood, Michael Shortland, and Robin Wilson, eds. 1988. *Let Newton Be!* Oxford: Oxford University Press.

Findlen, Paula. 1994. *Possessing Nature: Museums, Collecting, and Scientific Culture in Early Modern Italy.* London and Berkeley, University of California Press.

Hall, Rupert. 1954. *The Scientific Revolution, 1500–1800.* London: Longmans, Green.

Hessen, Boris. [1931] 1971. "The Social and Economic Roots of Newton's 'Principia,'" In *Science at the Cross-Roads,* edited by N. I. Bukharin et al. Reprint ed., edited by Gary Werskey. London: Frank Cass, 149–212.

Iliffe, Rob. 1992. "In the Warehouse: Privacy, Property and Propriety in the Early Royal Society." *History of Science* 30:29–68.

Koyré, Alexandre. 1953. *From the Closed World to the Infinite Universe.* Baltimore: Johns Hopkins University Press.

———. 1968. *Metaphysics and Measurement: Essays in Scientific Revolution.* Cambridge, MA: Harvard University Press.

Kuhn, Thomas. 1966. *The Copernican Revolution.* Cambridge, MA: Harvard University Press.

Lindberg, David, and Robert Westman, eds. 1990. *Reappraisals of the Scientific Revolution.* Cambridge: Cambridge University Press.

Hunter, Michael, and Simon Schaffer, eds. 1989. *Robert Hooke: New Studies.* Woodbridge: Boydell.

Lloyd, Geoffrey E. R. 1970. *Early Greek Science.* London: Chatto & Windus.

———. 1973. *Greek Science after Aristotle.* London: Chatto & Windus.

Mayr, Otto. 1986. *Authority, Liberty and Automatic Machinery.* Baltimore: Johns Hopkins University Press.

Martin, Julian. 1992. *Francis Bacon, the State, and the Reform of Natural Philosophy.* Cambridge: Cambridge University Press.

Redondi, Pietro. 1987. *Galileo Heretic.* Princeton, NJ: Princeton University Press.

Shapin, Steven. 1994. *A Social History of Truth: Civility and Science in Seventeenth-Century England.* Chicago: University of Chicago Press.

———. 1996. *The Scientific Revolution.* Chicago: University of Chicago Press.

Shapin, Steven, and Simon Schaffer. 1985. *Leviathan and the Air-Pump: Hobbes, Boyle and the Experimental Life.* Princeton, NJ: Princeton University Press.

Thoren, Victor. 1990. *Lord of Uraniborg: A Biography of Tycho Brahe.* Cambridge: Cambridge University Press.

Westfall, Richard. 1971. *The Construction of Modern Science: Mechanisms and Mechanics.* Cambridge: Cambridge University Press.

Westfall, Richard. 1980. *Never at Rest: A Biography of Isaac Newton.* Cambridge: Cambridge University Press.

Whiteside, D. Thomas, ed. 1969. *The Mathematical Papers of Isaac Newton.* Cambridge: Cambridge University Press.

Yates, Frances. 1964. *Giordano Bruno and the Hermetic Tradition.* London: Routledge.

Discussion Questions

1. In what aspects was clockwork the key analogy of the mechanical philosophy? In what ways is the working of a clock similar to the working of the natural world?

2. Descartes is famous for the most widely quoted philosophical statement *Cogito ergo sum* (I think, therefore I am). What does this statement mean and what is its significance?

3. What are the three laws and how do they pave a way to his universal law of gravitation?

4. The seventeenth-century natural philosophers held the view that knowledge is based on actual experience of the world rather than authority, and that the best approach to knowledge was to read in the book of nature. Which one is more trustworthy—experience or authority?

5. Many natural philosophers argued that the language in which the book of nature was written was the language of mathematics, and this attitude brought about a shift in the status of mathematics—from a practical instrument of counting numbers to a philosophical framework. Do we see the natural world itself as mathematical?

The Descent of Man

The Evidence of the Descent of Man from Some Lower Form

Charles Darwin

Nature of the evidence bearing on the origin of man—Homologous structures in man and the lower animals—Miscellaneous points of correspondence—Development—Rudimentary structures, muscles, sense-organs, hair, bones, reproductive organs, &c.—The bearing of these three great classes of facts on the origin of man.

He who wishes to decide whether man is the modified descendant of some pre-existing form, would probably first enquire whether man varies, however slightly, in bodily structure and in mental faculties; and if so, whether the variations are transmitted to his offspring in accordance with the laws which prevail with the lower animals; such as that of the transmission of characters to the same age or sex. Again, are the variations the result, as far as our ignorance permits us to judge, of the same general causes, and are they governed by the same general laws, as in the case of other organisms; for instance by correlation, the inherited effects of use and disuse, &c.? Is man subject to similar malconformations, the result of arrested development, of reduplication of parts, &c., and does he display in any of his anomalies reversion to some former and ancient type of structure? It might also naturally be enquired whether man, like so many other animals, has given rise to varieties and sub-races, differing but slightly from each other, or to races differing so much that they must be classed as doubtful species? How are such races distributed over the world; and how, when crossed, do they react on each other, both in the first and succeeding generations? And so with many other points.

The enquirer would next come to the important point, whether man tends to increase at so rapid a rate, as to lead to occasional severe struggles for existence, and consequently to beneficial variations, whether in body or mind, being preserved,

Charles Darwin, "The Evidence of the Descent of Man from Some Lower Form," *The Descent of Man and Selection in Relation to Sex*, pp. 9-17, 1891.

and injurious ones eliminated. Do the races or species of men, whichever term may be applied, encroach on and replace each other, so that some finally become extinct? We shall see that all these questions, as indeed is obvious in respect to most of them, must be answered in the affirmative, in the same manner as with the lower animals. But the several considerations just referred to may be conveniently deferred for a time; and we will first see how far the bodily structure of man shows traces, more or less plain, of his descent from some lower form. In the two succeeding chapters the mental powers of man, in comparison with those of the lower animals, will be considered.

The Bodily Structure of Man.—It is notorious that man is constructed on the same general type or model with other mammals. All the bones in his skeleton can be compared with corresponding bones in a monkey, bat, or seal. So it is with his muscles, nerves, blood-vessels and internal viscera. The brain, the most important of all the organs, follows the same law, as shewn by Huxley and other anatomists. Bischoff,[1] who is a hostile witness, admits that every chief fissure and fold in the brain of man has its analogy in that of the orang; but he adds that at no period of development do their brains perfectly agree; nor could this be expected, for otherwise their mental powers would have been the same. Vulpian[2] remarks: "Les differences réelles qui existent entre l'encéphale de l'homme et celui des singes supérieurs, sont bien minimes. Il ne faut pas se faire d'illusions à cet égard. L'homme est Men plus prèsdes singes anthropomorphes par les caractères anatomiques de son cerveau que ceux-ci ne le sont non-seulement des autres mammifères, mais mêmes de certains quadrumanes, des guenons et des macaques." But it would be superfluous here to give further details on the correspondence between man and the higher mammals in the structure of the brain and all other parts of the body.

It may, however, be worth while to specify a few points, not directly or obviously connected with structure, by which this correspondence or relationship is well shewn.

Man is liable to receive from the lower animals, and to communicate to them, certain diseases as hydrophobia, variola, the glanders, &c.; and this fact proves the close similarity of their tissues and blood, both in minute structure and composition, far more plainly than does their comparison under the best microscope, or by the aid of the best chemical analysis. Monkeys are liable to many of the same non-contagious diseases as we are; thus Rengger,[3] who carefully observed for a long time the *Cebus Azaræ* in its native land, found it liable to catarrh, with the usual symptoms, and which when often recurrent led to consumption. These monkeys suffered also from apoplexy, inflammation of the bowels, and cataract in the eye. The younger ones when shedding their milk-teeth often died from fever. Medicines produced the same effect on them as on us. Many kinds of monkeys have a strong taste for tea, coffee, and spirituous liquors: they will also, as I have myself seen, smoke tobacco with pleasure. Brehm asserts that the natives

---

1 'Grosshirnwindungen des Menschen,' 1868, s. 96.
2 'Leç. sur la Phys.' 1866, p. 890, as quoted by M. Dally, 'L'Ordre des Primates et le Transformisme,' 1868, p. 29.
3 'Naturgeschichte der Säugethiere von Paraguay,' 1830, s. 50.

of north-eastern Africa catch the wild baboons by exposing vessels with strong beer, by which they are made drunk. He has seen some of these animals, which he kept in confinement, in this state; and he gives a laughable account of their behaviour and strange grimaces. On the following morning they were very cross and dismal; they held their aching heads with both hands and wore a most pitiable expression: when beer or wine was offered them, they turned away with disgust, but relished the juice of lemons.[4] An American monkey, an Ateles, after getting drunk on brandy, would never touch it again, and thus was wiser than many men. These trifling facts prove how similar the nerves of taste must be in monkeys and man, and how similarly their whole nervous system is affected.

Man is infested with internal parasites, sometimes causing fatal effects, and is plagued by external parasites, all of which belong to the same genera or families with those infesting other mammals. Man is subject like other mammals, birds, and even insects, to that mysterious law, which causes certain normal processes, such as gestation, as well as the maturation and duration of various diseases, to follow lunar periods.[5] His wounds are repaired by the same process of healing; and the stumps left after the amputation of his limbs occasionally possess, especially during an early embryonic period, some power of regeneration, as in the lowest animals.[6]

The whole process of that most important function, the reproduction of the species, is strikingly the same in all mammals, from the first act of courtship by the male[7] to the birth and nurturing of the young. Monkeys are born in almost as helpless a condition as our own infants; and in certain genera the young differ fully as much in appearance from the adults, as do our children from their full-grown parents.[8] It has been urged by some writers as an important distinction, that with man the young arrive at maturity at a much later age than with any other animal: but if we look to the races of mankind which inhabit tropical countries the difference is not great, for

---

4   Brehm, 'Thierleben,' B. i. 1864, s. 75, 86. On the Ateles, s. 105. For other analogous statements, see 8. 25, 107.

5   With respect to insects see Dr. Laycock 'On a General Law of Vital Periodicity,' British Association, 1842. Dr. Macculloch, 'Silliman's North American Journal of Science,' vol. xvii. p. 305, has seen a dog suffering from tertian ague.

6   I have given the evidence on this head in my 'Variation of Animals and Plants under Domestication,' vol. ii. p. 15.

7   "Mares e diversis generibus Quadrumanorum sine dubio dignoscunt feminas humanas a maribus. Primum, credo, odoratu, postea aspectu. Mr. Youatt, qui diu in Hortis Zoologicis (Bestiariis) medicus animalium erat, vir in rebus observandis cautus et sagax, hoc mihi certissime probavit, et curatores ejusdem loci et alii e ministris confirmaverunt. Sir Andrew Smith et Brehm notabant idem in Cyno-cephalo. Illustrissimus Cuvier etiam narrat multa de hac re quâ ut opinor nihil turpius potest indicari inter omnia hominibus et Quadrumanis communia. Narrat enim Cynocephalum quendam in furorem incidere aspectu feminarum aliquarum, sed nequaquam accendi tanto furore ab omnibus. Semper eligebat juniores, et dignoscebat in turba, et advocabat voce gestuque."

8   This remark is made with respect to Cynocephalus and the anthropomorphous apes by Geoffroy Saint-Hilaire and F. Cuvier, 'Hist. Nat. des Mammifères,' tom. i. 1824.

the orang is believed not to be adult till the age of from ten to fifteen years.[9] Mam differs from woman in size, bodily strength, hairyness, &c., as well as in mind, in the same manner as do the two sexes of many mammals. It is, in short, scarcely possible to exaggerate the close correspon-dence in general structure, in the minute structure of the tissues, in chemical composition and in constitution, between man and the higher animals, especially the anthropomorphous apes.

Embryonic Development.—Man is developed from an ovule, about the 125th of an inch in diam-eter, which differs in no respect from the ovules of other animals. The embryo itself at a very early period can hardly be distinguished from that of other members of the vertebrate kingdom. At this period the arteries run in arch-like branches, as if to carry the blood to branchiæ which are not present in the higher vertebrata, though the slits on the sides of the neck still remain (*f, g,* fig. 10.1), marking their former position. At a somewhat later period, when the extremities are developed, "the feet of lizards and mammals," as the illustrious Von Baer remarks, "the wings and feet of birds, no less than the hands and feet of man, all arise from the same fundamental form." It is, says Prof. Huxley,[10] "quite in the later stages of development that the young human being presents marked differences from the young ape, while the latter departs as much from the dog in its developments, as the man does. Startling as this last assertion may appear to be, it is demonstrably true."

As some of my readers may never have seen a drawing of an embryo, I have given one of man and another of a dog, at about the same early stage of development, carefully copied from two works of undoubted accuracy.[11]

After the foregoing statements made by such high authorities, it would be superfluous on my part to give a number of borrowed details, shewing that the embryo of man closely resembles that of other mammals. It may, however, be added that the human embryo likewise resembles in various points of structure certain low forms when adult. For instance, the heart at first exists as a simple pulsating vessel; the excreta are voided through a cloacal passage; and the os coccyx projects like a true tail, "extending considerably beyond the rudimentary legs."[12] In the embryos of all air-breathing vertebrates, certain glands called the corpora Wolffiana, correspond with and act like the kidneys of mature fishes.[13] Even at a later embryonic period, some striking resemblances between man and the lower animals may be observed. Bischoff says that the

---

9   Huxley, 'Man's Place in Nature,' 1863, p. 34.

10   'Man's Place in Nature,' 1863, p. 67.

11   The human embryo (upper fig.) is from Ecker, 'Icones Phys.,' 1851–1859, tab. xxx. fig. 2. This embryo was ten lines in length, so that the drawing is much magnified. The embryo of the dog is from Bis-choff, 'Entwicklungsgeschichte des Hunde-Eies,' 1845, tab. xi. fig. 42 B. This drawing is five times magnified, the embryo being 25 days old. The internal viscera have been omitted, and the uterine appendages in both drawings removed. I was directed to these figures by Prof. Huxley, from whose work, 'Man's Place in Nature,' the idea of giving them was taken. Häckel has also given analogous drawings in his 'Schöpfungsgeschichte.'

12   Prof. Wyman in 'Proc. of American Acad. of Sciences,' vol. iv. 1860, p. 17.

13   Owen, 'Anatomy of Vertebrates,' vol. i. p. 533.

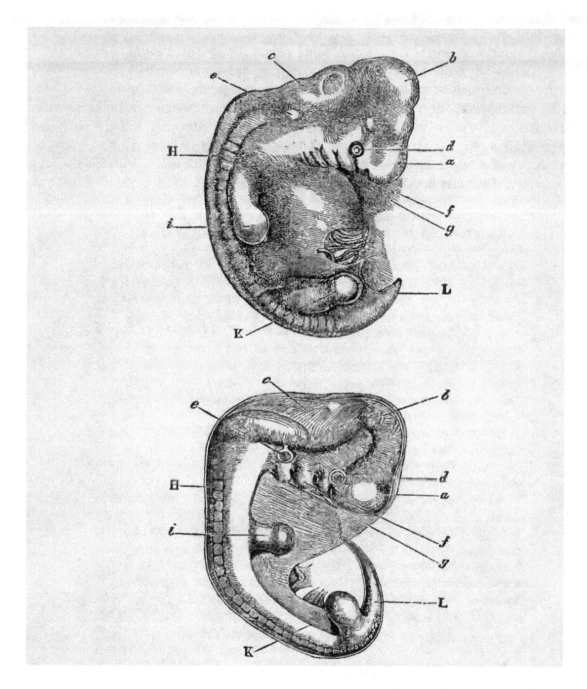

FIGURE 10.1   Upper figure human embryo, from Ecker. Lower figure that of a dog, from Bischoff.

a. Fore-brain, cerebral hemispheres, &c.
b. Mid-brain, corpora quadrigemina.
c. Hind-brain, cerebellum, medulla oblongata.
d. Eye.
e. Ear.
f. First visceral arch.

g. Second visceral arch.
H. Vertebral columns and muscles in process
   of development.
i. Anterior
K. Posterior } extremities.
L. Tail or os coccyx.

convolutions of the brain in a human foetus at the end of the seventh month reach about the same stage of development as in a baboon when adult.[14] The great toe, as Prof. Owen remarks,[15] "which forms the fulcrum when standing or walking, is perhaps the most characteristic peculiarity in the human structure;" but in an embryo, about an inch in length, Prof. Wyman [16] found "that the great toe was shorter than the others, and, instead of being parallel to them, projected at an angle from the side of the foot, thus corresponding with the permanent condition of this part in the quadrumana." I will conclude with a quotation from Huxley,[17] who after asking, does man originate in a different way from a dog, bird, frog or fish? says, "the reply is not doubtful for a moment; without question, the mode of origin and the early stages of the development of man are identical with those of the animals immediately below him in the scale: without a doubt in these respects, he is far nearer to apes, than the apes are to the dog."

---

14   'Die Grosshirnwindungen des Menschen,' 1868, s. 95.

15   'Anatomy of Vertebrates,' vol. ii. p. 553.

16   'Proc. Soc. Nat. Hist.' Boston, 1863, vol. ix. p. 185.

17   'Man's Place in Nature,' p. 65.

Discussion Questions

1. What are the two questions Darwin posed to answer the question whether humans are modified descendant of other animals?
2. What is Darwin's prediction on the possibility of human species extinction?
3. What are some homologous structures between men and lower animals that Darwin used as evidence for the evolution of human species?
4. What is the significance of the statement that the convolution of the brain in a human fetus at the end of the seventh month reaches about the same stage of development as in a baboon when adult?
5. Is it reasonable to think that scientific discovery and generalization has an implication on a moral judgment about how we should behave?

The Quest for Unification

Paul Halpern

This Einstein has proven a great comfort to us that always knew we didn't know much. He has shown us that the fellows that we thought was smart is just as dumb as we are.... I think this Dutchman [sic] is just having a quiet laugh at the world's expense.

—Will Rogers, "Will Rogers Takes a Look at the Einstein Theory"

Working in Berlin, Einstein was surrounded by constant activity. Not only was the city a major center for science and technology, it was also a haven for the arts. Unter den Linden, the main thoroughfare in central Berlin, offered in the late 1920s one of the most concentrated hubs of culture in the world. Stretching from the famous Brandenburg Gate to the central cathedral, city palace, and statue-packed Museum Island, it was home of the state library, state opera, and the main buildings of the University of Berlin.

Although inflation had racked Germany, Berlin had many bragging rights. The sprawling city boasted that it was the largest in area in the world. Pulsing new neighborhoods were popping up everywhere, packed with department stores, restaurants, jazz clubs, and other venues. Operetta companies were thriving, capturing from Vienna the title of best light opera scene. Bertolt Brecht and Kurt Weill skillfully mixed opera with street language and jazz in their masterpiece, *The Threepenny Opera,* which opened at the Theater am Schiffbauerdamm in August 1928.

Late in 1927, Planck retired from the University of Berlin. With the involvement of Einstein, Schrödinger was invited to fill the prestigious professorship. While Zurich held many attractions, particularly its proximity to the mountains, he was delighted to receive an offer. Returning to German soil once again, he and Anny happily moved to the bustling capital.

Anny recalled the excitement of those times: "Berlin was the most wonderful and absolutely unique atmosphere for all the scientists. They knew it all and they appreciated it all.... The theatre was at the height, the music was at the height and science with all the scientific institutes, the industry. And the most famous colloquium ... My husband liked it very much indeed."[1]

Situated in the German capital, not only did Schrödinger become a central figure in the scientific community and have easy access to lectures and discussions, but he also started to enjoy a measure of international publicity. It was just a smidgen of the monumental attention awarded to Einstein, but it still gave him a taste of fame.

For example, in July 1928, *Scientific American* published an article that presented Schrödinger's view as being the canonical replacement for the Bohr model.[2] The *New York Times* took note and informed its readership that Schrödinger's theory was the new fashion. Bohr's work, it reported, was as out of style as "ankle-length skirts"; savvy readers would need to acquaint themselves with Schrödinger's wave theory of the atom instead.[3]

While Schrödinger began to enjoy publicity, Einstein started to detest it, except when it proved useful to the charitable causes he supported or earned him extra pocket money from popular articles and books that he published. Although Einstein felt that the public should be informed about science, he was dubious that many people could really understand his theories. Perhaps his bluntest expression of this was an unfortunate set of remarks that he made right after his 1921 visit to the United States in which he accused Americans of being boorish. His odd speculations about why they were interested in his work produced this headline in the *New York Times:* "Einstein Declares Women Rule Here. Scientist Says He Found American Men the Toy Dogs of the Other Sex. People Colossally Bored."

Einstein was quoted as suggesting that American women "do everything which is the vogue and now quite by chance they have thrown themselves on the Einstein fashion.... [I]t is the mysteriousness of what they cannot conceive which places them under a magic spell." American men, on the other hand, "take an interest in absolutely nothing at all."[4]

Elsa generally welcomed publicity and saw one of her roles as controlling and promoting Einstein's image. Nevertheless, as she discovered during a chilling encounter on January 31, 1925, major public figures often attract the unwelcome attention of deranged individuals. That day a Russian widow, Marie Dickson, forced her way into their apartment building. Brandishing a weapon—by some accounts a loaded revolver, by others a hatpin—she threatened Elsa and demanded to see the professor. Reportedly, Dickson was under the delusion that Einstein had been an agent of the czar. She had previous threatened the Soviet ambassador in France, served three weeks in prison, and then been deported. She had headed straight to Berlin to target Einstein.[5]

Knowing that her husband was up in his study, Elsa concocted a clever subterfuge. She pretended he was not at home and offered to call him. Dickson calmed down, left the house, and said she would come back later. Once she stepped out, Elsa phoned the police. Five police detectives arrived and were waiting for Dickson when she returned. After a violent struggle they arrested her and sent her to an asylum. All the while, Einstein was safely up in his study, immersed in his theories, not knowing until afterward that Elsa may have saved his life.[6]

Although Einstein may have been indebted to his wife, they often quarreled. His lack of interest in his appearance rattled her. He famously hated haircuts, which she had to persuade him to sit through, and also refused to wear socks. Given their elite status, she wanted him to look reasonable for photographers, but he couldn't have cared less. Maintaining a certain public image was just added pressure for him, and he preferred to be alone with his projects. He complained to her, in turn, about the "folly" of her expensive clothes.[7]

By the time the Schrödingers arrived in Berlin, stress—mixed with lack of exercise, overindulgence, and a heavy pipe-smoking habit—had begun to take a toll on Einstein's health. In March 1928, while visiting Switzerland, he collapsed and was diagnosed with an enlarged heart. After returning to Berlin, he was put on bed rest and a strict salt-free diet. He was incapacitated for many months, using that quiet time as an opportunity to work on a new unified field theory. That May, Einstein excitedly informed a friend, "In the tranquility of my sickness, I have laid a wonderful egg in the area of general relativity. Whether the bird that will hatch from it will be vital and long-lived only the gods know. So far I am blessing my sickness that has endowed me with it."[8]

Secrets of the Old One

Einstein's jubilee birthday year of 1929 was celebrated both publicly and privately. Publicly, it roughly coincided with the announcement of his first widely reported attempt at a unified field theory, spawned during his time of incapacitation. He had previously published other attempts at unification, to little fanfare. Turning fifty, producing new work, and being Einstein would award his novel approach ample press coverage.

Throughout the 1920s, other researchers' unification theories had whetted Einstein's appetite for unraveling the secret formula of the "Old One" that would describe how all the forces of nature meshed together. Gravitation and electromagnetism seemed to have too many similarities to be independent. Both were forces that weakened with the square of the distances between objects. General relativity's limitation was that it could accommodate only one of the forces, gravity. Its equations needed extra terms on the geometric side to make room for the other force. Adding additional factors to a successful theory was not a step to be taken lightly. There needed to be clear justification—if not through physical principles, then through mathematical reasoning.

Einstein had dabbled with variations of Kaluza's, Weyl's, and Eddington's ideas, but was not happy with the results. Try as he might, he couldn't find physically realistic solutions that resembled particles. He even produced a paper similar to Klein's five-dimensional theory only to realize that Klein had beaten him to the punch. Pauli had told Einstein about the similarity, prompting him to include an awkward note at the end acknowledging that its contents were identical to Klein's.

Then, starting in mid-1928 and persisting for several years, he turned to an idea called "distant parallelism" (also known as "teleparallelism" and "absolute parallelism"). His new approach juxtaposed Riemannian geometry with Euclidean geometry, making it possible to define parallel lines between two distant points in space. Starting with general relativity's curved, non-Euclidean spacetime manifold, he associated with each point an extra Euclidean geometry called a tetrad. Because the tetrads have a simple, boxlike, Cartesian coordinate system, Einstein noted that it would be very straightforward to see if lines within those structures are parallel or not. Such comparisons of distant parallel lines would add extra information that is not present in standard general relativity—allowing for the geometric description of electromagnetism along with gravity.

In standard general relativity, because of spacetime's curvature, each point has a differently oriented coordinate system—tilted differently from place to place. It is like looking at Earth from space. You wouldn't expect a rocket blasting off from Australia to head in the same direction as one launched from Sweden. Similarly, the directional arrows in the vicinity of one region of spacetime would be different from those in another. Consequently, in standard general relativity, one cannot determine whether distant lines are parallel or not. One can define distances between lines but not their relative directions.

Distant parallelism, with its boxlike additional structure, makes it possible to specify the relative directions of any two straight lines, along with the distance between them. It adds a navigation system for the universe that supplements the basic road map supplied by standard general relativity. For that reason, Einstein judged it more comprehensive.

Einstein's initial goal with each of his unified field theories was to reproduce Maxwell's equations of electromagnetism in a geometric way, bringing them under the umbrella of general relativity. He was pleased he could accomplish that with distant parallelism, at least in the case of empty space. He didn't, however, make testable experimental predictions, as he did with general relativity, or identify credible physical solutions.

He also didn't achieve his goal of reproducing the quantum rules. Starting in the late 1920s, for each of his unified proposals, he hoped that the equations would be overdetermined—meaning more equations than independent variables. Such redundancy, he hoped, would force the solutions to have discrete types of behavior, something like quantum levels.

An example of overdetermination would be writing down the equations for the motion of a baseball and adding an extra condition that its vertical position must have a certain height. While without the condition the baseball would have continuous motion, tracing a curved path through the air, including the condition would restrict its position to only two discrete values. It would reach that height once on the way up and once on the way down. Thus the continuous equations, in tandem, would produce discontinuous values. Similarly, Einstein hoped that an overdetermined unified field theory would force electrons into particular orbits, similar to the Bohr-Sommerfeld model and the eigenstates found via the Schrödinger equation. However, he couldn't achieve that goal.

In general, distant parallelism failed to reproduce either the classical or quantum behavior of particles, as much as Einstein tried to do so. Therefore, his proposal was largely a mathematical exercise rather than a rigorous physical theory.

Even the math for his theory wasn't novel. As Einstein belatedly learned, French mathematician Élie Cartan and Austrian mathematician Roland Weitzenböck had already published on the topic. Cartan reminded Einstein that they had once discussed distant parallelism at a 1922 seminar—an encounter that Einstein apparently had forgotten. Einstein would eventually give Cartan credit for the mathematics underlying his theory.

As it turns out, it is relatively easy to tweak general relativity to include a version of Maxwell's equations by tampering with its rules about lengths, directions, dimensions, and other parameters. Einstein thought at the time that distant parallelism offered a reasonable modification. His criteria included simplicity, logic, and mathematical elegance. However, as Pauli and others advised him, discarding general relativity's successful predictions, such as the bending of starlight, was a radical move that shouldn't be taken lightly. To his colleagues' dismay, Einstein's growing interest in abstract notions had pushed aside the need to match experimental data.

Walking on Air

In January 1929, Einstein prepared to release a short paper describing his new scheme for unification. Despite the lack of physical evidence, he issued a short press statement emphasizing its scientific importance and highlighting its superiority to standard general relativity.[9] As soon as the international press learned of the imminent publication, more than a hundred journalists clamored for an interview, hounding him for a simple description of his novel idea. Not realizing how abstract and unphysical the paper was, they sensed a breakthrough akin to relativity. Einstein refused at first to offer further comment, hiding from reporters.[10] Eventually he offered more detailed popular explanations, published in the *Times* of London, the *New York Times, Nature,* and elsewhere. The *Nature* piece quoted him as stating: "Now, but only now, we know that the force which moves electrons in their ellipses about the nuclei of atoms is the same force which moves our earth in its annual course about the sun, and it is the same force which brings to us the rays of light and heat which make life possible upon this planet."[11]

The announcement of the theory set off an avalanche of publicity, comparable perhaps to the 1919 eclipse announcement. Given its abstruse, hypothetical nature and lack of experimental verification, the amount of press it received was staggering. Almost a dozen articles referring to the theory were published in the *New York Times* alone.

Scientists around the world were asked to comment on and interpret Einstein's results. Enthusiasm abounded, despite the dearth of proof. Among the unjustifiably eager reactions was that of Professor H. H. Sheldon, the chair of New York University's physics department, who speculated wildly that "such things as keeping airplanes aloft without engines or material support, as stepping out of a window into the air without fear of falling, or of making a trip to the moon … are avenues of investigation suggested by this theory."[12]

The theory also seemed to strike a cultural chord. A number of clergy members remarked about its theological implications. One pastor, the Reverend Henry Howard of Fifth Avenue Presbyterian Church in New York, compared its message to St. Paul's preachings about nature's unity.[13] Humorists, such as lasso-twirling satirist Will Rogers, joked about its incomprehensibility.[14] Another jested that the theory could be used to test golf balls.[15]

Massive media attention to a theoretical physics article was virtually unheard of before Einstein. Einstein made even the most abstract, far-flung theory seem sexy, mysterious, and earth-shattering. The fact that his hypothesis offered a lifeless set of equations lacking experimental vital signs did not scare off coverage. Einstein's moving hand as he carefully composed his mathematical arrangements provided the press with all the vital evidence it needed.

Einstein cringed at his celebrity status. He clearly wanted the spotlight to be on his theories and their implications, not on him personally. Needless to say, the press focused on the physicist himself, to which his only recourse was to try, often unsuccessfully, to hide out.

In stark contrast to the booming public hype, the reaction of the theoretical physics community was barely audible. By that time, largely because of the quantum revolution, Einstein's ideas were rapidly losing relevance to the mainstream physics community. Among the most active quantum theorists of the younger generation, only Pauli kept up a keen interest in his work. While Einstein remained respected personally, his rapid-fire production of seemingly irrelevant unification proposals became seen as a joke. For instance, young physicists in Copenhagen mocked his ideas in a humorous production of *Faust* in which a king (Einstein) was besieged by fleas (unified field theories).

Pauli was not an easy audience to please. Keeping up his reputation for bluntness, he threw a sobering splash of ice-cold water Einstein's way. Commenting on an essay published about distant parallelism, he wrote in a letter to the editor: "It is indeed a courageous deed of the editors to accept an essay on a new field theory of Einstein for the '*Results* in the Exact Sciences.' His never-ending gift for invention, his persistent energy in the pursuit of a fixed aim in recent years surprise us with, on the average, one such theory per year. Psychologically interesting is that the author normally considers his actual theory for a while as the 'definite solution.' Hence ... one could cry out: 'Einstein's new field theory is dead. Long live Einstein's new field theory!'"[16]

Privately, Pauli commented to Pascual Jordan that only American journalists would be gullible enough to accept Einstein's distant parallelism; not even American physicists, let alone European researchers, would be that naive. And Pauli bet Einstein that he would reverse course within a year.

Meanwhile, in contrast to the publicity granted to Einstein's results, little noticed at the time was Weyl's pivotal work at Göttingen showing that his old idea of gauge could be applied to electron wavefunctions and explain the electromagnetic interaction in a natural way. The reason is that including the extra gauge factor along with the electron's description mathematically requires the addition of a new "gauge field" that propagates through space. That extra field can be identified as the electromagnetic field, offering a gauge theory of electromagnetism. One can think of the gauge factor as a kind of fan that is free to point in any direction as it is spinning around. To keep it spinning requires the "wind" of an influx of electromagnetic field lines. Despite the brilliance of Weyl's quantum gauge theory of electromagnetism, it would take another two decades before the physics community began to make use of it. Pauli, who was very astute, would be one of the first to recognize its importance.

Rabbi Onion's Blessing for Unification

Once he got the word out to the public about his unification scheme, Einstein hastened to close the floodgates and push back the rising tide of paparazzi. His birthday was coming up soon, and he desperately needed to escape. Much to the confusion and dismay of the press, on March 12, two days before he would turn fifty, he elected to flee the official celebrations and hide out in a secret location. "Even his most intimate friends will not know his whereabouts," reported the *New York Times,* which pointed out that he had been "driven crazy" by questions about his unified field theory.[17]

Somehow, one anonymous reporter did locate Einstein's hideout and file a story about his private celebration. The savvy journalist found out that Einstein's wealthy friend Franz Lemm, known as "Berlin's shoe polish king," was lending out his villa in the woodsy district of Gatow for the occasion. Far from the glare of Berlin's city center, Einstein was celebrating his birthday quietly with his family.

When the reporter walked in, Einstein was peering intently through a gift microscope, gazing with wonder at a drop of blood that he had extracted from his own finger. Casually dressed in a floppy sweater, informal pants, and slippers, stopping on occasion to take a puff from a pipe, he exuded childlike contentment. Perhaps he recalled his childhood gift of a compass. Other presents he received included a silk gown, pipes, tobacco, and a sketch of a yacht friends were planning to have built for him.

Perhaps the most unusual tribute was a doll created by his stepdaughter, Margot, that depicted a rabbi holding an onion in each hand. Margot's passion was sculpture, and she specialized in mystical images of clerics. Shaping the rabbi figure for her dear stepfather was a labor of love. Proud of her work, she read him a poem about it, "Rabbi Onion."[18]

Rabbi Onion, Margot explained, was an extraordinary healer. Onions, according to traditional Jewish lore, are good for the heart. Einstein had attempted such a cure during his recovery the year before. She had fashioned the mystical sage with his magical onions to bless him with a long, healthy life. That way, he could compose many more unified field theories. Einstein winced at the thought of churning out more and more unification proposals—which turned out to be an accurate prediction.

When Einstein returned to his Berlin dwelling he found a mountain of gifts waiting for him. Foremost among his presents was a generous offer by the Berlin city government to obtain a house and land for him near the Havel River and the lakes it flows through so that he could enjoy the serene landscape and go sailing. The city offered him free use of a mansion on the Neu Cladow estate, recently procured from a wealthy gentleman. However, when Elsa arrived to inspect the residence, the former owner informed her that his sales agreement included the right for him to stay there indefinitely. Without mincing words, he asked her to get off the property.

Red-faced about the botched present, the city government scrambled to find a solution. After months of civic wrangling about the right plan for Einstein, the scientist decided to take matters into his own hands and buy his own property in Caputh, near Potsdam, right at the intersection of two lakes: Schwielow and Templin. He hired an ambitious young architect, Konrad Wachsmann, to design and build a comfortable wooden cottage for him and his family, just a short walk to forested trails and the lakes. During its construction his eagerly awaited sailboat arrived, called the *Tümmler* (porpoise). Once the house was finished and they moved in, he was truly in paradise.

By the Banks of Lake Schwielow

Caputh was a perfect place for Einstein to go hiking or sailing, which allowed him to escape into his thoughts and forget about the burgeoning demands on his time. In the sylvan retreat, he was as casual as possible, often going barefoot and either in pajamas or shirtless—never dressed formally. He deliberately didn't have a telephone, so those who visited him often stopped by unannounced. One time when a group of dignitaries was visiting, Elsa implored Albert to dress up. He refused, stating that if they wanted to see *him,* he was there, but if they had come to see his clothes, they were in the closet.

One of the frequent visitors to Einstein's cottage who didn't mind the casual atmosphere was Schrödinger, who similarly hated formal attire. While professors in German universities of that era were expected to wear a suit and tie to class, Schrödinger almost always wore a sweater. On sweltering days in summer, he would sometimes come in wearing just a short-sleeved shirt and pants. One time, a guard wouldn't even let him through the university gate because he looked so scruffy. A student had to rescue him by attesting that he really taught there.[19] In another incident, Dirac recalled that the hotel staff hesitated before letting Schrödinger into his fancy accommodations for the Solvay meeting because he looked like a backpacker.[20]

In July 1929, the Prussian Academy of Sciences honored Schrödinger by inducting him into its ranks. As the ceremony was a white-tie affair, Schrödinger dressed up. He gave a well-received talk about chance in physics, taking a balanced stance that did not either endorse or condemn the Heisenberg-Born view. He had learned to tread lightly around that touchy issue. In that way, he invited both the determinism and nondeterminism camps to use his equation the way they wished.

In general, Schrödinger was delighted to be part of such a prestigious organization as the Prussian Academy. However, he came to share with Einstein a feeling that the academy was rather stuffy. Both of them would much rather be hiking or sailing than suffering through dry meetings. Consequently, it was on the trails and waterways of Caputh that they truly bonded and became close friends.

In their walks in the woods and jaunts on the lake, Einstein and Schrödinger came to appreciate their common interests. Perhaps only Schrödinger's disdain for music prevented them from growing even closer; Einstein loved to perform chamber music with his dearest friends. At that point in the two men's lives, they shared a deep fascination with the philosophical ramifications of physics. Each was more at ease talking about how Spinoza's or Schopenhauer's views applied to modern science than about the latest experimental findings.

Einstein was much steadier in his opposition to the mainstream interpretation of quantum mechanics, though. Schrödinger's attitude was so changeable that in a talk held at a Munich museum in May 1930 he practically adopted the Heisenberg-Born interpretation of the wave equation, though he would retreat again several years later.

Einstein's firm position was expressed in a March 1931 interview in which he affirmed his belief in causality and opposition to indeterminacy. "I know very well," he stated wryly, "that my conception of causality as part of the nature of things will be interpreted as a sign of senility. I am convinced, however, that the concept of causality is instinct in matters related to natural science.... I believe that the Schroedinger-Heisenberg theory is a great advance and am convinced that this formulation of the relationships of quanta is nearer the truth than any previous attempts. I feel, however, that the essentially statistical character of this theory will eventually disappear because this leads to unnatural descriptions."[21]

The clash between the two friends' views on cause and effect was featured in a news story published in the *Christian Science Monitor* in November 1931.[22] The piece was likely the first to mention both physicists' outlooks. Describing talks about quantum mechanics each delivered around that time, it compared Einstein's steadfast opinion that the law of causality still applied with Schrödinger's nuanced belief that physicists needed to become more open-minded about various alternatives, such as the prospect of acausality. Evolving perspectives, Schrödinger argued, might transform our way of looking at nature's behavior, including the possibility of rendering the law of causality obsolete.

We see that while both maintained an interest in philosophy, Einstein was more inclined to favor Spinoza's rigid view that the world's laws were set from the beginning and might be logically deduced, while Schrödinger favored a more malleable perspective, shaped by Eastern beliefs in the veil of illusion, in which society's changing viewpoint molds truth. What appears true today, Schrödinger argued, might be seen tomorrow as a misconception. Therefore, it is possible that we might never find the ultimate truth.

Along with their mutual interests in philosophy and its application to science, the two physicists had more mundane woes in common. Neither had a happy domestic situation; each had multiple affairs. Finding Elsa controlling, Albert sought ways to escape. She was dismayed when he attended concerts and theater performances with a stunning heiress, Toni Mendel, who flamboyantly rode around in a chauffeur-driven limousine. He also went out regularly with a blond Austrian beauty, Margarete Lebach, whom Elsa couldn't stand.[23]

Erwin and Anny had a strong friendship but little sexual spark, and they would never have children together. They had decided not to divorce, but rather to maintain an open marriage. They continued to find too much comfort in each other's company to split up completely.

In contrast to Einstein, who expressed regrets about his failures in married life, Schrödinger romanticized his various trysts and kept a diary of his exploits. Some of the affairs would last for many years. At one point he became smitten with a young woman whom he tutored in math, Ithi Junger. Their liaison led to her having an unplanned pregnancy. Though he strongly wanted a child, he wouldn't leave Anny. Against his wishes, Ithi had an abortion and left him.[24] While that affair was cooling down, Schrödinger began a relationship with Hildegunde "Hilde" March, the young wife of a physicist he knew from Innsbruck, Arthur March. Their passionate bond would end up becoming something like a second marriage.

Einstein and Schrödinger could not have realized how fragile and special their time together in Berlin and Caputh would turn out to be. The mirth, relaxed attitudes, and open-mindedness of those days would vanish without a trace once Nazi boots trampled the Weimar Republic. Accustomed to a cozy, celebrated life, both scientists would be forced into exile, never to sail the Havel lakes together again.

Ill Winds and Ocean Breezes

The early 1930s in Germany were marked by massive unemployment and unrest. The 1929 stock market crash set off a chain reaction that toppled a succession of teetering economies around the world, including the fragile German postwar engine. With the Nazi movement and other far-right groups stirring the pot of nationalism, German resentment of the armistice terms became a rallying cry for vengeance. Communists and socialists responded with calls for worker power, frightening many business owners and mainstream conservatives—some of whom came to see the Nazis as the lesser evil and a bulwark against communism. In Berlin, hundreds of thousands of unemployed laborers with nothing else to do were ripe for recruitment to political movements on both ends of the spectrum. A massive rally in Alexanderplatz, one of Berlin's main squares, was quashed by the police, using tanks to round up the demonstrators. The right and left battled for votes and supporters as weak coalition governments rose and fell.

While he wasn't active in any particular party, Einstein generally supported the progressive socialist movement and favored greater worker rights. He considered himself an internationalist, seeing nationalism as a dangerous force. As a pacifist, he supported the War Resisters' League. Generally straightforward about his views, he had no qualms about openly condemning the Nazis. While at first he saw the support for them as an aberration, he soon came to realize—even before they took power—the dire threat they posed. Schrödinger, in contrast, had no interest in politics and tended to avoid such discussions. He didn't take the Nazi movement seriously until it was too late.

During the economic crisis, both physicists worried about their finances and were open to opportunities to work abroad, at least temporarily. Einstein's chance came first. He was pleased to get a invitation to travel to Caltech, in Pasadena, California, in the winter of 1931 and visit Mount Wilson Observatory, where Hubble had discovered the expansion of the universe. The stipend of $7,000 that Einstein was promised for just two months was incredibly generous for the time—about a full professor's yearly pay.

By then, Einstein had the help of two paid assistants: Helen Dukas, his secretary, and Walther Mayer, his "calculator" (mathematical aide). Dukas handled Einstein's flood of correspondence and extensive calendar of speaking engagements. Mayer performed the routine mathematical manipulations required for Einstein's research, particularly in unified field theories. Einstein had started to realize that Pauli was right and that distant parallelism would not be physically viable. Therefore, he began to pursue other avenues for unification.

Before departing for the West Coast of the United States, Einstein published the *New York Times Magazine* commentary piece mentioned in Chapter Three, declaring his views on science and religion and advocating the Spinozan concept of a deity. The essay generated heated debate and helped focus public attention on Einstein's upcoming visit.

Massive crowds like those that would greet a visiting king or queen welcomed the arrival of Einstein and his entourage in the port of San Diego on December 30, 1930. His companions disembarking from the great ship *Belgenland* included his wife, Dukas, and Mayer. Elsa proved a critical translator; her English was far better than Albert's. Mayer was always on hand whenever Einstein had a free moment for calculations.

Once at Caltech, the physics faculty, led by famed experimentalist Robert Millikan, began to discuss with him the possibility of a permanent position. But given his attachment to Berlin—and the Caputh lifestyle in particular—the discussions were premature. Nevertheless, Einstein loved Southern California, especially Pasadena's beautiful gardens and mild weather. One highlight of his stay was meeting Hubble and seeing the Mount Wilson telescope. He and Elsa also took some time to hobnob with Hollywood stars such as Charlie Chaplin. A great fan of his movies, Einstein was honored to be his guest at the world premiere of *City Lights*.

The following winter, Einstein was invited to Caltech again for another two-month visit. The question of a permanent appointment resurfaced. Given all the problems in Germany and the frightening prospect of a Nazi-led government, Einstein was starting to consider emigrating. However, by then he had begun to receive other offers, including the possibility of an Oxford professorship.

In Millikan's wooing of Einstein, he made one fatal mistake. He introduced Einstein to educator Abraham Flexner, who had come to Caltech to discuss the establishment of an Institute for Advanced Study (IAS) in Princeton, funded by wealthy benefactors and dedicated to fundamental research. Flexner ended up recruiting Einstein for a position that was meant, at first, to be only part-time. He offered Einstein a whopping salary of $15,000 a year, which would make him one of the highest-paid physics professors in the country. Einstein insisted, as an added condition, that Mayer be established in a second permanent position for assistance with his unified field theory calculations. Flexner was stunned by Einstein's demand but eventually relented. Einstein, in turn, committed to the Institute appointment.

Around the same period, Einstein took the time to nominate Schrödinger and Heisenberg, in that order, for the Nobel Prize in Physics. As a Nobelist, Einstein had the privilege of suggesting candidates for that high honor. In his nomination he ranked Schrödinger first because, in his opinion, Schrödinger's findings were more far-reaching than Heisenberg's. Still, Einstein was generous to nominate Heisenberg at all, considering his opposition to Heisenberg's probabilistic views. He realized that many physicists placed the two of them on par, as co-founders of quantum mechanics. Therefore, he felt that it was logical to include both, with his personal preference duly noted.

In December 1932, the Einsteins and their companions set sail to Southern California for their third and final visit to Caltech. The visit was bittersweet, partly because Millikan was miffed about Einstein's new commitment and partly due to the growing realization that Adolf Hitler, who was then deputy chancellor in a coalition between a conservative party and the Nazis, was on the brink of leading Germany. As they stepped out the door of the Caputh cottage, Albert reportedly told Elsa it was the last time she would see it. Still, part of him must have thought there was a chance they would return, as he had written his colleagues in Berlin about plans there for the following year.

Ironically, Millikan had earlier booked Einstein to give a speech shortly after his arrival extolling German-American relations. The purpose was to court a donor. Not wanting to disappoint his host, Einstein delivered the speech, which he read in English from a translation of his own text. He used the opportunity to promote the idea of tolerance for opposing political views and religious beliefs, both in the United States and in Germany.

The mention of the United States alluded to public complaints by a right-wing group called the Woman Patriot Corporation that a known "revolutionary" such as Einstein was allowed into the country. Although nothing would come of it, the FBI began a file on him that for decades accumulated similar questions about his patriotism.

In stark contrast to Einstein's message of tolerance, about one week later, on January 30, 1933, Paul von Hindenburg, the president of Germany, appointed Hitler as chancellor. With a notorious racist and anti-Semite, backed by hundreds of thousands of brown-shirted paramilitary thugs called the Sturmabteilung (SA) or "storm troopers," grasping the reins of the German state, opponents braced themselves for caustic rhetoric at the very least. People wondered if Hitler would turn his hateful words into actions—or were they just political poses designed to attract bands of hooligan supporters?

Fire in the Reichstag

German politics was so changeable in the early 1930s that many pundits thought Hitler's chancellorship would be a passing phase. Moderate conservatives quietly expected that he would trump labor's support for the communists and move toward the center. As the economy improved, many thought that voters would come to their senses, elect more sensible politicians, and temper extremism. Even right after Hitler assumed his post, Einstein still harbored some hope of returning to Berlin. Schrödinger, though despising the Nazis and their intolerance, wasn't even concerned at first.

Then came a turn of events that no pundit had anticipated. On February 27, arsonists set fire to the Reichstag, the German parliament building. Although historians believe that the culprits were probably members of the SA, Hitler immediately pointed a finger at the communists. Parliament passed a law suspending civil rights and permitting indefinite detention of suspects. Communist politicians and other members of left-wing movements were summarily arrested and eventually sent to concentration camps. A new election was held on March 5, in which the Nazis became the largest parliamentary group.

Around the time of the Reichstag fire, Einstein came to realize that he couldn't return to Germany while the Nazis were in power. He wrote to Margarete Lebach that he had canceled a talk he was supposed to give to the Prussian Academy because he was afraid to set foot in the country. After leaving Pasadena by train and traveling to New York, newspaper reports that the Nazis had rummaged through his Caputh house horrified him further. In Manhattan, he gave speeches to various organizations decrying the Nazi assault on freedom. These were picked up by the German press, which slammed him for disloyalty.

In New York, Einstein and his entourage boarded the *Belgenland* for the return voyage to Europe. During the ocean journey, he wrote a polite letter to the Prussian Academy thanking them for their previous support but asking to withdraw his membership, citing the political situation as a reason to step down. Then, upon arrival at the port of Antwerp, Belgium, Einstein handed over his German passport to the consulate and renounced all of his ties to that country. For the second time in his life (the first being when he was a student in Switzerland), he was a man without a country.

Luckily, Einstein had many friends in Belgium and neighboring Holland who offered him assistance. Queen Elisabeth, who had been born in Bavaria and married into the Belgian royal family, was particularly supportive. Einstein held bank accounts in Leiden and New York that proved indispensable after the Nazis confiscated the money he had deposited in Berlin banks. Though homeless and stateless, he had a secure future abroad.

Einstein was fortunate to have left Germany in time. The Enabling Act, passed on March 23 by the German parliament, suspended all right to dissent, effectively granting Hitler complete power. The Nazis soon dissolved all provincial assemblies, solidifying their iron rule. The twelve-year dictatorship would be the most brutal the world has ever seen.

The Einsteins searched for a place to live temporarily until the IAS appointment was ready. They found a small house in Le Coq sur Mer, on the North Sea, to rent for the time being. The seaside cottage, though not as comfortable as Caputh, proved a cozy refuge for his months in Belgium, until he could leave for America.

It was a sad period for Einstein in many ways. Around the time he had been forced to flee his native land, two of his dear ones met tragic fates. His son Eduard, nicknamed "Tete," who had done brilliantly in school and wanted to be a psychiatrist, began to suffer from schizophrenia and was committed to a mental institution in Zurich. Having corresponded with him about the world of psychology and the works of Sigmund Freud, Einstein had high hopes for his career and was devastated when it was cut short. Then in September 1933, Paul Ehrenfest, who had been one of Einstein's best friends, committed suicide. Before Ehrenfest killed himself, he had shot his own son Wassik, who had Down syndrome, with the delusional motive of sparing his wife the expense of caring for the child.

The cold, blue Atlantic would soon separate Einstein from Europe and its suffering. He would watch the situation from abroad, observing the lives of his former compatriots go from bad to worse. Never would he forget their plight, even when permanently exiled in the New World. Although he would never return to Europe, his pained heart and anguished thoughts would always remain there.

Notes

1   Interview with Annemarie Schrödinger by Thomas S. Kuhn in Vienna, Austria, April 5, 1963, Archive for the History of Quantum Physics, American Philosophical Society, Philadelphia, PA.
2   Paul Heyl, "What Is an Atom?," *Scientific American* 139 (July 1928): 9–12.
3   "Current Magazines," *New York Times*, July 1, 1928.
4   Albert Einstein, quoted in "Einstein Declares Women Rule Here," *New York Times*, July 8, 1921.
5   "Woman Threatens Prof. Einstein's Life," *New York Times*, February 1, 1925.
6   "A Deluded Woman Threatens Krassin and Professor Einstein," *The Age* (Melbourne, Australia), February 3, 1925, 9.
7   Wythe Williams, "Einstein Distracted by Public Curiosity," *New York Times*, February 4, 1929.
8   Einstein to Zangger, end of May 1928, Einstein Archives, Hebrew University of Jerusalem, call no. 40-069, translated and quoted in Tilman Sauer, "Field Equations in Teleparallel Spacetime: Einstein's *Fernparallelismus* Approach Towards Unified Field Theory," *Historia Mathematica* 33 (2006): 404–405.
9   "Einstein Extends Relativity Theory," *New York Times*, January 12, 1929, 1.
10 Albert Einstein, quoted in "Einstein Is Amazed at Stir over Theory; Holds 100 Journalists at Bay for a Week," *New York Times*, January 19, 1929.
11 Albert Einstein, quoted in "News and Views," *Nature,* February 2, 1929, reprinted in Hubert Goenner, "On the History of Unified Field Theories," in *Proceedings of the Sir Arthur Eddington Centenary Symposium,* edited by V. de Sabbata and T. M. Karade, 1:176–196 (Singapore: World Scientific, 1984).
12 H. H. Sheldon, quoted in "Einstein Reduces All Physics to 1 Law," *New York Times*, January 25, 1929.
13 "Einstein Is Viewed as Near the Mystic," *New York Times*, February 4, 1929.
14 Will Rogers, "Will Rogers Takes a Look at the Einstein Theory," *New York Times*, February 1, 1929.
15 "Byproducts: Some Parallel Vectors," *New York Times*, February 3, 1929.
16 Wolfgang Pauli, "[Besprechung von] Band 10 der Ergebnisse der exakten Naturwissenschaften," *Ergebnisse der exakten Naturwissenschaften* 11 (1931): 186, quoted and translated in Goenner, "On the History of Unified Field Theories."
17 "Einstein Flees Berlin to Avoid Being Feted," *New York Times*, March 13, 1929.
18 "Einstein Is Found Hiding on Birthday," *New York Times*, March 14, 1929.
19 Walter Moore, *Schrödinger: Life and Thought* (New York: Cambridge University Press, 1982), 242.
20 Paul Dirac, quoted in "Erwin Schrödinger," Archive for the History of Quantum Physics.
21 Albert Einstein, quoted in "Einstein Affirms Belief in Causality," *New York Times*, March 16, 1931, 1.

22 "Physicists Scan Cause to Effect with Skepticism," *Christian Science Monitor*, November 13, 1931, 8.

23 Albrecht Fölsing, *Albert Einstein: A Biography*, trans. Ewald Osers (New York: Penguin, 1997), 617.

24 Moore, *Schrödinger*, 255.

Discussion Questions

1. What was Einstein's goal in establishing unified filed theories? What was the role of distant parallelism in achieving this goal?

2. Why was Pauli reluctant to accept Einstein's public success as genuine scientific triumph ("only an American journalist would be gullible enough to accept Einstein's distant parallelism")?

3. What explains Einstein's distaste toward the quantum indeterminacy and his stubborn adherence to the causality in matters?

4. What are the striking differences in the philosophical outlook on the universe between Einstein and Schrödinger underlying their starkly different theories of nature?

5. Do you believe in causality: that nature is governed by universal law of cause and effect, or accept quantum indeterminacy: that things in nature are explained only statistically and never in terms of fixed laws?

Indigenous and Scientific Knowledge

Anne Ross, Richard Sherman, and Jeffrey G. Snodgrass

> The whole of science is nothing more than a refinement of everyday thinking.
> (Einstein, quoted in Ellen 2004: 425)

In his book *A Forest of Time*, Nabokov (2002) describes a meeting between an archaeologist and an elderly Navajo man. The archaeologist was keen to know what the Navajo man thought of archaeological descriptions of the past. The elder began to explain that, for Navajo, one could not understand the origin of people on the land without first knowing about insects and corn kernels and their place in the creation of people and the landscape. The archaeologist, mystified by these stories, tried asking his questions in different ways. He laid out maps of migration routes across the Bering Strait and held up pictures of Folsom points and Clovis arrowheads. The Navajo elder, however, indicated that horny toads had made these stone tools. At this point, the archaeologist appears to have given up his quest for Navajo corroboration of scientific knowledge (Nabokov 2002: 29–31).

Nabokov uses this vignette to demonstrate the nature of Indigenous modes of narrating history and imparting knowledge about the past. For the Navajo and other Indigenous communities, according to Nabokov, objects and archaeological sites are not just neutral and 'objective' records of past human events (cf. Appadurai 1986; Bradley 2008; Byrne 2005). They are locales that document interactions between those human and nonhuman persons who have come before the present generation and, as importantly, who continue to interact in contemporary times. History for these communities is thus a living entity that documents but also *maintains* past and present relationships of dependency between humans and nonhuman persons such as insects, corn kernels, and horny toads. In Indigenous worldviews, as Nabokov explains, these relationships have structured the naming of places and the creation of such material artifacts as arrowheads; but they continue to structure the contemporary production of places and artifacts (Nabokov 2002: 126–149; see also Bradley 2008). For Indigenous communities, as Nabokov elaborates, the narration of history is a multimedia production involving the communal creation of stories, songs, dances, music, and visual art. For Indigenous groups to separate the past from these contemporary performative and social contexts, like separating the past from human relations with corn kernels and horny toads, would entail killing history by robbing it of most of its power to evoke commitment and passion in living human beings (Nabokov 2002: 29–57).

For Nabokov, the uniqueness of Indigenous epistemologies points to the fundamentally different understandings of time and space, landscape, and the past held by Indigenous peoples on the one hand and scientists on the other. In framing the past by evoking and paying homage to the 'subjectivities' of human and nonhuman persons, Indigenous peoples personify history in a way that cannot be easily heard or fathomed by archaeologists pursuing purely 'objective' forms of analysis (cf. Bradley 2008; Godwin 2005; Nabokov 2002: 150–171; Ross 2008; Rowlands 1994). It is not surprising, then, that the interaction between the archaeologist and Navajo elder described above, informed as it is by these individuals' contrasting assumptions and priorities regarding the past that literally 'crackle off the page', is characterized by 'halting exchanges' that never quite take off (Nabokov 2002: 31).

Solomon Islands nationals, Gegeo and Watson-Gegeo, discuss this and other related issues in the context of their comparative analysis of Indigenous and Western (scientific) epistemologies. They define Indigenous epistemology as 'a cultural *group's* way of thinking and of creating, reformulating, and theorizing about knowledge via traditional discourses' (2001: 58, emphasis added). Scientific epistemologies, in contrast, are rarely recognized as having this social and communal context, despite anthropological discourse to the contrary (Nabokov 2002; Nadasdy 1999; Sillitoe 2002; Stevenson 2006). To most Western-trained academics, science is based on an objective 'knowledge without a knower' that is usually foreign to Indigenous peoples for whom knowledge is very much personalized and social (Gegeo and Watson-Gegeo 2001: 62). Although Indigenous knowledge is owned and shared asymmetrically (Ellen and Harris 2000: 4–5)—often only certain individuals have the right to speak about certain aspects of local knowledge (Rose 1996a)—such knowledge is put back together as a whole when the community gathers together on practical and ritual occasions (Gegeo and Watson-Gegeo 2001: 62).

At this general level, then, Western scientific and Indigenous ways of knowing would seem to constitute distinctive modes of thought. In this chapter we analyze the nature of both difference and similarity between these two knowledge systems, dealing not so much with *what* is known but rather with *how* different ways of knowing are valorized and institutionalized in modern scientific and Indigenous contexts. In grappling with these epistemological issues we realize that we are in illustrious and daunting company. Anthropological luminaries from Frazer to Tylor, from Malinowski to Evans-Pritchard and Tambiah have all wrestled with the separation or lack of separation between science and magic, which we see as a proxy discussion for the relationship between scientific and Indigenous knowledge more generally. Further, an immense literature spanning most of the social sciences as well as philosophy and history has attempted to define the nature of science and thus, by extension, the nature of nonscientific forms of knowing. Indeed, this literature has been polarized into what has been termed the 'science wars' (Anderson 2000; Ellen 2004). In this discursive 'war', one side argues for the distinctive and superior nature of scientific forms of understanding: scientists discover 'truths' about the way the world really works. The other side, in a position with roots in extreme 'postmodernist' forms of cultural relativism, denies any special status for scientific forms of understanding: 'science' is merely a label used to privilege certain forms of knowledge and thus to denigrate and marginalize other nonscientific modes of thought (see the discussion on constructivism in the Introduction).

We are not under the illusion that we will resolve all the contentious issues related to how scientists and nonscientists understand the world. However, in this chapter we sketch a position that lies between the two poles of this debate, a position that frames the arguments of this book. We do believe that there are good reasons to separate scientific from Indigenous modes of thought. We argue, however, that such differences lie primarily on the level of cultural ideals and methodological prescriptions: scientists privilege impersonal and decontextualized knowledge, for example, in a way that Indigenous peoples generally do not; they strive to follow a method that seeks to eliminate observer bias and the peculiarity of context in a way, again, that Indigenous peoples usually do not. Nevertheless, we still see important continuities between scientific and Indigenous ways of knowing, especially on the level of actual epistemological practice: for example, we accept that scientific knowledge, like Indigenous ways of knowing, 'draws its form from its social and cultural roots' (Nader 1996b: xi; see also Ede and Cormack 2004; Peloquin and Berkes 2009). To decontextualize science from its social roots is to grant science a privileged status and an unfounded superiority over other ways of knowing (Agrawal 1995; Nadasdy 1999; Nader 1996a; Sillitoe 2002). Alternatively, to argue that only Indigenous knowledge has a social context tends to produce views of Indigenous peoples as 'ecological savages' (Krech 1999; Milton 1996; Redford 1990) with no 'objective' knowledge of value in a modern political world (Kuper 2003). These are positions we cannot support.

Overall, we hope this chapter introduces some important differences between scientific and Indigenous ways of knowing without essentializing these differences or implying that they are absolute. To argue for an insurmountable 'cognitive divide' between scientists and nonscientists would in fact defeat one of the primary aims of this book, which is to show how barriers become *constructed* between government-based resource managers and Indigenous peoples and thus also how such barriers, as social *constructs*, might be bridged.

Indigenous Knowledge versus Scientific Knowledge

From our field experiences, we have learned that Indigenous know-how is a form of '*local* knowledge', intricately bound to particular communities and places as well as to whole ways of life. Such knowledge is often learned through informal trial and error processes and thus comes from direct personal experiences. Despite the highly personal and even individualized character of this knowledge, however, the acquisition and preservation of Indigenous understandings are usually mediated by social others in informal apprentice relationships. Such apprenticeships, in turn, are structured by highly repetitive and often unspoken demonstrations by, and silent imitations of, local experts. In similar terms, Indigenous knowledge is often pragmatic rather than abstractly theoretical—a *knowledge how* rather than an abstract *knowledge of* or *knowledge about*. Likewise, Indigenous knowledge, as suggested above, is orally preserved not only in the living memories of individuals but also within the textures of local songs, stories, and other performance traditions. Further, Indigenous knowledge is almost invariably informed by references to elusive spiritual beings such as gods, ghosts, and ancestors. Such knowledge, again as indicated above, interconnects local human communities with nonhuman societies of animals and plants (Feit 1987; Gadgil, Berkes, and Folke 1993; Nadasdy 1999; Posey 1992, 2000; Scott 1996; Sillitoe 2002; Snodgrass, Sharma, et al. 2007, 2008; Snodgrass, Lacy, et al. 2008) and with past-human realms of spirit and creator beings and ancestors (Bradley 2001, 2008; Merlan 1998; Nabokov 2002; Povinelli 1993; Rose 1996b; Snodgrass and Tiedje 2008; Tiedje and Snodgrass 2008). Overall, such knowledge is explicitly acknowledged as partaking in local 'traditions' that build on the know-how of multiple preceding generations. And such 'traditional' knowledge, it is argued, has helped its practitioners to manage their lands relatively sustainably across large expanses of time (but see Chapter 2).

By contrast, scientists are said to pursue knowledge that is replicable across contexts that are strictly controlled, making such knowledge more abstract and universalizing, rigorously empirical and experimental rather than simply experiential (Ede and Cormack 2004; Kalland 2000; Lindberg 1990; Nader 1996a; Schafersman 1997). Scientific knowledge is also preserved in impersonal institutional networks such as written and digital texts rather than only in the minds and bodies of living persons and in the fluid and unpredictable language of story (Ede and Cormack 2004: 147; Goody 1977, 1986, 1987; Nadasdy 1999; Wallerstein 2003: 459). Further, scientists are certainly interested in gaining technological *knowledge how* to control and manipulate the world. Nevertheless, such practical know-how is often subordinated to abstract *knowledge of* in the form of coherent systems of explanation, even logical syllogisms and proofs, statistical tables and rigorous taxonomies, and mathematical equations. Modern scientists, more than Indigenous peoples, seem to be interested in consciously coding their knowledge in formalized representations that can be manipulated according to the rules of logical inference to retrieve such knowledge. Such a coding, it is sometimes argued, also makes knowledge easier to critique and thus facilitates the critical distance that prevents irrational and blind commitment to traditional authority. Mathematics and formal logic, then, not narrative, performance, and social authority, are the watchwords of modern scientific practice. In this same vein, scientists are committed to the generation of testable hypotheses that are systematic, logically coherent, and empirically grounded (Schafersman 1997), not to mercurial spiritual beings. And scientific knowledge, owing to the institutional and technological forms it has engendered and in seeming direct contrast to Indigenous forms of knowing, has led to an unprecedented control over, and even exploitation and degradation of, the planet. Indeed, many social scientists preserve the distinction between these two forms of knowledge on precisely these grounds (Gegeo and

Watson-Gegeo 2001, 2002; Hunn 2003; Hunn et al. 2003; Kalland 2000; Nadasdy 1999; Scott 1996; Silberbauer 1994; Sillitoe 1998, 2002).

Indigenous knowledge, we would thus argue, is eminently social as well as *integrated*. Here we wish to be careful, however, not to occlude the personalized, and even individualized, nature of such knowledge. Institutional structures such as totems, kinship relationships, proprietary stories/myths, political status, and so on influence the construction and indeed *ownership* of Indigenous knowledge and therefore the exclusive right to speak about and regulate certain resources. This individual ownership, it should be pointed out, makes Indigenous knowledge potentially unstable: important traditions can be lost with the death of a single expert; like-wise, such knowledge can be acquired, or re-acquired, with the help of a single Native genius. Indigenous knowledge, then, can be said to be fragmented in a certain sense. Nevertheless, one typically finds Indigenous mechanisms that ensure that knowledge, even when shared asymmetrically, is available to many. This sharing of knowledge can occur through the bringing together of specialists at appropriate times to address important resource problems, to direct the extraction of resources, and/or to grant rights of access over these resources. In addition, much Indigenous ownership of knowledge is not limited to specific individuals; instead, it is spread over entire clans or communities, or it is distributed over categories of persons based on their age or their gender. This form of knowledge management adds to the understanding that Indigenous knowledge is social, and indeed redundant, rather than merely individualized (see Basso 1996; Bradley 2001; Feit 1987, 1994; Kearney 2008; Mearns 1994; Merculieff 1994; Pickering and Jewell 2008; Povinelli 1993; Rose 1996b; Silberbauer 1994; Williams and Mununggurr 1989).

To elaborate on the social nature of Indigenous knowledge, Feit (1994) and Nadasdy (1999) argue that the ritual and political nature of Indigenous knowledge is central to the successful sharing of knowledge within a Native community as well as between Indigenous peoples, on the one hand, and scientists and resource managers, on the other. For Feit, local relations of power are particularly important in the praxis of hunting. Passing on the hunting culture from one generation to the next not only regenerates the hunt, it also 'reproduces the social system of relations, including social differentiations that both hierarchically separate and link gener-ations' (Feit 1994: 436). For Nadasdy (1999), power lies in the choices made about the kinds of information brought to the management table. Local experience is the key to understanding management problems and to developing solutions, and social networks inform experience. Indigenous resource managers combine their knowledge and experience in a social context that ensures that all relevant elements of knowledge can come together regularly. Because Indigenous peoples form communities, their social structures ensure that they interrelate on a regular (often daily) basis, coming together for a range of social activities—including but not limited to the stewardship of natural resources and the resolution of ecological crises—as part of normal community activities.

In contrast to Indigenous peoples' 'holistic' distribution of knowledge, scientists' knowledge tends to be specialized, with research concentrated on narrow fields of knowledge. This highly specialized way of knowing, which is the dominant tendency of science, is often experienced by outsiders to the scientific enterprise—or to certain narrowly demarcated dimensions of the scientific enterprise—as the extremely esoteric nature of certain kinds of scientific knowledge and expertise. In 2003 one of us (AR) attended a workshop presenting scientific research undertaken in national parks in Queensland (Australia) as a collaborative venture of university and other scientists and national parks staff. Dr. Don Sands, from the Australian Commonwealth Scientific Industrial and Research Organisation (CSIRO) Division of Entomology discussed his work in communicating scientific research into *Lepidoptera* (butterflies) to the general public. His was the only paper relating to invertebrates. Most of the other speakers discussed research into ecosystems supporting rare and threatened plant and animal species, with large vertebrate mammals dominating the day's proceedings. In speaking about butterflies and moths, Sands distinguished himself from his colleagues by referring to the other speakers at the gathering as 'you vertebrate people'. He then outlined why his talk was only about *Lepidoptera*, explaining that he was interested only in collecting and researching butterflies and moths: 'although I will do ants if someone needs me to'.

Suzuki documents a similar experience while on a visit to the Amazon rainforest: 'Three scientists, frog experts, were there at the time, and their knowledge of their subject was impressive. One of them took us on a night hike and in pitch dark, could find frogs that were barely half an inch long. But when I asked about a bird we scared up and a strange plant on a tree, he shrugged his shoulders. "Don't ask me, I'm a herpetologist", he said' (1992: xxxvi).

Kalland (2000) argues that this sometimes myopic knowledge bind of scientists is due to a one-dimensional focus on causation that is at the heart of the separation of scientific disciplines. As a result, scientists like Nabokov's archaeologist often cannot understand the complex interconnections between different animal species that characterize Indigenous explanations of problems (Feit 1987; Nadasdy 1999; Scott 1996; Silberbauer 1994; Sillitoe 2002; Stevenson 2006). This problem is not so marked in those scientific fields that adopt a holistic approach to the environment, such as ecology, but even here there are some ecologists who take a narrow perspective on the discipline and therefore fail to realize the level of holism that is characteristic of so many nonscientific communities (Taylor 2001).

Such myopia is often evident in resource management. In most management agencies, especially those dealing with the protection of important—often endangered—species, individual species management plans are the most common instrument of fauna and flora conservation. Although holistic management of the entire protected area is desired and even required by legislation, holistic management is achieved by the separation of each element of the protected area and the development of individual management plans on a species-by-species basis. A review of any plan of management for a national park, for example, demonstrates this point. The plan is divided into separate management components, with a separate, individual, isolated set of policies and procedures for each compartment. Management of the whole is simply the sum of the individual, isolated parts (Golschewski 2004; Nadasdy 1999).

The segregation of knowledge and understanding, as we have argued, is not entirely foreign to most Indigenous communities. Indigenous experts, too, maintain technical and esoteric knowledge that is unequally distributed within a community. However, we would suggest that Indigenous experts must continually translate their knowledge into terms that are meaningful and practical to the community as a whole. Western scientists also participate in communal gatherings—academic conferences, for example. And interdisciplinary gatherings are increasingly common. We would suggest, however, that these more holistically defined occasions have been precipitated by a perceived failure of or crisis within normative science which is, by its nature, fragmenting and compartmentalized.

Disentangling Simplistic Distinctions I: Indigenous Peoples Thinking Like Scientists

Despite these examples, ample anthropological research breaks down simplistic distinctions between Indigenous and scientific knowledge. Bourdieu (1960, 1972), for example, has demonstrated that knowledge that is usually presented as characteristic of Indigenous societies—knowledge that is context-bound, practical, largely unspoken and unsystematic, often beyond challenge, and deeply embodied rather than abstractly theorized—is also characteristic of communities as diverse as Algerian peasants and the French bourgeoisie.

Simplistic distinctions between Indigenous and scientific knowledge tend to occlude important features of Indigenous thought that we have all encountered in our various field-sites. For example, an emphasis on Indigenous knowledge as 'traditional' knowledge handed down from generation to generation, tends to suggest that Indigenous peoples inhabit 'closed' epistemological systems, thus denying them their creativity and ability to learn and respond flexibly to new situations (Berkes 2008; Hunn 1993; Merlan 1998; Nadasdy 1999). Belying such assumptions, we have all witnessed Indigenous incorporations of scientific knowledge into local Indigenous systems of land management (cf. Stevenson 2006). Similarly, the emphasis on Indigenous knowledge as experiential and sacred rather than experimental and purely empirical—the fact that Indigenous peoples are willing to be guided by unseen forces and entities—can obscure the reality that Indigenous peoples may produce accounts of their environments that are just as objective, detailed, rigorously grounded, and coherent as those of ecologists. And the suggestion that Indigenous knowledge is largely informal, pragmatic rather than abstract, again denies the fact that Indigenous peoples often speculate in the most nuanced and conscious of manners not only about their environments but also about what they know about their environments, even if such speculations are often encoded in folktales and myths rather than abstract propositions.

Berkes (2008; Berkes and Kislalioglu Berkes 2009; Peloquin and Berkes 2009) has documented careful empirical quantitative thought among his Cree hunter research collaborators. Although hunters' and Indigenous land managers' knowledge is experiential, shared, and communal (Peloquin and Berkes 2009), the complexity of variables involved in decision making about hunting requires highly complex ecological knowledge and 'direct immersion in and constant observation of countless elements' (Peloquin and Berkes 2009: 538). Berkes likens Cree and Inuit resources management to the adaptive management regimes and 'fuzzy logic' of Western science, arguing that 'some indigenous groups have resource-use practices that suggest a sophisticated understanding of ecological relationships and dynamics' (Berkes and Kislalioglu Berkes 2009: 6; see also Peloquin and Berkes 2009).

Other researchers have drawn similar analogies between Indigenous knowledge and scientific methods. Nadasdy (1999) describes Kluane First Nation Canadians working with scientists to count Dall sheep using rigorous monitoring and counting techniques. According to Nadasdy, the difference between the scientists and the Kluane was not in the methods used to achieve the quantitative data but in the readiness to rely on small sample sizes as well as the eventual use made of these observations. Nadasdy demonstrates that knowledge that Kluane believed was significant in the management of the sheep was ignored by the scientists, because the total count, by scientific standards, was too low for meaningful statistical analysis. Kluane felt the data were important, because they demonstrated a serious decline in total sheep population numbers, observations that were born out in other contexts, such as Indigenous oral history (Nadasdy 1999: 9).

None of us would deny that our Indigenous research collaborators, like us, can and do think inductively and deductively. Native peoples certainly think abstractly and build hypotheses. For example, the Dandrubin Gorenpul Aboriginal people of Moreton Bay in southeastern Queensland, observing numbers of rainbow lorikeets (a small, brightly colored bird) will know that large numbers (as one variable) portend a large haul of sea mullet (as a second variable), which will lead the Aboriginal community to invite kin and trading partners from neighboring areas for the forthcoming feast. Alternatively, low numbers of lorikeets will lead to hypotheses of a lean fishing season and a consequent cancellation of plans for festivities. Western scientists have not, as yet, accounted for the causal chain that explains this connection between variables, although the correlation is evident.

Likewise, although Indigenous knowledge is often characterized as holistic and thus in contrast to the compartmentalization of science, it still supports the existence of specialists among Indigenous resource managers. In Rajasthan, for example, where another of us works (JS), we sometimes find compartmentalization of knowledge occurring among, say, herbalists specializing in curing a particular stomach affliction in cattle and who are consulted and paid for their services. These specialists typically know little to nothing about, for example, how to treat children's flu or even such human stomach ailments as common indigestion.

Disentangling Simplistic Distinctions II: Scientists Thinking Like Indigenous Peoples

Some philosophers do continue to argue for the special character of scientific knowledge and continue to conceptualize the scientific enterprise as a search for universal and objective 'Truth'. Here we are especially thinking of certain neo-Popperian philosophers of science who seek to identify and define the formal method and logic that separates scientific thought from everyday or Indigenous thought. Still, formal definitions of science—for example, in terms of an idealized hypothetico-deductive method—are increasingly difficult to defend and have been largely abandoned (Ellen 2004: 420). And a new consensus among philosophers of science has emerged that suggests that we should look more closely at the social and cultural roots of science and thus at the way science is actually performed rather than at scientific knowledge as simply 'true', 'objective', or 'accurate' knowledge of the world (Ellen 2004: 420–421; see also Bruner 1996; Dunbar 1995).

Indeed, anthropologists have for some time now been studying scientific 'tribes': biologists in the Pasteur Institute in Paris; high-energy physicists; and employees of the CETUS Corporation busily piecing together the human genome (respectively, Latour 1988; Traweek 1988; Rabinow 1996). If these 'science studies' are to be believed, scientists are also story-tellers: laboratory folklore serves to transmit knowledge within the scientific community as well as to cement social networks; stories also work to render scientific knowledge compelling as well as understandable both to insiders and outsiders to scientific endeavors. More generally, ethnographic and historical studies of laboratories and real scientific practice suggest that science is as much an irrational Weberian 'calling' as an objective enterprise. Scientists, it seems, are driven as much by hunches, inspirations, quirks of personality, and irrational passions as by the numbers. Furthermore, the answers to scientific questions may be as much structured by local oral traditions, culturally peculiar definitions of 'nature', hidden assumptions about what are valuable and testable, networks of patronage and tutelage, the next paycheck, ritualized relationships of jesting and familiarity, and worries over reputations as by cool reason.

One example of the social dimension of science comes from our sister subdiscipline of archaeology. For many years, archaeologists in most parts of the world have asserted the primary place of 'science' and scientific methods to their discipline (Cole 1993; Hiscock 1996, 2008; Loy and Wood 1989). As early as 1973, David Clarke argued:

> In the new era of critical self-consciousness the discipline [of archaeology] recognizes that its domain is as much defined by the characteristic forms of its reasoning, the intrinsic nature of its knowledge and information, and its competing theories of concepts and their relationships [i.e., its scientific methods]—as by the elementary specification of raw material, scale of study, and methodology. (Clarke 1973: 7)

Yet it is clear that archaeology does not, and cannot, operate outside a sociopolitical framework, especially when the past of Indigenous others is the focus of research (see arguments in Fforde, Hubert, and Turnbull 2002; Swidler et al. 1997). At the first World Archaeological Congress in Southampton in 1986, Indigenous owners of heritage vocally challenged the findings of 'scientific archaeology' conducted outside an Indigenous construction of the past (Rowlands 1994). In response to concerns raised by Indigenous peoples, and by archaeologists working closely with traditional owners, we have since seen numerous nations develop Codes of Ethics that recognize that archaeology has a social place and that Indigenous ways of understanding the past have a legitimate role in the interpretation of archaeological remains. In response to the re-emergence of archaeology as a 'soft' as well as a 'hard' science, genuinely collaborative projects between archaeologists and Indigenous heritage managers have grown. Termed 'community archaeology', such research recognizes Indigenous explanations of the past even when such interpretations may not always concur with the analytical models and specialist language of standard scientific investigations (Clarke 2002; Cole et al. 2002; Field et al. 2000; Greer, Harrison, and McIntyre-Tamwoy 2002; Harrison 2002; Marshall 2002; Ross 2008; Ross and Coghill 2000; Smith and Burke 2003, 2004).

Increasingly, archaeologists are redefining their discipline as an enterprise that cannot put aside passions, politically driven purposes, and collective imaginations of the past (Rowlands 1994: 133; see also Nabokov 2002; Perkins 2001). Neither can this discipline ignore the fact that some methodological choices are unscientifically arbitrary, linked as they are to certain historically specific developments. As one critic puts it:

> The social construction of archaeological pasts is more than personal values getting involved in the academic enterprise. In the differing contexts of nationalism, development and the postmodern, we encounter the silences and gaps in archaeological explanations that determine which sites are excavated, what kinds of artefacts are privileged in the legitimizing of expert archaeological knowledges. (Rowlands 1994: 141; see also Byrne 2005)

Archaeologists and other 'scientists', to put it bluntly and to summarize, also inhabit communities and possess cultures (Nader 1996a; Rowlands 1994). Or, in Kuhn's terms (1962), scientists possess 'paradigms' to which they are largely blind but that nevertheless guide inquiry, structuring the kinds of questions scientists ask, the way they interpret their data, and indeed the very way they inhabit the world (Hytten and Burns 2007). Ellen (2004) refers to these Kuhnian paradigms as 'framework theories', which he believes contrasts with Popperian-like methodologies for testing more context-dependent and narrowly defined hypotheses. One can certainly define science in terms of its formal methods of hypothesis-testing rather than in terms of its paradigms, framework theories, and social practices. Likewise, one can remove from one's definitions the messy, unplanned, and contingent side of science and instead focus on an idealized methodology and program by which hypotheses are generated and tested against objective 'data'—although, as Ellen (2004) and other observers of science point out, the elimination of the social and cultural dimensions of science may remove features of science that are absolutely integral to our understanding of the way science actually works and thus critical to our understanding of the way scientific knowledge is generated and validated.

We noted in the previous section that Indigenous people sometimes make generalizations based on small samples. Yet, scientists, too, sometimes draw conclusions based on small samples and slim data. Brower (1991), for example, describes the case of a fine but narrow ecological study of slope processes in Sagarmatha National Park in Nepal. A Western-trained researcher studied one slope for one season, observed vegetation decline and erosion, and blamed Sherpa grazing and juniper harvesting as the cause of degradation without any further assessment. As a consequence of these observations the researcher advised adoption of 'strict land-use policies' (Brower 1991: 177). However, Brower notes that a more in-depth and longer-term study would have demonstrated that the local micro-environment of the slope was drier than nearby areas. Long-term sampling of the area by Brower indicated the ecological resilience of the Khumbu region, including diversity of grasses and juniper regeneration, despite this dry micro-climate. She argued that the relatively sparse distribution of juniper on the slope compared to elsewhere may be because, unlike adjacent areas, Sherpas live near the slope year round and thus harvest the slope's juniper for fuel more regularly than elsewhere (Brower 1991: 178). She argued that the scientific study's conclusions, although highly compartmentalized and based on a narrow base of data, were accepted because they fitted the dominant view of Himalayan ecosystems as fragile and under serious threat from human occupation (1991: 5–7).

References

Agrawal, A. 1995. Dismantling the divide between Indigenous and scientific knowledge. *Development and Change* 26: 413–439.

Anderson, E. N. 2000. Maya knowledge and 'science wars'. *Journal of Ethnobiology* 20(2): 129–158.

Appadurai, A. 1986. Introduction: Commodities and the politics of value. In A. Appadurai (Ed.), *The social life of things: Commodities in cultural perspective*, pp. 3–63. Cambridge University Press, Cambridge.

Basso, K. 1996. *Wisdom sits in places: Landscape and language among the Western Apache*. University of New Mexico Press, Albuquerque.

Berkes, F. 2008. *Sacred ecology* (2nd edition). Routledge, New York.

Berkes, F., and M. Kislalioglu Berkes. 2009. Ecological complexity, fuzzy logic, and holism in Indigenous knowledge. *Futures* 41: 6–12.

Bourdieu, P. 1960. *Algeria* (1979 translation). Cambridge University Press, Cambridge.

———. 1972. *Outline of a theory of practice* (1977 translation). Cambridge University Press, Cambridge.

Bradley, J. 2001. Landscapes of the mind, landscapes of the spirit: Negotiating a sentient landscape. In R. Baker, J. Davies, and E. Young (Eds.), *Working on country: Contemporary Indigenous management of Australia's lands and coastal regions,* pp. 295–307. Oxford University Press, Melbourne.

———. 2008. When a stone tool is a dingo: Country and relatedness in Australian Aboriginal notions of landscape. In B. David and J. Thomas (Eds.), *Handbook of landscape archaeology,* pp 633–637. Left Coast Press, Walnut Creek, CA.

Brower, B. 1991. *Sherpa of Khumbu: People, livestock, and landscape*. Oxford University Press, New Delhi.

Bruner, J. 1996. Frames for thinking: Ways of making meaning. In D. R. Olson and N. Torrance (Eds.), *Modes of thought: Explorations in culture and cognition*, pp. 189–215. Cambridge University Press, Cambridge.

Byrne, D. 2005. Messages to Manilla. In I. Macfarlane with M-J. Mountain and R. Paton (Eds.), *Many exchanges: Archaeology, history, community and the work of Isabel McBryde*, pp. 53–62. Aboriginal History Monograph 11.

Clarke, A. 2002. The ideal and the real: Cultural and personal transformations of archaeological research in Groote Eylandt, northern Australia. In Y. Marshall (Ed.), *Community Archaeology*, pp. 249–264. *World Archaeology* 34(2).

Clarke, D. 1973. Archaeology: The loss of innocence. *Antiquity* 47: 6–18.

Cleveland, D. A., and D. Soleri (Eds.). 2002. *Farmers, scientists and plant breeding: Integrating knowledge and practice*. CABI Publishing, Wallingford.

Cole, J. R. 1993. Cult archaeology and unscientific method and theory. *Advances in Archaeological Method* 3: 1–33.

Cole, N., G. Musgrave, L. George, T. George, and D. Banjo. 2002. Community archaeology at Laura, Cape York Peninsula. In S. Ulm, C. Westcott, J. Reid, A. Ross, I. Lilley, J. Prangnell, and L. Kirkwood (Eds.), *Barriers, borders, boundaries: Proceedings of the 2001 Australian Archaeological Association Annual Conference*, pp. 137–150. Tempus 7. Anthropology Museum, The University of Queensland, Brisbane.

Dunbar, K. 1995. How scientists really reason: Scientific reasoning in real-world laboratories. In R. J. Steinberg and J. Davidson (Eds.), *Mechanisms of insight*, pp. 365–395. MIT Press, Cambridge, MA.

Ede, A., and L. B. Cormack. 2004. *A History of science in society: From philosophy to utility*. Broadview Press, Peterborough, Ontario.

Ellen, R. 2004. From ethno-science to science, or 'What the indigenous knowledge debate tells us about how scientists define their project.' *Journal of Cognition and Culture* 4(3–4): 409–450.

Ellen, R., and H. Harris. 2000. Introduction. In R. Ellen, P. Parkes, and A. Bicker (Eds.), *Indigenous environmental knowledge and its transformations: Critical anthropological perspectives*, pp. 1–33. Overseas Publishers Association, Harwood Academic Publishers, Amsterdam.

Feit, H. A. 1987. Waswanipi Cree management of land and wildlife: Cree ethnoecology revisited. In B. A. Cox (Ed.), *Native people, native lands: Canadian Indians, Inuit and Metis*, pp. 75–91. Carleton Library Series No. 142, Carleton University Press, Ottowa, Canada.

———. 1994. The enduring pursuit: Land, time, and social relationships in anthropological models of hunter-gatherers and in hunters' images. In E. S. Burch and L. J. Ellanna (Eds.), *Key issues in hunter-gatherer research*, pp. 421–439. Berg Publishers, Oxford.

Fforde, C., J. Hubert, and P. Turnbull (Eds.). 2002. *The dead and their possessions: Repatriation in principle, policy and practice*. Routledge, New York.

Field, J., J. Barker, R. Barker, E. Coffey, L. Coffey, E. Crawford, L. Darcy, T. Fields, G. Lord, B. Steadman, and S. Colley. 2000. 'Coming back': Aborigines and archaeologists at Cuddie Springs. *Public Archaeology* 1(1): 35–38.

Gadgil, M., F. Berkes, and C. Folke. 1993. Indigenous knowledge for biodiversity conservation. *Ambio* XXII(2–3): 151–156.

Gegeo, D. W., and K. A. Watson-Gegeo. 2001. 'How we know': Kwara'ae rural villagers doing Indigenous epistemology. *The Contemporary Pacific* 13(1): 55–88.

———. 2002. Whose knowledge? Epistemological collisions in Solomon Islands community development. *The Contemporary Pacific* 14(2): 377–409.

Godwin, L. 2005. 'Everyday archaeology': Archaeological heritage management and its relationship to native title in development-related processes. *Australian Aboriginal Studies* 2005(1): 74–83.

Golschewski, K. 2004. Expanding concepts of heritage: An investigation into the concept of cultural landscape and its inclusion into heritage management practice and legislation. Unpublished B.A. Honours thesis, The University of Queensland, Brisbane.

Goody, J. 1977. *The domestication of the savage mind.* Cambridge University Press, Cambridge.

———. 1986. *The logic of writing and the organisation of society.* Cambridge University Press, Cambridge.

———. 1987. *The interface between the written and the oral.* Cambridge University Press, Cambridge.

Greer, S., R. Harrison, and S. McIntyre-Tamwoy. 2002. Community-based archaeology in Australia. In Y. Marshall (Ed.), *Community Archaeology*, pp. 265–287. *World Archaeology* 34(2).

Hardin, G. 1968. The tragedy of the commons. *Science* 162: 1243–1248.

———. 1991. The tragedy of the unmanaged commons: Population and the disguises of providence. In R. V. Anderson (Ed.), *Commons without tragedy: Protecting the environment from overpopulation –A new approach*, pp. 162–185. Shepheard-Walwyn, London.

———. 1993. *Living within limits: Ecology, economics, and population taboos.* Oxford University Press, New York.

Harrison, R. 2002. Shared histories and the archaeology of the pastoral industry in Australia. In R. Harrison and C. Williamson (Eds.), *After Captain Cook: The archaeology of the recent Indigenous past in Australia*, pp. 37–58. Sydney University Archaeological Methods Series 8. Archaeological Computing Laboratory, University of Sydney, Sydney.

Hiscock, P. 1996. The New Age of alternative archaeology of Australia. *Archaeology in Oceania* 31(3): 152–164.

———. 2008. *Archaeology of ancient Australia.* Routledge, New York.

Hunn, E. S. 1993. What is traditional ecological knowledge? In N. M. Williams and G. Baines (Eds.), *Traditional ecological knowledge: Wisdom for sustainable development*, pp. 13–15. Centre for Resource and Environmental Studies, Australian National University, Canberra.

———. 2003. Epiphenomenal conservation reconsidered. Paper delivered to American Anthropological Society Annual Meeting, Chicago, November 20, 2003.

Hunn, E. S., D. R. Johnson, P. N. Russell, and T. F. Thornton. 2003. Huna Tlingit traditional environmental knowledge, conservation, and the management of a 'wilderness' park. *Current Anthropology* 44(Supplement): S79, S103.

Hytten, K., and G. L. Burns. 2007. Deconstructing dingo management on Fraser Island: The significance of social constructionism for effective wildlife management. *Australian Journal of Environmental Management* 14: 48–57.

Igoe, J. 2004. *Conservation and globalization: A study of national parks and Indigenous communities from East Africa to South Dakota.* Wadsworth, Belmont, CA.

Kalland, A. 2000. Indigenous knowledge: Prospects and limitations. In R. Ellen, P. Parkes, and A. Bicker (Eds.), *Indigenous environmental knowledge and its transformations: Critical anthropological perspectives*, pp. 319–335. Overseas Publishers Association, Harwood Academic Publishers, Amsterdam.

Kearney, A. 2008. Gender in landscape archaeology. In B. David and J. Thomas (Eds.), *Handbook of landscape archaeology*, pp. 247–255. Left Coast Press, Walnut Creek, CA.

Krech, S. 1999. *The ecological Indian: Myth and history*. W. W. Norton and Company, New York.

Kuhn, T. 1962. *The structure of scientific revolutions*. University of Chicago Press, Chicago.

Kuper, A. 2003. The return of the native. *Current Anthropology* 44(3): 389–412.

Latour, B. 1988. *The pasteurization of France*. Harvard University Press, Cambridge, MA.

Lindberg, D. C. 1990. Conceptions of the scientific revolution from Bacon to Butterfield: A preliminary sketch. In D. C. Lindberg and R. S. Westman (Eds.), *Reappraisals of the scientific revolution*, pp. 1–26. Cambridge University Press, Cambridge.

Loy T. H., and A. R. Wood. 1989. Blood residue analysis at Çayönü Tepesi, Turkey. *Journal of Field Archaeology* 16: 451–460.

Marshall, Y. 2002. What is community archaeology? In Y. Marshall (Ed.), *Community Archaeology*, pp. 211–219. *World Archaeology* 34(2).

Mearns, L. 1994. To continue the Dreaming: Aboriginal women's traditional responsibilities in a transformed world. In E. S. Burch and L. J. Ellanna (Eds.), *Key issues in hunter-gatherer research*, pp. 263–288. Berg Publishers, London.

Merculieff, I. L. 1994. Western society's linear systems and aboriginal cultures: The need for two-way exchanges for the sake of survival. In E. S. Burch and L. J. Ellanna (Eds.), *Issues in hunter-gatherer research*, pp. 405–415. Berg Publishers, Oxford.

Merlan, F. 1998. *Caging the rainbow: Places, politics, and Aborigines in a North Australian town*. University of Hawai'i Press, Honolulu.

Milton, K. 1996. *Environmentalism and cultural theory: Exploring the role of anthropology in environmental discourse*. Routledge, New York.

Nabokov, P. 2002. *A forest of time: American Indian ways of history*. Cambridge University Press, Cambridge.

Nadasdy, P. 1999. The politics of TEK: Power and the 'integration' of knowledge. *Arctic Anthropology* 36: 1–18.

Nader, L. 1996a. Anthropological inquiry into boundaries, power and knowledge: Introduction. In L. Nader (Ed.), *Naked science: Anthropological inquiry into boundaries, power and knowledge*, pp. 1–25. Routledge, New York.

Nader, L. 1996b. Preface in L. Nader (Ed.), *Naked science: Anthropological inquiry into boundaries, power and knowledge*, pp. xi–xv. Routledge, New York.

Peloquin, C., and F. Berkes. 2009. Local knowledge, subsistence harvests, and social-ecological complexity in James Bay. *Human Ecology* 37(5): 533–545.

Perkins, M. 2001. *The reform of time*. Pluto Press, London.

Pickering, K. A., and B. Jewell. 2008. Nature is relative: Religious affiliation, environmental attitudes, and political constraints on the Pine Ridge Indian Reservation. *Journal for the Study of Religion, Nature and Culture* 2(1): 135–158.

Posey, D. A. 1992. Interpreting and applying the 'reality' of Indigenous concepts: What is necessary to learn from the natives? In K. H. Redford and C. Padoch (Eds.), *Conservation of neotropical forests: Working from traditional resource use*, pp. 21–34. Columbia University Press, New York.

———. 2000. Ethnobiology and ethnoecology in the context of national laws and international agreements affecting Indigenous and local knowledge, traditional resources and intellectual property rights. In R. Ellen, P. Parkes, and A. Bicker (Eds.), *Indigenous environmental knowledge and its transformations: Critical anthropological perspectives*, pp. 35–54. Overseas Publishers Association, Harwood Academic Publishers, Amsterdam.

Povinelli, E. 1993. 'Might be something': The language of indeterminacy in Australian Aboriginal land use. *Man* (New series) 28: 679–704.

Rabinow, P. 1996. *Making PCR: A story of biotechnology.* University of Chicago Press, Chicago.

Redford, K. 1990. The ecologically noble savage. *Orion Nature Quarterly* 9: 24–29.

Richards, P. 1985. *Indigenous agricultural revolution: Ecology and food-crop farming in West Africa.* Hutchison, London.

Rose, D. B. 1996a. Land rights and deep colonizing: The erasure of women. *Aboriginal Law Bulletin* 3(85): 6–13.

———. 1996b. *Nourishing terrains: Australian Aboriginal views of landscape and wilderness.* Australian Heritage Commission, Canberra.

Ross, A. 2008. Managing meaning at an ancient site in the 21st century: The Gummingurru Aboriginal stone arrangement on the Darling Downs, southern Queensland. *Oceania* 78: 91–108.

Ross, A., and S. Coghill. 2000. Conducting a community-based archaeological project: An archaeologist's and a Koenpul man's perspective. *Australian Aboriginal Studies* 2000(1&2): 76–83.

Rowlands, M. 1994. The politics of identity in archaeology. In G. Bond and A. Gilliam (Eds.), *Social construction of the past: Representation as power,* pp. 131–135. Unwin Hyman, London.

Schafersman, S. 1997. An introduction to science, scientific thinking and the scientific method, http://pbisotopes.ess.sunysb.edu/esp/files/scientific-method.html. Accessed October 2004.

Scott, C. 1996. Science for the West, myth for the rest? The case of James Bay Cree knowledge construction. In L. Nader (Ed.), *Naked science: Anthropological inquiries into boundaries, power and knowledge,* pp. 69–86. Routledge, London.

Silberbauer, G. 1994. A sense of place. In E. S. Burch and L. J. Ellanna (Eds.), *Key issues in hunter-gatherer research*, pp. 119–146. Berg Publishers, Oxford.

Sillitoe, P. 1998. The development of Indigenous knowledge: A new applied anthropology. *Current Anthropology* 39(2): 223–235.

Sillitoe, P. 2002. 'Maggots in their ears': Hunting incantations and Indigenous knowledge in development. *Journal of Ritual Studies* 16(2): 64–77.

Smith, C., and H. Burke. 2003. In the spirit of the code. In L. Zimmerman, K. Vitelli, and J. Howell-Zimmer (Eds.), *Ethical issues in archaeology*, pp. 177–197. AltaMira Press, Walnut Creek, CA.

———. 2004. Joining the dots: Managing the land and seascapes of Indigenous Australia. In I. Krupnik and R. Mason (Eds.), *Northern ethnographic landscapes: Perspectives from the circumpolar nations*, pp. 379–400. Smithsonian Institution Press, Washington, D.C.

Snodgrass, J. G., and K. Tiedje. 2008. Introduction to JSRNC theme issue. Indigenous nature reverence and conservation: Seven ways of transcending an unnecessary dichotomy. *Journal for the Study of Religion, Nature, and Culture* 2(1): 6–29.

Snodgrass, J. G., M. G. Lacy, S. K. Sharma, Y. Singh Jhala, M. Advani, N. K. Bhargava, and C. Upadhyay. 2008. Witch hunts, herbal healing, and discourses of indigenous 'eco-development' in North India: Theory and method in the anthropology of environmentality. *American Anthropologist* 110(3): 299–312.

Snodgrass, J. G., S. K. Sharma, Y. Singh Jhala, M. G. Lacy, M. Advani, N. K. Bhargava, and C. Upadhyay. 2007. Beyond self-interest and altruism: Herbalist and Leopard Brothers in an Indian wildlife sanctuary. *Human Dimensions of Wildlife* 12(5): 375–387.

———. 2008. Lovely leopards, frightful forests: The environmental ethics of indigenous Rajasthani shamans. *Journal for the Study of Religion, Nature, and Culture* 2(1): 30–54.

Stevenson, M. G. 2006. The possibility of difference: Rethinking co-management. *Human Organization* 65(2): 167–180.

Suzuki, D. 1992. A personal forward: The value of native ecologies. In D. Suzuki and P. Knudtson, *Wisdom of the elders: Sacred native stories of nature,* pp. xxvii–xliv. Bantam Books, New York.

Swidler, N., K. E. Dongoske, R. Anyon, and A. S. Downer (Eds.). 1997. *Native Americans and Archaeologists: Stepping stones to common ground.* AltaMira Press, Walnut Creek, CA.

Taylor, K. 2001. Trees, farms, ecosystems and 'places': A constructivists approach to an ecological problem. Unpublished Honours Project, School of Natural and Rural Systems, The University of Queensland, Gatton Campus.

Tiedje, K., and J. G. Snodgrass (Eds.). 2008. Indigenous nature reverence and environmental degradation: Exploring critical intersections of animism and conservation. Special theme issue of the *Journal for the Study of Religion, Nature, and Culture* 2(1): 5–159.

Traweek, S. 1988. *Beamtimes and lifetimes: The world of high energy physicists.* Harvard University Press, Cambridge, MA.

Wallerstein, I. 2003. Anthropology, sociology, and other dubious disciplines. *Current Anthropology* 44(4): 453–465.

Williams, N. M., and D. Mununggurr. 1989. Understanding Yolngu signs of the past. In R. Layton (Ed.), *Who needs the past? Indigenous values and archaeology,* pp. 70–83. Unwin Hyman, London.

Discussion Questions

1. How does Navokov describe the indigenous modes of narrating history among the Navajo and other indigenous communities?
2. What are distinctive characteristics of indigenous epistemology that make it a form of local knowledge?
3. What are the functions of formal logic and mathematics in modern scientific practice and how do they shape the ideal of objective and universal scientific truths?
4. What are the merits and demerits of holistic distribution of knowledge and highly specialized concentration of knowledge, respectively? Which mode of knowledge do you think is more effective in yielding important knowledge we seek in our time?
5. Do you agree with the authors that indigenous people think like scientists despite their tendency to hand down traditional knowledge in a practical setting, to rely on experiential and sacred dimension in informal and pragmatic languages and rituals?

UNIT IV

MAKING SENSE OF PHILOSOPHY

In the thirteenth chapter from a Platonic Dialogue of a perennial importance, Socrates presents a defense argument against the criminal charges against him by addressing the accusations with an appeal to his divine vocation of awakening the fellow Athenian citizen from complacent ignorance. In the fourteenth chapter, Spinoza, believed to be the first modern philosopher, provides in geometrical order an argument for human freedom as the highest good attainable with the supremacy of human intellect. In the fifteenth chapter, Graham Bird presents his interpretation of Kant's philosophy in the *Critique of Pure Reason*, according to which Kant's critical philosophy is a progress over his modern predecessors' skepticism as well as Scholastic dogmatism. In the sixteenth chapter, Marie McGinn explains the unique philosophical style of Wittgenstein's *Philosophical Investigations* by carefully probing the intentions and aims of the book.

Apology

Plato; ed. John M. Cooper; trans. G. M. A. Grube

Because of this occupation, I do not have the leisure to engage in public affairs to any extent, nor indeed to look after my own, but I live in great poverty because of my service to the god.

Furthermore, the young men who follow me around of their own free will, those who have most leisure, the sons of the very rich, take pleasure in hearing people questioned; they themselves often imitate me and try to question others. I think they find an abundance of men who believe they have some knowledge but know little or nothing. The result is that those whom they question are angry, not with themselves but with me. They say: "That man Socrates is a pestilential fellow who corrupts the young." If one asks them what he does and what he teaches to corrupt them, they are silent, as they do not know, but, so as not to appear at a loss, they mention those accusations that are available against all philosophers, about "things in the sky and things below the earth," about "not believing in the gods" and "making the worse the stronger argument"; they would not want to tell the truth, I'm sure, that they have been proved to lay claim to knowledge when they know nothing. These people are ambitious, violent, and numerous; they are continually and convincingly talking about me; they have been filling your ears for a long time with vehement slanders against me. From them Meletus attacked me, and Anytus and Lycon, Meletus being vexed on behalf of the poets, Anytus on behalf of the craftsmen and the politicians, Lycon on behalf of the orators, so that, as I started out by saying, I should be surprised if I could rid you of so much slander in so short a time. That, men of Athens, is the truth for you. I have hidden or disguised nothing. I know well enough that this very conduct makes me unpopular, and this is proof that what I say is true, that such is the slander against me, and that such are its causes. If you look into this either now or later, this is what you will find.

Let this suffice as a defense against the charges of my earlier accusers. After this I shall try to defend myself against Meletus, that good and patriotic man, as he says he is, and my later accusers. As these are a different lot of accusers, let us again take up their sworn deposition. It goes something like this: Socrates is guilty of corrupting the young and of not believing in the gods in whom the city believes, but in other new spiritual things. Such is their charge. Let us examine it point by point.

He says that I am guilty of corrupting the young, but I say that Meletus is guilty of dealing frivolously with serious matters, of irresponsibly bringing people into court, and of professing to be seriously concerned with things about none of which he has ever cared, and I shall try to prove that this is so. Come here and tell me, Meletus. Surely you consider it of the greatest importance that our young men be as good as possible?[1]—Indeed I do.

Come then, tell these men who improves them. You obviously know, in view of your concern. You say you have discovered the one who corrupts them, namely me, and you bring me here and accuse me to these men. Come, inform these men and tell them who it is who improves them. You see, Meletus, that you are silent and know not what to say. Does this not seem shameful to you and a sufficient proof of what I say, that you have not been concerned with any of this? Tell me, my good sir, who improves our young men?—The laws.

That is not what I am asking, but what person who has knowledge of the laws to begin with?—These jurymen, Socrates.

How do you mean, Meletus? Are these able to educate the young and improve them?—Certainly.

All of them, or some but not others?—All of them.

Very good, by Hera. You mention a great abundance of benefactors.

But what about the audience? Do they improve the young or not?

—They do, too.

What about the members of Council?[2]—The Councillors, also. But, Meletus, what about the assembly? Do members of the assembly corrupt the young, or do they all improve them?—They improve them.

All the Athenians, it seems, make the young into fine good men, except me, and I alone corrupt them. Is that what you mean?—That is most definitely what I mean.

You condemn me to a great misfortune. Tell me: does this also apply to horses, do you think? That all men improve them and one individual corrupts them? Or is quite the contrary true, one individual is able to improve them, or very few, namely, the horse breeders, whereas the majority, if they have horses and use them, corrupt them? Is that not the case, Meletus, both

---

1   Socrates here drops into his usual method of discussion by question and answer. This, no doubt, is what Plato had in mind, at least in part, when he made him ask the indulgence of the jury if he spoke "in his usual manner."

2   The Council was a body of 500 men, elected annually by lot, that prepared the agenda for meetings of the assembly and together with the magistrates conducted the public business of Athens. (On the assembly, see note to *Euthyphro* 3c.)

with horses and all other animals? Of course it is, whether you and Anytus say so or not. It would be a very happy state of affairs if only one person corrupted our youth, while the others improved them.

You have made it sufficiently obvious, Meletus, that you have never had any concern for our youth; you show your indifference clearly; that you have given no thought to the subjects about which you bring me to trial.

And by Zeus, Meletus, tell us also whether it is better for a man to live among good or wicked fellow citizens. Answer, my good man, for I am not asking a difficult question. Do not the wicked do some harm to those who are ever closest to them, whereas good people benefit them?—Certainly.

And does the man exist who would rather be harmed than benefited by his associates? Answer, my good sir, for the law orders you to answer. Is there any man who wants to be harmed?—Of course not.

Come now, do you accuse me here of corrupting the young and making them worse deliberately or unwillingly?—Deliberately.

What follows, Meletus? Are you so much wiser at your age than I am at mine that you understand that wicked people always do some harm to their closest neighbors while good people do them good, but I have reached such a pitch of ignorance that I do not realize this, namely that if I make one of my associates wicked I run the risk of being harmed by him so that I do such a great evil deliberately, as you say? I do not believe you, Meletus, and I do not think anyone else will. Either I do not corrupt the young or, if I do, it is unwillingly, and you are lying in either case. Now if I corrupt them unwillingly, the law does not require you to bring people to court for such unwilling wrongdoings, but to get hold of them privately, to instruct them and exhort them; for clearly, if I learn better, I shall cease to do what I am doing unwillingly. You, however, have avoided my company and were unwilling to instruct me, but you bring me here, where the law requires one to bring those who are in need of punishment, not of instruction.

And so, men of Athens, what I said is clearly true: Meletus has never been at all concerned with these matters. Nonetheless tell us, Meletus, how you say that I corrupt the young; or is it obvious from your deposition that it is by teaching them not to believe in the gods in whom the city believes but in other new spiritual things? Is this not what you say I teach and so corrupt them?—That is most certainly what I do say.

Then by those very gods about whom we are talking, Meletus, make this clearer to me and to these men: I cannot be sure whether you mean that I teach the belief that there are some gods—and therefore I myself believe that there are gods and am not altogether an atheist, nor am I guilty of that—not, however, the gods in whom the city believes, but others, and that this is the charge against me, that they are others. Or whether you mean that I do not believe in gods at all, and that this is what I teach to others.—This is what I mean, that you do not believe in gods at all.

You are a strange fellow, Meletus. Why do you say this? Do I not believe, as other men do, that the sun and the moon are gods?—No, by Zeus, gentlemen of the jury, for he says that the sun is stone, and the moon earth.

My dear Meletus, do you think you are prosecuting Anaxagoras? Are you so contemptuous of these men and think them so ignorant of letters as not to know that the books of Anaxagoras[3] of Clazomenae are full of those theories, and further, that the young men learn from me what they can buy from time to time for a drachma, at most, in the bookshops, and ridicule Socrates if he pretends that these theories are his own, especially as they are so absurd? Is that, by Zeus, what you think of me, Meletus, that I do not believe that there are any gods?

—That is what I say, that you do not believe in the gods at all.

You cannot be believed, Meletus, even, I think, by yourself. The man appears to me, men of Athens, highly insolent and uncontrolled. He seems to have made this deposition out of insolence, violence, and youthful zeal. He is like one who composed a riddle and is trying it out: "Will the wise Socrates realize that I am jesting and contradicting myself, or shall I deceive him and others?" I think he contradicts himself in the affidavit, as if he said: "Socrates is guilty of not believing in gods but believing in gods," and surely that is the part of a jester!

Examine with me, gentlemen, how he appears to contradict himself, and you, Meletus, answer us. Remember, gentlemen, what I asked you when I began, not to create a disturbance if I proceed in my usual manner.

Does any man, Meletus, believe in human activities who does not believe in humans? Make him answer, and not again and again create a disturbance. Does any man who does not believe in horses believe in horsemen's activities? Or in flute-playing activities but not in flute-players? No, my good sir, no man could. If you are not willing to answer, I will tell you and these men. Answer the next question, however. Does any man believe in spiritual activities who does not believe in spirits?—No one.

Thank you for answering, if reluctantly, when these gentlemen made you. Now you say that I believe in spiritual things and teach about them, whether new or old, but at any rate spiritual things according to what you say, and to this you have sworn in your deposition. But if I believe in spiritual things I must quite inevitably believe in spirits. Is that not so? It is indeed. I shall assume that you agree, as you do not answer. Do we not believe spirits to be either gods or the children of gods? Yes or no?—Of course.

Then since I do believe in spirits, as you admit, if spirits are gods, this is what I mean when I say you speak in riddles and in jest, as you state that I do not believe in gods and then again that I do, since I do believe in spirits. If, on the other hand, the spirits are children of the gods, bastard children of the gods by nymphs or some other mothers, as they are said to be, what man would believe children of the gods to exist, but not gods? That would be just as absurd as to believe the young of horses and asses, namely mules, to exist, but not to believe in the existence of horses and asses. You must have made this deposition, Meletus, either to test us

---

3   Anaxagoras of Clazomenae, born about the beginning of the fifth century B.C., came to Athens as a young man and spent his time in the pursuit of natural philosophy. He claimed that the universe was directed by Nous (Mind) and that matter was indestructible but always combining in various ways. He left Athens after being prosecuted for impiety.

or because you were at a loss to find any true wrongdoing of which to accuse me. There is no way in which you could persuade anyone of even small intelligence that it is possible for one and the same man to believe in spiritual but not also in divine things, and then again for that same man to believe neither in spirits nor in gods nor in heroes.

I do not think, men of Athens, that it requires a prolonged defense to prove that I am not guilty of the charges in Meletus' deposition, but this is sufficient. On the other hand, you know that what I said earlier is true, that I am very unpopular with many people. This will be my undoing, if I am undone, not Meletus or Anytus but the slanders and envy of many people. This has destroyed many other good men and will, I think, continue to do so. There is no danger that it will stop at me.

Someone might say: "Are you not ashamed, Socrates, to have followed the kind of occupation that has led to your being now in danger of death?" However, I should be right to reply to him: "You are wrong, sir, if you think that a man who is any good at all should take into account the risk of life or death; he should look to this only in his actions, whether what he does is right or wrong, whether he is acting like a good or a bad man." According to your view, all the heroes who died at Troy were inferior people, especially the son of Thetis who was so contemptuous of danger compared with disgrace.[4] When he was eager to kill Hector, his goddess mother warned him, as I believe, in some such words as these: "My child, if you avenge the death of your comrade, Patroclus, and you kill Hector, you will die yourself, for your death is to follow immediately after Hector's." Hearing this, he despised death and danger and was much more afraid to live a coward who did not avenge his friends. "Let me die at once," he said, "when once I have given the wrongdoer his deserts, rather than remain here, a laughingstock by the curved ships, a burden upon the earth." Do you think he gave thought to death and danger?

This is the truth of the matter, men of Athens: wherever a man has taken a position that he believes to be best, or has been placed by his commander, there he must I think remain and face danger, without a thought for death or anything else, rather than disgrace. It would have been a dreadful way to behave, men of Athens, if, at Potidaea, Amphipolis, and Delium, I had, at the risk of death, like anyone else, remained at my post where those you had elected to command had ordered me, and then, when the god ordered me, as I thought and believed, to live the life of a philosopher, to examine myself and others, I had abandoned my post for fear of death or anything else. That would have been a dreadful thing, and then I might truly have justly been brought here for not believing that there are gods, disobeying the oracle, fearing death, and thinking I was wise when I was not. To fear death, gentlemen, is no other than to think oneself wise when one is not, to think one knows what one does not know. No one knows whether death may not be the greatest of all blessings for a man, yet men fear it as if they knew that it is the greatest of evils. And surely it is the most blameworthy ignorance to believe that one knows what one does not know. It is perhaps on this point and in this respect, gentlemen, that I differ from the majority of men, and if I were to claim that I am wiser than anyone in anything, it would

---

4   The scene between Thetis and Achilles is from the *Iliad* xviii.94 ff.

be in this, that, as I have no adequate knowledge of things in the underworld, so I do not think I have. I do know, however, that it is wicked and shameful to do wrong, to disobey one's superior, be he god or man. I shall never fear or avoid things of which I do not know, whether they may not be good rather than things that I know to be bad. Even if you acquitted me now and did not believe Anytus, who said to you that either I should not have been brought here in the first place, or that now I am here, you cannot avoid executing me, for if I should be acquitted, your sons would practice the teachings of Socrates and all be thoroughly corrupted; if you said to me in this regard: "Socrates, we do not believe Anytus now; we acquit you, but only on condition that you spend no more time on this investigation and do not practice philosophy, and if you are caught doing so you will die"; if, as I say, you were to acquit me on those terms, I would say to you: "Men of Athens, I am grateful and I am your friend, but I will obey the god rather than you, and as long as I draw breath and am able, I shall not cease to practice philosophy, to exhort you and in my usual way to point out to any one of you whom I happen to meet: 'Good Sir, you are an Athenian, a citizen of the greatest city with the greatest reputation for both wisdom and power; are you not ashamed of your eagerness to possess as much wealth, reputation, and honors as possible, while you do not care for nor give thought to wisdom or truth, or the best possible state of your soul?' Then, if one of you disputes this and says he does care, I shall not let him go at once or leave him, but I shall question him, examine him, and test him, and if I do not think he has attained the goodness that he says he has, I shall reproach him because he attaches little importance to the most important things and greater importance to inferior things. I shall treat in this way anyone I happen to meet, young and old, citizen and stranger, and more so the citizens because you are more kindred to me. Be sure that this is what the god orders me to do, and I think there is no greater blessing for the city than my service to the god. For I go around doing nothing but persuading both young and old among you not to care for your body or your wealth in preference to or as strongly as for the best possible state of your soul, as I say to you: Wealth does not bring about excellence, but excellence makes wealth and everything else good for men, both individually and collectively."[5]

Now if by saying this I corrupt the young, this advice must be harmful, but if anyone says that I give different advice, he is talking nonsense. On this point I would say to you, men of Athens: "Whether you believe Anytus or not, whether you acquit me or not, do so on the understanding that this is my course of action, even if I am to face death many times." Do not create a disturbance, gentlemen, but abide by my request not to cry out at what I say but to listen, for I think it will be to your advantage to listen, and I am about to say other things at which you will perhaps cry out. By no means do this. Be sure that if you kill the sort of man I say I am, you will not harm me more than yourselves. Neither Meletus nor Anytus can harm me in any way; he could not harm me, for I do not think it is permitted that a better man be harmed by a worse; certainly he might kill me, or perhaps banish or disfranchise me, which

---

5 Alternatively, this sentence could be translated: "Wealth does not bring about excellence, but excellence brings about wealth and all other public and private blessings for men."

he and maybe others think to be great harm, but I do not think so. I think he is doing himself much greater harm doing what he is doing now, attempting to have a man executed unjustly. Indeed, men of Athens, I am far from making a defense now on my own behalf, as might be thought, but on yours, to prevent you from wrongdoing by mistreating the god's gift to you by condemning me; for if you kill me you will not easily find another like me. I was attached to this city by the god—though it seems a ridiculous thing to say—as upon a great and noble horse which was somewhat sluggish because of its size and needed to be stirred up by a kind of gadfly. It is to fulfill some such function that I believe the god has placed me in the city. I never cease to rouse each and every one of you, to persuade and reproach you all day long and everywhere I find myself in your company.

Another such man will not easily come to be among you, gentlemen, and if you believe me you will spare me. You might easily be annoyed with me as people are when they are aroused from a doze, and strike out at me; if convinced by Anytus you could easily kill me, and then you could sleep on for the rest of your days, unless the god, in his care for you, sent you some-one else. That I am the kind of person to be a gift of the god to the city you might realize from the fact that it does not seem like human nature for me to have neglected all my own affairs and to have tolerated this neglect now for so many years while I was always concerned with you, approaching each one of you like a father or an elder brother to persuade you to care for virtue. Now if I profited from this by charging a fee for my advice, there would be some sense to it, but you can see for yourselves that, for all their shameless accusations, my accusers have not been able in their impudence to bring forward a witness to say that I have ever received a fee or ever asked for one. I, on the other hand, have a convincing witness that I speak the truth, my poverty.

It may seem strange that while I go around and give this advice privately and interfere in private affairs, I do not venture to go to the assembly and there advise the city. You have heard me give the reason for this in many places. I have a divine or spiritual sign which Meletus has ridiculed in his deposition. This began when I was a child. It is a voice, and whenever it speaks it turns me away from something I am about to do, but it never encourages me to do anything. This is what has prevented me from taking part in public affairs, and I think it was quite right to prevent me. Be sure, men of Athens, that if I had long ago attempted to take part in politics, I should have died long ago, and benefited neither you nor myself. Do not be angry with me for speaking the truth; no man will survive who genuinely opposes you or any other crowd and prevents the occurrence of many unjust and illegal happenings in the city. A man who really fights for justice must lead a private, not a public, life if he is to survive for even a short time.

I shall give you great proofs of this, not words but what you esteem, deeds. Listen to what happened to me, that you may know that I will not yield to any man contrary to what is right, for fear of death, even if I should die at once for not yielding. The things I shall tell you are commonplace and smack of the lawcourts, but they are true. I have never held any other office in the city, but I served as a member of the Council, and our tribe Antiochis was presiding at the time when you wanted to try as a body the ten generals who had failed to pick up the survivors of the naval battle.[6] This was illegal, as you all recognized later. I was the only member of the presiding committee to oppose your doing something contrary to the laws, and I voted against it. The orators were ready to prosecute me and take me away, and your shouts were egging them on, but I thought I should run any risk on the side of law and justice rather than join you, for fear of prison or death, when you were engaged in an unjust course.

This happened when the city was still a democracy. When the oligarchy was established, the Thirty[7] summoned me to the Hall, along with four others, and ordered us to bring Leon from Salamis, that he might be executed. They gave many such orders to many people, in order to implicate as many as possible in their guilt. Then I showed again, not in words but in action, that, if it were not rather vulgar to say so, death is something I couldn't care less about, but that my whole concern is not to do anything unjust or impious. That government, powerful as it was, did not frighten me into any wrongdoing. When we left the Hall, the other four went to Salamis and brought in Leon, but I went home. I might have been put to death for this, had not the government fallen shortly afterwards. There are many who will witness to these events.

Do you think I would have survived all these years if I were engaged in public affairs and, acting as a good man must, came to the help of justice and considered this the most important thing? Far from it, men of Athens, nor would any other man. Throughout my life, in any public activity I may have engaged in, I am the same man as I am in private life. I have never come to an agreement with anyone to act unjustly, neither with anyone else nor with any one of those who they slanderously say are my pupils. I have never been anyone's teacher. If anyone, young or old, desires to listen to me when I am talking and dealing with my own concerns, I have never begrudged this to anyone, but I do not converse when I receive a fee and not when I do not. I am equally ready to question the rich and the poor if anyone is willing to answer my questions and listen to what I say. And I cannot justly be held responsible for the good or bad conduct of these people, as I never promised to teach them anything and have not done so. If anyone says that he has learned anything from me, or that he heard anything privately that the others did not hear, be assured that he is not telling the truth.

Why then do some people enjoy spending considerable time in my company? You have heard why, men of Athens; I have told you the whole truth. They enjoy hearing those being questioned who think they are wise, but are not. And this is not unpleasant. To do this has, as I say, been

---

6   This was the battle of Arginusae (south of Lesbos) in 406 B.C., the last Athenian victory of the war. A violent storm prevented the Athenian generals from rescuing their survivors. For this they were tried in Athens and sentenced to death by the assembly. They were tried in a body, and it is this to which Socrates objected in the Council's presiding committee which prepared the business of the assembly. He obstinately persisted in his opposition, in which he stood alone, and was overruled by the majority. Six generals who were in Athens were executed.

7   This was the harsh oligarchy that was set up after the final defeat of Athens by Sparta in the Pelopon-nesian War in 404 B.C. and that ruled Athens for some nine months in 404–3 before the democracy was restored.

enjoined upon me by the god, by means of oracles and dreams, and in every other way that a divine manifestation has ever ordered a man to do anything. This is true, gentlemen, and can easily be established.

If I corrupt some young men and have corrupted others, then surely some of them who have grown older and realized that I gave them bad advice when they were young should now themselves come up here to accuse me and avenge themselves. If they were unwilling to do so themselves, then some of their kindred, their fathers or brothers or other relations should recall it now if their family had been harmed by me. I see many of these present here, first Crito, my contemporary and fellow demesman, the father of Critobulus here; next Lysanias of Sphettus, the father of Aeschines here; also Antiphon the Cephisian, the father of Epigenes; and others whose brothers spent their time in this way; Nicostratus, the son of Theozotides, brother of Theodotus, and Theodotus has died so he could not influence him; Paralius here, son of Demo-docus, whose brother was Theages; there is Adeimantus, son of Ariston, brother of Plato here; Aeantodorus, brother of Apollodorus here.

I could mention many others, some one of whom surely Meletus should have brought in as witness in his own speech. If he forgot to do so, then let him do it now; I will yield time if he has anything of the kind to say. You will find quite the contrary, gentlemen. These men are all ready to come to the help of the corruptor, the man who has harmed their kindred, as Meletus and Anytus say. Now those who were corrupted might well have reason to help me, but the uncorrupted, their kindred who are older men, have no reason to help me except the right and proper one, that they know that Meletus is lying and that I am telling the truth.

Very well, gentlemen. This, and maybe other similar things, is what I have to say in my defense. Perhaps one of you might be angry as he recalls that when he himself stood trial on a less dangerous charge, he begged and implored the jurymen with many tears, that he brought his children and many of his friends and family into court to arouse as much pity as he could, but that I do none of these things, even though I may seem to be running the ultimate risk. Thinking of this, he might feel resentful towards me and, angry about this, cast his vote in anger. If there is such a one among you—I do not deem there is, but if there is—I think it would be right to say in reply: My good sir, I too have a household and, in Homer's phrase, I am not born "from oak or rock" but from men, so that I have a family, indeed three sons, men of Athens, of whom one is an adolescent while two are children. Nevertheless, I will not beg you to acquit me by bringing them here. Why do I do none of these things? Not through arrogance, gentlemen, nor through lack of respect for you. Whether I am brave in the face of death is another matter, but with regard to my reputation and yours and that of the whole city, it does not seem right to me to do these things, especially at my age and with my reputation. For it is generally believed, whether it be true or false, that in certain respects Socrates is superior to the majority of men. Now if those of you who are considered superior, be it in wisdom or courage or whatever other virtue makes them so, are seen behaving like that, it would be a disgrace. Yet I have often seen them do this sort of thing when standing trial, men who are thought to be somebody, doing amazing things as if they thought it a terrible thing to die, and as if they were to be immortal if you did not execute them. I think these men bring shame upon the city so that a stranger, too, would assume that those who are outstanding in virtue among the Athenians, whom they themselves select from themselves to fill offices of state and receive other honors, are in no way better than women. You should not act like that, men of Athens, those of you who have any reputation at all, and if we do, you should not allow it. You should make it very clear that you will more readily convict a man who performs these pitiful dramatics in court and so makes the city a laughingstock, than a man who keeps quiet.

Quite apart from the question of reputation, gentlemen, I do not think it right to supplicate the jury and to be acquitted because of this, but to teach and persuade them. It is not the purpose of a juryman's office to give justice as a favor to whoever seems good to him, but to judge according to law, and this he has sworn to do. We should not accustom you to perjure yourselves, nor should you make a habit of it. This is irreverent conduct for either of us.

Do not deem it right for me, men of Athens, that I should act towards you in a way that I do not consider to be good or just or pious, especially, by Zeus, as I am being prosecuted by Meletus here for impiety; clearly, if I convinced you by my supplication to do violence to your oath of office, I would be teaching you not to believe that there are gods, and my defense would convict me of not believing in them. This is far from being the case, gentlemen, for I do believe in them as none of my accusers do. I leave it to you and the god to judge me in the way that will be best for me and for you.

Discussion Questions

1. What were the reasons Socrates was accused for by Meletus?
2. What are the arguments Socrates presented to the court to defend himself against the accusation?
3. For what reason does Socrates believe that to fear death is to think oneself wise when one is not, to think one knows what one does not know?
4. What is the response to Socrates' statement: "You are wrong if you think that a man who is any good at all should take into account the risk of life or death; he should look to this only in his actions, whether what he does is right or wrong, whether he is acting a good man or a bad man." Can you relate Socratic confidence to your personal experience of facing a danger while standing firmly on your ground?
5. According to Socrates, it is not the purpose of a juryman's office to give justice as a favor to whoever seems good to him, but to judge according to the law. Do you think laws always serve justice? How do we make sense of unjust laws and what can we do about them?

Of the Power of the Intellect, or of Human Freedom

Baruch Spinoza; ed. Seymour Feldman; trans. Samuel Shirley

Preface

I pass on finally to that part of the *Ethics* which concerns the method, or way, leading to freedom. In this part, then, I shall be dealing with the power of reason, pointing out the degree of control reason has over the emotions, and then what is freedom of mind, or blessedness, from which we shall see how much to be preferred is the life of the wise man to the life of the ignorant man. Now we are not concerned here with the manner or way in which the intellect should be perfected, nor yet with the science of tending the body so that it may correctly perform its functions. The latter is the province of medicine, the former of logic. Here then, as I have said, I shall be dealing only with the power of the mind or reason. Above all I shall be showing the degree and nature of its command over the emotions in checking and controlling them. For I have already demonstrated that we do not have absolute command over them.

Now the Stoics thought that the emotions depend absolutely on our will, and that we can have absolute command over them. However, with experience crying out against them they were obliged against their principles to admit that no little practice and zeal are required in order to check and control emotions. One of them tried to illustrate this point with the example of two dogs, if I remember correctly, one a house-dog, and the other a hunting-dog; in the end he succeeded in training the house-dog to hunt and the hunting-dog to refrain from chasing hares.

This view is much favoured by Descartes. He maintained that the soul or mind is united in a special way with a certain part of the brain called the pineal gland, by means of which the mind senses all movements that occur in the body, as well as external objects, and by the mere act of willing it can move the gland in various ways.

He maintained that this gland is suspended in the middle of the brain in such a way that it can be moved by the slightest motion of the animal spirits. He further maintained that the number of different ways in which the gland can be suspended in the middle of the brain corresponds with the number of different ways in which the animal spirits can impinge upon it, and that, furthermore, as many different marks can be imprinted on the gland as there are external objects impelling the animal spirits towards it. As a result, if by the will of the soul, which can move it in various ways, the gland is later suspended in that particular way in which it had previously been suspended by a particular mode of agitation of the spirits, then the gland will impel and determine the animal spirits in the same way as they had previously been acted upon by a similar mode of suspension of the gland. He furthermore maintained that every single act of willing is by nature united to a particular motion of the gland. For example, if anyone wills to gaze at a distant object, this act of willing will bring about the dilation of the pupil. But if he thinks only of dilating the pupil, it will be useless for him to will this, because the motion of the gland which serves to impel the spirits towards the optic nerve in a manner that will bring about dilation or contraction of the pupil has not been joined by nature to the act of willing its contraction or dilation, but only to the act of willing to gaze at distant or near objects. Finally, he maintained that although each motion of this gland seems to have been connected through nature from the beginning of our lives to particular thoughts, these motions can be joined to other thoughts through training, and this he endeavors to prove in Article 50, Part I of *On the Passions of the Soul*. From this he concludes that there is no soul so weak that it cannot, through good guidance, acquire absolute power over its passions. For these passions are defined by him as "perceptions, or feelings, or disturbances of the soul, which are related to the soul as species, and which are produced (note well!), preserved and strengthened through some motion of the spirits." (See Article 27, Part I, *On the Passions of the Soul.*) But as we are able to join any motion of the gland, and consequently of the spirits, to any act of willing, and as the determination of the will depends only on our own power, if therefore we determine our will by the sure and firm decisions in accordance with which we want to direct the actions of our lives, and if to these decisions we join the movements of the passions which we want to have, we shall acquire absolute command over our passions.

Such is the view of this illustrious person (as far as I can gather from his own words), a view which I could scarcely have believed to have been put forward by such a great man, had it been less ingenious. Indeed, I am lost in wonder that a philosopher who had strictly resolved to deduce nothing except from self-evident bases and to affirm nothing that he did not clearly and distinctly perceive, who had so often censured the Scholastics for seeking to explain obscurities through occult qualities, should adopt a theory more occult than any occult quality. What, I ask, does he understand by the union of mind and body? What clear and distinct conception does he have of thought closely united to a certain particle of matter? I should have liked him, indeed, to explain this union through its proximate cause. But he had conceived mind as so distinct from body that he could assign no one cause either of this union or of mind itself, and found it necessary to have recourse to the cause of the entire universe, that is, God. Again, I should like to know how many degrees of motion mind can impart to that pineal gland of his, and by what force it can hold it suspended. For I know not whether this gland can be moved about more slowly or more quickly by the mind than by animal spirits, and whether the movements of the passions which we have joined in a close union with firm decisions cannot again be separated from those decisions by corporeal causes, from which it would follow that, although the mind firmly decides to face danger and joins to that decision the motions of boldness, when the danger appears, the gland may assume such a form of suspension that the mind can think only of flight. And surely, since will and motion have no common standard, there cannot be any comparison between the power or strength of the mind and body, and consequently the strength of the latter cannot possibly be determined by the strength of the former. There is the additional fact that this gland is not to be found located in the middle of the brain in such a way that it can be driven about so easily and in so many ways, nor do all nerves extend as far as the cavities of the brain.

Finally, I omit all Descartes' assertions about the will and its freedom, since I have already abundantly demonstrated that they are false. Therefore, since the power of the mind is defined solely by the understanding, as I have demonstrated above, we shall determine solely by the knowledge of the mind the remedies for the emotions—remedies which I believe all men experience but do not accurately observe nor distinctly see—and from this knowledge we shall deduce all that concerns the blessedness of the mind.

AXIOMS

1. If two contrary actions are instigated in the same subject, a change must necessarily take place in both or in the one of them until they cease to be contrary.
2. The power of an effect is defined by the power of the cause in so far as its essence is explicated or defined through the essence of its cause.
   This Axiom is evident from Pr.7,III.

PROPOSITION 1
The affections of the body, that is, the images of things, are arranged and connected in the body in exactly the same way as thoughts and the ideas of things are arranged and connected in the mind.

Proof
The order and connection of ideas is the same (Pr.7,II) as the order and connection of things, and, vice versa, the order and connection of things is the same (Cor.Pr.6 and Pr.7,II) as the order and connection of ideas. Therefore, just as the order and connection of ideas in the mind occurs in accordance with the order and connection of the affections of the body (Pr.18,II), so vice versa (Pr.2,III) the order and connection of the affections of the body occurs in just the way that thoughts and the ideas of things are arranged and connected in the mind.

PROPOSITION 2

If we remove an agitation of the mind, or emotion, from the thought of its external cause, and join it to other thoughts, then love or hatred towards the external cause, and also vacillations, that arise from these emotions will be destroyed.

Proof

That which constitutes the form of love or hatred is pleasure or pain accompanied by the idea of an external cause (Def. of Emotions 6 and 7). So when the latter is removed, the form of love or hatred is removed with it; and thus these emotions, and those that arise from them, are destroyed.

PROPOSITION 3

A passive emotion ceases to be a passive emotion as soon as we form a clear and distinct idea of it.

Proof

A passive emotion is a confused idea (Gen. Def. of Emotions). So if we form a clear and distinct idea of the emotion, this idea is distinguishable only in concept from the emotion in so far as the latter is related only to mind (Pr.21,H and Sch.); and so the emotion will cease to be passive (Pr.3,III).

Corollary

So the more an emotion is known to us, the more it is within our control, and the mind is the less passive in respect of it.

PROPOSITION 4

There is no affection of the body of which we cannot form a clear and distinct conception.

Proof

What is common to all things can only be conceived adequately (Pr.38,II), and thus (Pr.12 and Lemma 2 which comes after Sch.Pr.13, II) there is no affection of the body of which we cannot form a clear and distinct conception.

Corollary

Hence it follows that there is no emotion of which we cannot form a clear and distinct conception. For an emotion is the idea of an affection of the body (Gen. Def. of Emotions), which must therefore involve some clear and distinct conception (preceding Pr.).

Scholium

Since there exists nothing from which some effect does not follow (Pr.36,I), and all that follows from an idea that is adequate in us is understood by us clearly and distinctly (Pr.40,II), it therefore follows that everyone has the power of clearly and distinctly understanding himself and his emotions, if not absolutely, at least in part, and consequently of bringing it about that he should be less passive in respect of them. So we should pay particular attention to getting to know each emotion, as far as possible, clearly and distinctly, so that the mind may thus be determined from the emotion to think those things that it clearly and distinctly perceives, and in which it finds full contentment. Thus the emotion may be detached from the thought of an external cause and joined to true thoughts. The result will be that not only are love, hatred, etc. destroyed (Pr.2,V) but also that the appetites or desires that are wont to arise from such an emotion cannot be excessive (Pr.61,IV). For it is very important to note that it is one and the same appetite through which a man is said both to be active and to be passive. For example, we have shown that human nature is so constituted that everyone wants others to live according to his way of thinking (Cor. Pr.31,III). Now this appetite in a man who is not guided by reason is a passive emotion which is called ambition, and differs to no great extent from pride. But in a man who lives according to the dictates of reason it is an active emotion, or virtue, which is called piety (Sch.1, Pr.37,IV and second proof of that same proposition). In this way all appetites or desires are passive emotions only in so far as they arise from inadequate ideas, and they are accredited to virtue when they are aroused or generated by adequate ideas. For all desires whereby we are determined to some action can arise both from adequate and from inadequate ideas (Pr.59,IV). To return to the point from which I digressed, there is available to us no more excellent remedy for the emotions than that which consists in a true knowledge of them, since there is no other power of the mind than the power of thought and of forming adequate ideas, as I have shown above (Pr.3,III).

PROPOSITION 5
An emotion towards a thing which we imagine merely in itself, and not as necessary, possible or contingent, is the greatest of all emotions, other things being equal.

Proof
An emotion towards a thing that we imagine to be free is greater than an emotion towards a necessary thing (Pr.49,III), and consequently still greater than an emotion towards a thing that we imagine to be possible or contingent (Pr.11,IV). But to imagine some thing as free can be nothing else than to imagine it merely in itself, while we are ignorant of the causes by which it has been determined to act (Sch.Pr.35,II). Therefore, an emotion towards a thing that we imagine merely in itself is greater, other things being equal, than an emotion towards a necessary, possible, or contingent thing, and consequently it is the greatest of all emotions.

PROPOSITION 6
In so far as the mind understands all things as governed by necessity, to that extent it has greater power over emotions, i.e. it is less passive in respect of them.

Proof
The mind understands all things to be governed by necessity (Pr.29,I) and to be determined to exist and to act by an infinite chain of causes (Pr.28,I). And so (preceding Pr.) to that extent the

mind succeeds in becoming less passive to the emotions that arise from things, and (Pr.48,III) less affected towards the things themselves.

Scholium

The more this knowledge (namely, that things are governed by necessity) is applied to particular things which we imagine more distinctly and more vividly, the greater is this power of the mind over the emotions, as is testified by experience. For we see that pain over the loss of some good is assuaged as soon as the man who has lost it realises that that good could not have been saved in any way. Similarly, we see that nobody pities a baby because it cannot talk or walk or reason, and because it spends many years in a kind of ignorance of self. But if most people were born adults and only a few were born babies, then everybody would feel sorry for babies because they would then look on infancy not as a natural and necessary thing but as a fault or flaw in Nature. There are many other examples of this kind that we might note.

PROPOSITION 7

Emotions which arise or originate from reason are, if we take account of time, more powerful than those that are related to particular things which we regard as absent.

Proof

We do not look on a thing as absent by reason of the emotion with which we think of it, but by reason of the body being affected by another emotion which excludes the existence of the said thing (Pr.17,II). Therefore the emotion that is related to a thing that we regard as absent is not of a kind to overcome the rest of man's activities and power (see Pr.6,IV). On the contrary, its nature is such that it can be checked in some way by those affections which exclude the existence of its external cause (Pr.9,IV). But an emotion that arises from reason is necessarily related to the common properties of things (see Def. of Reason in Sch.2,Pr.40,II) which we regard as being always present (for there can be nothing that excludes their present existence) and which we always think of in the same way (Pr.38,II). Therefore such an emotion always remains the same. Consequently (Ax.1,V) emotions which are contrary to it and are not fostered by their external causes must adapt themselves to it more and more until they are no longer contrary; and to that extent an emotion that arises from reason is more powerful.

PROPOSITION 8

The greater the number of causes that simultaneously concur in arousing an emotion, the greater the emotion.

Proof

Several causes acting together are more effective than if they were fewer (Pr.7,III). So (Pr.5,IV) the more simultaneous causes there are in arousing an emotion, the stronger will be the emotion.

Scholium

This Proposition is also obvious from Ax.2,V.

PROPOSITION 9

An emotion that is related to several different causes, which the mind regards together with the emotion itself, is less harmful, and we suffer less from it and are less affected towards each individual cause, than if we were affected by another equally great emotion which is related to only one or to a few causes.

Proof

An emotion is bad or harmful only in so far as the mind is thereby hindered from being able to think (Pr.26 and 27,IV). Thus an emotion whereby the mind is determined to regard several objects simultaneously is less harmful than another equally great emotion which so keeps the mind in the contemplation of only one or few objects that it cannot think of anything else. This is the first point. Again, because the essence of the mind, that is (Pr.7,III), its power, consists only in thought (Pr.11,II), it follows that the mind is less passive through an emotion by which it is determined to regard several things all together than through an equally great emotion which keeps the mind engrossed in the contemplation of only one or few objects. This is the second point. Finally, this emotion (Pr.48,III), in so far as it is related to several external causes, is also less towards each cause.

PROPOSITION 10

As long as we are not assailed by emotions that are contrary to our nature, we have the power to arrange and associate affections of the body according to the order of the intellect.

Proof

Emotions that are contrary to our nature, that is (Pr.30,IV), which are bad, are bad to the extent that they hinder the mind from understanding (Pr.27,IV). Therefore as long as we are not assailed by emotions contrary to our nature, the power of the mind whereby it endeavors to understand things (Pr.26,IV) is not hindered, and thus it has the ability to form clear and distinct ideas, deducing them from one another (Sch.2, Pr.40 and Sch. Pr.47,II). Consequently (Pr.1,V) in this case we have the ability to arrange and associate affections of the body according to the order of the intellect.

Scholium

Through the ability to arrange and associate rightly the affections of the body we can bring it about that we are not easily affected by bad emotions. For (Pr.7,V) greater force is required to check emotions arranged and associated according to intellectual order than emotions that are uncertain and random. Therefore the best course we can adopt, as long as we do not have perfect knowledge of our emotions, is to conceive a right method of living, or fixed rules of life, and to commit them to memory and continually apply them to particular situations that are frequently encountered in life, so that our casual thinking is thoroughly permeated by them and they are always ready to hand. For example, among our practical rules, we laid down (Pr.46,IV and Sch.) that hatred should be conquered by love or nobility, and not repaid with reciprocal hatred. Now in order that we may have this precept of reason always ready to hand we should think about and frequently reflect on the wrongs that are commonly committed among mankind, and the best way and method of warding them off by nobility of character. For thus we shall associate the image of a wrong with the presentation of this rule of conduct, and it will always be at hand for us (Pr.18,II) when we suffer a wrong. Again, if we always have in readiness consideration of our true advantage and also of the good that follows from mutual friendship and social rela-tions, and also remember that supreme contentment of spirit follows from the right way of life (Pr.52,IV), and that men, like everything else, act from the necessity of their nature, then the wrong, or the hatred that is wont to arise from it, will occupy just a small part of our imagina-tion and will easily be overcome. Or if the anger that is wont to arise from grievous wrongs be not easily overcome, it will nevertheless be overcome, though not without vacillation, in a far shorter space of time than if we had not previously reflected on these things in the way I have described, as is evident from Prs.6,7, and 8,V. We ought, in the same way, to reflect on courage to banish fear; we should enumerate and often picture the everyday dangers of life, and how they can best be avoided and overcome by resourcefulness and strength of mind.

But it should be noted that in arranging our thoughts and images we should always concen-trate on that which is good in every single thing (Cor. Pr.63,IV and Pr.59,III) so that in so doing we may be determined to act always from the emotion of pleasure. For example, if anyone sees that he is devoted overmuch to the pursuit of honour, let him reflect on its proper function, and the purpose for which it ought to be pursued, and the means by which it can be attained, and not on its abuse and hollowness and the fickleness of mankind and the like, on which nobody reflects except from a morbid disposition. It is by thoughts like these that the most ambitious especially torment themselves when they despair of attaining the honour that they covet, and in vomiting forth their anger they try to make some show of wisdom. It is therefore certain that those who raise the loudest outcry about the abuse of honour and about worldly vanity are most eager for honour. Nor is this trait confined to the ambitious: it is shared by all who meet with adverse fortune and are weak in spirit. For the miser, too, who is in poverty, does not cease to talk of the abuse of money and the vices of the rich, with the result that he merely torments himself and makes it clear that he resents not only his own poverty but also the wealth of others. So, too, those who have been ill-received by a sweetheart are obsessed by thoughts of the fickleness and deceitfulness of women and the other faults commonly attributed to them, but immediately forget about all this as soon as they again find favour with their sweetheart. Therefore he who aims solely from love of freedom to control his emotions and appetites will strive his best to familiarise himself with virtues and their causes and to, fill his mind with the joy that arises from the true knowledge of them, while refraining from dwelling on men's faults and abusing mankind and deriving pleasure from a false show of freedom. He who diligently follows these precepts and practises them (for they are not difficult) will surely within a short space of time be able to direct his actions for the most part according to reason's behest.

Discussion Questions

1. Why is Spinoza using a mathematical order (axiom, proposition, proof) to present a theory of human emotion and ways to control them?

2. Spinoza defines freedom as a form of self-determination as opposed to compelled or coerced action—a thing is free if and only if it acts according to its own nature. What is it to act according to one's own nature in a way to become the cause of one's own action?

3. What are the two types of knowledge we are required to have in order to master the power of emotions, according to Spinoza?

4. "That which constitutes the form of love or hatred is pleasure or pain accompanied by the idea of an external cause. So when the latter is removed, the form of love or hatred is removed with it, and thus these emotions, and those that arise from them, are destroyed." What does this statement purport to prove?

5. According to Spinoza, emotions are contrary to our nature when they hinder the mind from understanding and obstruct the function of the intellect. Do you agree with Spinoza that some emotions are contrary to our nature, or think that all emotions are reflections of our nature?

Kant and Skepticism

Graham Bird

Despite the fact that Kant has been frequently taken to be a normative episte-mologist with the *primary* aim of challenging or refuting skepticism, he would certainly have qualified and probably rejected such an interpretation. Kant's attitude to skepticism is more complicated than that naïve interpretation suggests for at least two reasons. His own revolutionary project, as a descriptive metaphysics of experi-ence, does not directly address traditional skepticism, and traditional skepticism is itself a complex network of ideas covering diverse topics and different grounds for doubt.[1] That descriptive project can be pursued without directly involving *any* forms of skepticism, and it is not clear how it is intended to engage with traditional skep-ticism, or which versions of skepticism are targeted. It is not clear that Kant wished to refute a general skepticism about knowledge, or that his own positive account of experience was intended to *guarantee* scientific or everyday beliefs against skeptical attack. Nevertheless, one influential account of his philosophy represents its principal goal as offering such a guarantee by means of distinctive transcendental arguments.

Kant undoubtedly addresses *some* skeptical issues in the *Critique* but also, as I indicate, dismisses some traditional versions of skepticism out of hand. These compli-cations make it necessary to separate the two kinds of case, and to understand how Kant attempts to deal with the forms of skepticism he *does* take seriously. Because the issue involves the notions of "objectivity" and "objective reality" in the Transcen-dental Deduction I offer a preliminary survey of the issue at this early point, but it has implications for Kant's overall project and for all major sections of the *Critique*. I consider in 1 Kant's complex attitude to skepticism and "skeptical method,"; in 2 his view of skepticism and common sense; in 3 the supposed role of transcendental arguments against the skeptic; and in 4 a summary account of his strategy against empiricist skepticism.

1. Skepticism and Skeptical Method

Kant's general view of philosophical skepticism has already been expressed through his *reversal* of a philosophical skepticism in which doubt is cast by philosophy on knowledge in other areas or disciplines. Kant *accepts* knowledge in science and directs *his* doubts against the authority of philosophy to question knowledge in other areas. There are for Kant serious and resolvable issues about the *character* of knowledge in the sciences which carry over to the character of similar, a priori, knowledge in philosophy, but this is not a traditional skeptical doubt. The serious issues for him concern the structure, articulation, and classification of scientific and philosophical claims and systems. Kant accepts a genuine status for scientific knowledge in order to make the comparison with, and provide a model for, a reformed philosophy itself. Consider these passages:

> There is no need of a critique of reason in its empirical employment because in this field its principles are always subject to the test of experience. Nor is it needed in mathematics where the concepts of reason must be exhibited forthwith in concreto in pure intuition so that everything unfounded and arbitrary in them is at once exposed. But where neither empirical nor pure intuition keeps reason to a visible track, when, that is to say, reason is being considered in its transcendental employment in accordance with mere concepts it stands so greatly in need of a discipline to restrain its tendency towards extension beyond the narrow limits of possible experience, and to guard it against extravagance and error, that the whole philosophy of pure reason has no other than this strictly negative utility. (B739; see Bxxv–xxvi; B858–859[2])
>
> Geometry … proceeds with security in knowledge that is completely a priori and has no need to beseech philosophy for any certificate of the pure and legitimate descent of its fundamental concept of space. (B120)
>
> Pure mathematics and pure natural science had no need, for *their* security and certainty, of such a deduction as we have just completed. The former is based on its own self-evidence, and the latter, despite its origin in pure sources of the understanding, is based on experience and its thoroughgoing confirmation…. Both sciences had no need of the investigation to be undertaken for themselves; it was carried out for another science, namely metaphysics. (*Prolegomena* §40; Ak. 4.327)

These quotations make plain that for Kant what is in doubt, and what needs to be validated, is philosophy itself. It is part of his belief in the need for reform in philosophy that it should undergo an examination in order to establish and circumscribe its legitimate authority.

Kant's reversal of that skeptical tradition is not the result of some argument, but expresses his dissatisfaction with the lack of progress and clarity in school metaphysics and his wish for a more fruitful program in philosophy. It points to the need for reform and guides his revolutionary project and its method of investigation. His view is that philosophy cannot proceed in its customary way until *its* credentials and authority have been properly examined in a comparison between science and philosophy. The point is made forcefully in a quotation cited earlier from the *Prolegomena* preface.

> My intention is to convince all those who find it worth-while to pursue metaphysics: that it is unconditionally necessary to set aside all their previous work, to disregard everything in it that has been done up to now, and before anything else to ask the question: "Is any such thing as metaphysics even possible?" (Ak. 4.255)

The passage testifies to the radical nature of Kant's proposed revolution in metaphysics, and underlines his legitimate complaint against Garve that he never looked beyond the standards of a "school metaphysics" endorsed by both traditional dogmatists and skeptics (chapter 1). The authority claimed by dogmatic rationalists was their insight into truths beyond any possible sense experience through reason alone, and the authority claimed by skeptical empiricists is their right to question, and reject, claims to knowledge in the established sciences. Kant was not prepared to accept either authority, although he had more sympathy with the empiricists (B513–14, B788–89).

Kant does not dismiss *all* forms of skepticism in that programmatic and unargued way. An idealist skepticism about the external world *is* explicitly addressed and formally rejected in the Refutation of Idealism at B274–79, but the quotations already indicate that Kant has a generally dismissive attitude to a general philosophical skepticism. In some places the clear message is that skepticism is a wholly futile exercise not worth dignifying with an argumentative response.

> There is a principle of doubt, consisting in the maxim of considering knowledge with the aim of ... showing the impossibility of achieving certainty. This is the sceptical mode of thinking or scepticism. It is opposed to the dogmatic mode, or dogmatism, which places a blind trust in the capacity of reason to spread itself a priori through mere concepts without criticism in the hope of apparent success. Both methods ... are faulty. There are many types of knowledge which we cannot treat dogmatically, and on the other side scepticism inhibits all our efforts to achieve certainty by casting its doubt on all claims to knowledge. The more damaging such scepticism is the more useful ... is the sceptical method, by which I understand the manner of treating something as uncertain, bringing it to the highest pitch of uncertainty in the hope of getting on the track of truth. This method is properly a suspension of judgement. It is valuable to critical thought as a means of investigating the sources of our claims or objections and the grounds on which they rest. It is a method which holds out the hope of achieving certainty. There is no place for scepticism in mathematics and physics. Only that knowledge is vulnerable which is neither mathematical nor empirical, that is, pure philosophy. Absolute scepticism represents everything as illusion. It thus distinguishes illusion from truth, presupposes a criterion for the difference, and so some knowledge of truth, and thus contradicts itself. (*Logic*, Ak. 9.83–84)

Kant reinforces his priority of questioning philosophy before allowing skepticism a free rein to question other knowledge, but also importantly distinguishes "skepticism" and a "skeptical method." The former is treated as damaging in its exclusively negative aim of denying knowledge or certainty, and is dismissed with the brusque claim that it contradicts itself. That dismissal is all the more peremptory since the argument in support of it is not obviously valid.[3] That summary response is agreeably robust in rejecting one form of philosophical excess and indicates that it does not deserve a more carefully argued refutation. Skeptical method on the other hand is commended as Kant's own technique not for arbitrarily denying but attaining knowledge by refining and strengthening current beliefs in specific ways.

The same points are underlined in the *Critique*.

> This is the great utility of the sceptical mode of dealing with the questions pure reason puts to pure reason itself. By its means we can deliver ourselves at but a small cost from a great body of sterile dogmatism, and set in its place a sober critique, which as a true cathartic, will effectively guard us against groundless beliefs.... (B513–54)
>
> While the Transcendental Dialectic does not by any means favour scepticism it certainly favours the skeptical method. (B535)
>
> To allow ourselves simply to acquiesce in these doubts and thereupon to set out to commend the conviction and admission of our ignorance not merely as a remedy against the complacency of the dogmatists but likewise as the right method of putting an end to the conflict of reason with itself is a futile procedure.... (B785)

For Kant a method of doubt is valuable in rejecting dogmatism and as the basis for Kant's proposed therapy in the Dialectic, but what might be called "philosophical" skepticism itself is idle and futile. In other passages Kant has more pointed objections to skepticism.

> All objections divide into dogmatic, sceptical, and critical.... Dogmatic and sceptical objections alike lay claim to such insight into their object as is required to assert or deny something in regard to it. (A388)

For Kant both dogmatist and skeptic claim knowledge where they can have none, in the realm of things in themselves beyond any possible experience of ours, and the difference between them is that the former *asserts* claims in that realm while the latter *denies* them. Kant's critical view is that in such speculative cases we cannot know either way and should reject *both* dogmatic *and* skeptical claims and this is a basic Kantian strategy in the Dialectic for diagnosing and treating philosophical illusions.[4] In the Dialectic an important proviso is made for the practical and moral, rather than the speculative and theoretical, Ideas of reason, and that is considered in discussion of the Dialectic. For the present I focus exclusively on the speculative claims.[5]

If we call the general skepticism that Kant dismisses a specifically "philosophical" skepticism, then the passages express a refusal to take philosophical skepticism seriously, not because its arguments are inadequate or refutable, but because it is absurdly motivated and yields unwelcome, counterproductive consequences. Its motivation is represented as the arbitrary and exclusively negative denial of *any* knowledge or certainty, and its futile and counterproductive consequences are to inhibit genuine enquiry by focusing attention on issues which are in principle undecidable and not worth debating. It distinguishes what has been called an "idle" skepticism from the more useful skeptical method.[6]

The two criteria for "idle" skepticism, a negative *motivation* to reject every form of knowledge and a *method* of achieving that goal by making knowledge unattainable, have the consequence of rejecting *any* claim to knowledge. Perhaps few philosophers in the tradition have consciously adopted such a motive, but there is no doubt that some have committed themselves to its negative consequences. It might be thought that contemporary philosophers endorse neither such motives nor their consequences, and yet it is not difficult to find cases where the latter criterion is satisfied. Anyone who canvasses skepticism about knowledge in general by requiring that it is justified only where all possibilities of error have been eliminated is at least in danger of falling into that category.[7] It is quite evident that in empirical circumstances there simply is no way in which that criterion can be met *whatever* kind of possibility is canvassed. To require that it must be satisfied in *genuine* knowledge is inevitably to deny the achievement of any empirical knowledge. With that background, Stroud's claim that "the sceptic will always win going away"[8] is bound to hold. I consider in 3 some recent responses to these skeptical issues.

Kant's point indicates that the skeptic's victory in this case is hollow and futile, and he underlines that attitude in his comments on Leibniz in the Amphiboly. Skeptics might say that to disregard the requirement of eliminating every possibility of error just shows how slipshod our ordinary standards are, and bemoan the failure ever to achieve genuine knowledge. Others may take the view that the standard proposed is inappropriate and unachievable, think it foolish to bemoan our inability to achieve it, and regard a skepticism which canvasses it as "idle." Kant comments on this in the following passage: "If by the complaints—that we have no insight whatever into the inner *nature* of things—it be meant that we cannot conceive by pure understanding what the things which appear to us may be in themselves, they are entirely illegitimate and unreasonable" (B333). He recognizes that we may, like Leibniz, be tempted by the goal and be "eager to explore" those hidden inner natures (B334), but he insists throughout the passage that it is futile to aim at such an unachievable goal. When he talks at B517 of empirical experience as *setting* the standard for truth or knowledge he implicitly rejects the skeptical standard of eliminating every possible error. These remarks, coupled with his dismissive attitude to "philosophical skepticism," indicate that he did not take these issues as seriously as the tradition or some contemporary philosophers. I think he is right in this but the point has not been demonstrated.

To reject these forms of philosophical skepticism is, as Kant insists, not to reject all forms of philosophical enquiry. If the enquiry is designed to find a satisfactory analysis of some concept, or to resolve an issue about concept dependence in a transcendental topic with the prospect of a determinate outcome, no such objection can be raised. If questions are raised in a context where either the criterion for their resolution is already clear, or where attention focuses on finding agreement about such a criterion, there is a hope of such an outcome. Because these cases focus on the *prior* question of agreeing on the criteria for resolving the problems they would be included in Kant's approved deployment of "skeptical method." His point about idle skepticism is that it may seem profound and unanswerable *because* it offers no clear criterion to determine what *would* justify knowledge or settle the doubt. The objection is to cases where either the criterion to be satisfied is evidently impossible to achieve, or where no clear criterion is in prospect so that the issue becomes confused and oscillates between dogmatism and skepticism without ever finding a resolution. Such a situation and such an outcome are what Kant describes in the Prefaces (Bxv), the Dialectic (B492), and the Doctrine of Method (B775) as the "mock debates" and futile arguments into which metaphysics has disreputably fallen.[9] Idle skepticism is a paradigm case for Kant of the disreputable character of a routine school metaphysics.

2. Kant's View of Skepticism and Common Sense

Any philosophical argument characteristically involves questions of justification, and any such question may be said implicitly to cast doubt on the questioned item. Kant's interest in both skepticism and skeptical method is more pointed, and two skeptical issues already identified mark that more pointed interest. Kant is certainly concerned with a traditional idealist skepticism about our knowledge of the external world in the Refutation of Idealism, and he is concerned with a skeptical issue about philosophy's authority to raise doubts about the sciences. Though he is interested in both issues he approaches them from opposite directions. The former idealist issue is addressed with the aim of *refuting* a skepticism about our knowledge of the external world, but in the latter he *endorses* a skepticism towards traditional philosophy. In the former he argues consciously against skepticism but in the latter he supports a skeptical doubt.

Both issues concern peculiarly philosophical issues, but Kant also raises the question of their relation to common sense and everyday belief. In the *Prolegomena* preface he makes clear that an appeal to common sense, to what he calls "common human understanding," is not *sufficient* to refute a Humean skepticism, and he makes unflattering remarks about both common sense and those who deployed it against Hume (Ak. 4.258–62).[10] I have separated that appeal to common sense against Hume, which Kant rejects, from his evident appeal to ordinary experience for the purposes of his own metaphysical project. In order to identify and isolate the salient features of experience in a transcendental topic, as a priori or a posteriori, as fundamental *Grundelemente* or not, as belonging to sense or to understanding, Kant *has* to take experience as it is. This is not to use it as an antiskeptical resource but only as a datum from which his philosophical enquiry derives its basic material. His project, understood in these terms as a descriptive metaphysics of experience with its "inventory" of the a priori elements in experience, is skeptically *neutral*. Understood as an endorsement of common sense in order to criticize Hume's skepticism, it begs the question and conflicts with his objections to Reid, Oswald, and Beattie.

In the two cited cases, skepticism about outer objects and science, Kant identifies issues of a peculiarly philosophical kind. Ordinary common sense is not much exercised by an idealist skepticism about the external world or by the issue of philosophy's authority to raise doubts about the sciences.[11] Kant's intended reform of philosophy might interest those already concerned with metaphysics but it marks only a distant relation and oblique threat to commonsense beliefs. Such an account is partly disputed by Paul Guyer in his "Kant on Common Sense and Scepticism"

(2003, 1–37).[12] His view is that Kant's interest in skepticism engages even common sense and is governed by what Kant calls a "natural dialectic of reason." I consider only the speculative and theoretical, and not the practical and moral, issues and summarize his central claims:

> Kant organises the exposition of his entire philosophy as a response to scepticism as he understands it....
>
> [In the Dialectic the target is a] Pyrrhonian scepticism engendered by the natural dialectic of human reason....
>
> [These issues are] ... never a product of mere philosophical theory (as empiricism's scepticism about the concept of causation might be thought to be) but are natural and unavoidable products of human reason.
>
> This account will certainly be part of philosophy, not common sense, although it must be accessible and ultimately acceptable to common sense. (Guyer 2003, 3–7)

Guyer is right to stress the Dialectic's discussion of skeptical issues in the Antinomies, the conflicts of reason with itself, and he is right to say that those issues are not *purely* philosophical. The cosmological Antinomies arise out of physical science and exercise theoretical scientists as well as philosophers. But their scientific origin, and the dogmatic belief in the power of reason to provide definitive answers to their questions about the beginning of the universe or the infinite divisibility of matter, do not make them matters of commonsense belief. Common sense rarely has convictions on these matters, and Kant's interest in the issues is in part to be determinedly *skeptical* about the power of reason to provide *any* such resolution. In chapter 26, I show that Kant's resolution of the Antinomies does not deny the ability of *science* to raise and answer *their* cosmological questions, but turns on the mistaken attempt of *philosophers* to answer the questions by reason alone. What is spurious is the dogmatic understanding and purported resolution of the issues, not the scientific issues themselves. A properly critical reason can show in this way why the philosophical issues are unresolvable, but this is itself a higher-order philosophical enterprise. Reason in this context is not a common sense faculty but one involved in high-level theoretical thinking, whether scientific or philosophical.

Much of what Guyer says is undeniably correct and yet it puts the skeptical issues, and Kant's antiskeptical response, at the forefront of the *Critique*'s interests in a way which I have denied in the speculative sphere. I have argued that Kant's central project is not that of an attack on skepticism in general but of a descriptive metaphysics which discloses the a priori structure of our immanent experience. The project has implications for skepticism, but it is not driven solely or primarily by that goal, is targeted at specific skeptical issues, and draws a clear distinction between the practical and the speculative contexts. Guyer claims that the same relation holds between common human reason in both speculative and practical contexts, but in the passage from which he quotes in the *Grundlegung* Kant separates them quite sharply: "In this way common human reason is impelled not by some need of speculation (which never touches it so long as it is content to be mere sound reason) but on practical grounds ... to take a step into practical philosophy ..." (Ak. 4.405). The suggestion is that in the practical context there is a serious skepticism about moral principles affecting ordinary experience and conduct which is not matched in speculative matters. In both cases Kant allows that the philosophical issues arise for "common human reason *when it cultivates itself*," but it seems that the interest in such cultivation is closer to ordinary practical than to speculative experience. Ordinary people naturally sometimes wonder about the ground for supposed moral demands made on them in a way in which they do not wonder about the indivisibility of matter or the existence of an external world.

It is trivially true that if philosophy offers an account, skeptical or nonskeptical, of our ordinary or scientific experience then this will make claims about that experience, but it doesn't follow that those claims are commonly endorsed by ordinary experiencers themselves. Guyer is right to stress that such claims are part of philosophy rather than common sense, but he seems to hold that philosophical skepticism will have implications for, and seriously threaten, our common sense beliefs. It is not clear that even philosophers *should* accept that implication, but it is clear that common sense does not. Does anyone, even among philosophers, really believe that idealist skepticism seriously threatens our ordinary beliefs about the external world? Typically such lurid skeptical claims are interpreted to mean not that our common beliefs *are* seriously dubious, but that we are unclear how to analyze or explain them philosophically. That uncertainty belongs to philosophers rather than to common sense, and it doesn't follow from the philosophers' uncertainty that the common sense beliefs are uncertain.

Kant's own account of the philosophical commitments of common sense is more complex than, and rather different from, Guyer's account. When Kant considers the "interest of reason" in the conflicts of the Antinomies he draws a sharp distinction between the speculative and practical concerns of common sense and in the former represents common sense as thoroughly dogmatic and hostile to an empiricist skepticism. The former claim is surely right: common sense typically may have an interest in a supernatural God as creator of the universe, or in applied moral issues, where it has little in philosophical controversies about idealism or physical cosmology. The points are well expressed at B500–502:

> The common understanding, it might be supposed, would eagerly adopt a program which promises to satisfy it through exclusively empirical knowledge … in preference to the transcendental dogmatism which compels it to rise to concepts far outstripping the insight and rational faculties of the most practiced thinkers. But this is precisely what commends such dogmatism to the common understanding. For it is then in a position in which the most learned can claim no advantage over it. (B500–501)
>
> Thus indolence and vanity [on the part of common understanding] combine in sturdy support of those principles … (mere Ideas about which no one knows anything) … although the philosopher finds it extremely hard to accept a principle for which he can give no justification, still more to employ concepts the objective reality of which he is unable to establish, nothing is more usual in the case of the common understanding.... it never occurs to it to reflect upon the assumption; and accepts as known whatever is familiar to it through frequent use. For the common understanding … all speculative interests pale before the practical.... (B502)

Throughout the section Kant admits that common sense and common understanding do not have much interest in the natural dialectic of human reason, but he also goes beyond that claim. Common sense is said to accept *dogmatic rationalist principles* because they offer an apparent foundation to cling to in support of religious and moral convictions and put ordinary folk on an equal level with the learned. Insofar as common sense *has* preferences in these philosophical matters they are, according to Kant, in favor of dogmatism and against skepticism. The commonsense beliefs themselves are not dogmatic, but common sense has a natural tendency to impose a dogmatic gloss on them for the given discreditable reasons. Philosophy is of use to common sense not in order to guard ordinary folk *against* skepticism, but to protect them from their natural dogmatism. If philosophy is needed to correct their views, it is needed as a *skeptical* antidote to, rather than as a justification for, those dogmatic tendencies.[13]

The passage reinforces Kant's tripartite distinction between dogmatist infancy, skeptical adolescence, and Critical maturity in philosophy.

> The first step in matters of pure reason, marking its infancy, is *dogmatic*. The second step is *sceptical*; and indicates that experience has rendered our judgement wiser and more circumspect. But a third step, such as can be taken only by a fully matured judgement, based on assured principles of proved universality, is now necessary, namely to subject to examination, not the facts of reason, but reason itself in the whole extent of its powers.... This is not the censorship but the *criticism* of reason, in which not its present bounds [*Schranken*] but its determinate limits [*Grenzen*] ... are demonstrated from principles. (B789)

It confirms the view that to disentangle those tempting alternatives requires a complex contribution from a more critical philosophy than "school metaphysics." Kant's *central* interests are not in justifying common beliefs against philosophical skepticism both because his primary project is a descriptive metaphysical inventory and because not all common sense beliefs are defensible (B883[14]). The primary project *has* more remote implications for traditional skepticism, and these are considered in 4, but the project itself is not directed at normative skeptical issues.

Notes

1   Skepticism is not a single issue but involves diverse arguments and targets. Kant is skeptical about traditional philosophers but not skeptical about science, and his inventory and transcendental topic are descriptive of experience rather than normative or justificatory. The principal targets of Kant's criticism in the theoretical context are (i) idle general skepticism, (ii) Cartesian idealist skepticism about the outer world in the Refutation of Idealism, and (iii) Humean "universal empiricism" and the skepticism it encourages about the character of experience. Stroud's extensive discussion of skepticism and Kant focuses on (ii).

2   At B858–59 Kant considers the complaint that his philosophical outcome is so modest that it could have been achieved without philosophy. He counterattacks by implying that philosophers have no special insight into ultimate truths: "Do you really require that a mode of

knowledge which concerns all men should transcend the common understanding and should only be revealed to you by philosophers? For we have revealed ... what could not at the start have been foreseen that in regard to the essential ends of human nature philosophy can advance no further than is possible under the guidance which nature has bestowed on even the most ordinary understanding." This is not an appeal to common sense against skepticism but acceptance of experience as a datum for his metaphysical inventory.

3   The debate is pointless, but a skeptic might say that in casting doubt on truth he is not *assuming* a dubious truth for his own claims but merely raising the question and implying that without an answer our beliefs remain unjustified.

4   Kant insists throughout the Dialectic, but especially in his distinction between analytical and dialectical opposites at B530–32, that strictly we can neither assert nor deny transcendent claims. Kant's resolution of the mathematical Antinomies and the free will–determinism debate turn essentially on this claim.

5   Kant represents ordinary believers as responding differently to practical and speculative (theoretical) skepticism. Ordinary believers sometimes engage with moral skepticism but hardly at all with speculative skepticism. They recognize that there are difficulties about establishing moral conclusions which they do not take seriously in many matters of fact.

6   Kant's distinction separates two kinds of contemporary philosophers. Some, like Barry Stroud, reject the general claim that skepticism is just an idle philosophical game and regard it, in some forms, as a fundamental philosophical issue. Others, like Austin, regard a distinctively philosophical skepticism as "idle," as a "family of diseases."

7   Stroud's central arguments in *The Significance of Philosophical Scepticism*, as I indicate in 3.2, reject justifications for claimed knowledge on the ground that the possibility of error has not been eliminated.

8   Stroud in "Scepticism, Externalism, and the Goal of Epistemology," *Proceedings of the Aristotelian Society*, suppl. vol 68, (1994), said of the skeptical issue: "In that tough competition ... scepticism will always win going away." It is difficult *not* to feel suspicious of such a guaranteed success.

9   Kant refers to the mock battles and pseudo-disputes of school metaphysics throughout the *Critique*, e.g., Bxv, B492, B775. The futility of disputes in a routine "school metaphysics" evidently alerted him to the need for reform in philosophy.

10   In the *Prolegomena* preface (Ak. 4.258–62), the commonsense theorists who criticized Hume are firmly put in their place. "One cannot notice without some pain how Hume's opponents, Reid, Oswald, Beattie, and even Priestley, missed the point of his project, assumed what he doubted and sought to prove what he had never doubted."

11   Ordinary people nowadays question the *uses* of science in many areas from warfare to farming, but these are moral or utilitarian queries about the application of science and not about its establishment of truths. Anyone with postmodern tendencies might query science's achievement of objective truth, but at that stage the question has moved into philosophy of an unclear kind.

12   Paul Guyer's immediate target in outlining Kant's attitude to skepticism is Karl Ameriks's book *Kant and the Fate of Autonomy* (Cambridge: Cambridge University Press, 2000). Ameriks's view interprets Kant's relation to skepticism as one of trying to balance what Sellars called "manifest" and "scientific" images. The account offered here differs from that of both Guyer and Ameriks. It rests on Kant's project as a descriptive metaphysics of experience which broadly accepts ordinary and scientific beliefs as a datum for investigating the structure, and especially a priori factors, in experience. It does not distinguish the manifest and scientific images, at least for these skeptical purposes.

13   Kant does not think ordinary beliefs dogmatic in designating supposed transcendent objects. His objection is to untestable speculative arguments which ordinary folk indulge in, where they are at no disadvantage against the better educated, since no progress can be made in the issues. These are likely to be most evident in cases where speculative and moral issues overlap as in beliefs in the existence of God.

14   B883: "The naturalist of pure reason adopts as his principle that through common reason, without science, what he calls 'sound reason', he is able in the most sublime questions which form the problem of metaphysics, to achieve more than is possible through speculation. Thus he is virtually asserting that we can determine the size and distance of the moon with greater certainty by the naked eye than by mathematical devices." Kant's conception of a commonsense "naturalist" is different from contemporary naturalism, but he evidently regards appeals to the best available science as indispensable.

Bibliography

References to the *Critique of Pure Reason* are given to the B edition except for passages which occur only in A. Other references to Kant's works are given to the Akademie edition of *Kant's Gesammelte Schriften* (Berlin: De Gruyter, 1902–).

I have used, and sometimes slightly deviated from, Norman Kemp Smith's 1929 translation of the *Critique of Pure Reason* (London: Macmillan). Passages from the *Inaugural Dissertation* are from *Kant's Latin Writings*, edited and translated by Lewis White Beck, with collaboration from Mary J. Gregor, Ralf Meerbote, and John Reuscher (New York: Peter Lang, 1986).

Passages from the moral philosophy—*Critique of Practical Reason*, *Groundwork of the Metaphysics of Morals*, and so forth—are from the Cambridge edition translations: *Practical Philosophy*, edited and translated by Mary J. Gregor (Cambridge: Cambridge University Press, 1996); and *Religion and Rational Theology*, edited and translated by Allen Wood, and George Di Giovanni (Cambridge: Cambridge University Press, 1996). Page numbers refer to the Akademie edition.

All other translations (*Prolegomena*, *Anthropologie*, the Eberhard polemic, *Metaphysical Foundations of Natural Science*, and so forth) are mine.

Ameriks, Karl. 2000. *Kant and the Fate of Autonomy*. Cambridge: Cambridge University Press.
Austin, J. L. 1961. *Philosophical Papers*. Edited by G. Warnock, and J. O. Urmson. Oxford: Clarendon Press.

———.1962. *Sense and Sensibilia*. Oxford: Clarendon Press.

Bonk, Thomas, ed. 2003. *Language, Truth and Knowledge*. Vienna Circle Institute Library. Dordrecht: Kluwer.

Carnap, Rudolf. 1956. "Empiricism, Semantics and Ontology." Reprinted in his *Meaning and Necessity*, Chicago, University of Chicago Press.

Förster, Eckart. 1989a. "Kant's Transcendental Arguments." In Schaper and Vossenkuhl, *Reading Kant*.

Glock, H.-J., ed. 2003. *Strawson and Kant*. Oxford: Clarendon Press.

Guyer, Paul. 2003. "Kant on Common Sense and Scepticism." *Kantian Review* 7: 1–37.

Harrison, Ross. 1989. "Atemporal Necessities of Thought: or, How Not to Bury Philosophy by History." In Schaper and Vossenkuhl, *Reading Kant*.

Parrini, P., ed. 1994. *Kant and Contemporary Epistemology*. Dordrecht: Kluwer.

Pereboom, Derk. 2001. "Assessing Kant's Master Argument." Review of *Kant's Transcendental Deduction*, by Robert Howell. *Kantian Review* 5.

Stern, R., ed. 1999. *Transcendental Arguments; Problems and Prospects*. Oxford: Clarendon Press.

Strawson, P. F. 1959. *Individuals*. London: Routledge.

———. 1985. *Skepticism and Naturalism*. London: Methuen.

Stroud, Barry. 1968. "Transcendental Arguments." *Journal of Philosophy*.

———. 1984. *The Significance of Philosophical Scepticism*. Oxford: Clarendon Press.

———. 1994a. "Kantian Arguments, Conceptual Capacities, and Invulnerability." In *Kant and Contemporary Epistemology*, edited by P. Parrini. Dordrecht: Kluwer.

———. 1994b. "Scepticism, Externalism, and the Goal of Epistemology." *Proceedings of the Aristotelian Society*. Suppl. vol. 68.

———. 2000. *The Quest for Reality*. Oxford: Oxford University Press.

Williams, Bernard. 1978. *Descartes: The Project of Pure Enquiry*. London: Penguin.

READING 15

Discussion Questions

1. What is dogmatism and what is skepticism? Why do we want to avoid both dogmatism and skepticism in the pursuit of knowledge?
2. What is the difference between skepticism and skeptical method? Why does Kant take skeptical method but not accept skepticism?
3. For what reason is skepticism self-contradictory? Does it prove that skepticism is never a reasonable position and that skepticism has a self-refuting conclusion?
4. Kant, according to Bird, was interested in a "descriptive metaphysics" that discloses the "a priori structure of our immanent experiences." How can we have a system of knowledge that captures ordinary sense experiences built on concepts that are not dependent on experiences (a priori)? Is it a possible project?
5. Do you think that common sense has a tendency to impose a dogmatic gloss on beliefs for questionable reasons? Do you agree with Kant that skeptical doubt can be an antidote to such a dogmatic tendency of ordinary beliefs?

Style and Method

Philosophical Investigations §§89–133

Marie McGinn

Introduction

Wittgenstein's *Philosophical Investigations* is concerned with two principal topics: the philosophy of language and philosophical psychology. As soon as we open the book it is apparent that Wittgenstein's way of treating these topics is quite unlike that of any other philosopher. First of all, the form of the book is quite unique. Instead of the usual chapters with titles indicating the topics to be discussed, the work is made up of distinct, numbered remarks, varying in length from one line to several paragraphs. Moreover, instead of presenting arguments and clearly stated conclusions, these remarks reflect on a wide range of topics—many of which recur throughout the work—without ever producing a clear, final statement on any of them. The punctuation that Wittgenstein uses is complex and distinctive; many of the remarks take the form of a conversation between Wittgenstein and an interlocutor, and it is not always clear whether we are to take the words on the page as an assertion of Wittgenstein's, or of his interlocutor, or simply as the expression of a thought to be considered. Remarks often include questions for which Wittgenstein appears to provide no answer, or analogies whose point we cannot immediately see. Many more remarks include descriptions of concrete examples, both real and imaginary, which are quite unlike the examples in other works of philosophy, and which Wittgenstein never seems to use as the basis of a generalization.

It is Wittgenstein's unique way of treating the topics he deals with that makes the *Investigations* so difficult to understand. It is not that his style is technical or abstract, but rather it is just not possible to see, in the style of the book, what Wittgenstein's method is or how it is supposed to work. Yet understanding Wittgenstein's method and its connection with the form of the text is the key to understanding the *Investigations*. This is so not merely because it is only by means of such understanding that we can know how to read the remarks that make up the work, but because Wittgenstein himself emphasizes over and over again that it is a method or a style of thought, rather than doctrines, which characterizes his later philosophy. It is, moreover, his insistence that his philosophical aims do not involve him in putting forward 'any kind of theory' (*PI* §109) that makes the question of method, and of how to read his remarks, such a difficult one, for it suggests that we cannot approach the book in the usual way, with a view to finding and extracting the claims which are made in it.

Wittgenstein himself is alive to the difficulty involved in understanding the remarks that make up the *Investigations*. In the Preface to the book, he expresses pessimism as to its being understood, and he frequently speaks of our being somehow resistant to thinking or approaching problems in the way he recommends:

> I am trying to recommend a certain sort of investigation ... [T]his investigation is immensely important and very much *against the grain* of some of you.

(*WL*, p. 103)

> One difficulty was that [his method] required a 'sort of thinking' to which we are not accustomed and to which we have not been trained—a sort of thinking very different from what is required in the sciences.

(*WLFM*, p. 44)

We should not be surprised, therefore, if on first reading the book we cannot see the point of Wittgenstein's remarks, or if we cannot see how we are supposed to make use of the examples he presents. At first sight, the book may well seem fragmentary and diffuse, so that it remains obscure precisely how Wittgenstein's observations are to be brought to bear on the sort of problems about language and subjectivity which we are familiar with from traditional philosophy. The same sense of difficulty and disorientation is described by students who attended his lectures, in which the pattern of discussion closely mirrored the form of Wittgenstein's written remarks:

> The considerable difficulty in following the lectures arose from the fact that it was hard to see where all this often rather repetitive concrete detailed talk was leading to—how the examples were interconnected and how all this bore on the problems which one was accustomed to put oneself in abstract terms.

(Gasking and Jackson, 1978:51)

Faced with these difficulties, it may be tempting to treat the apparent fragmentariness of the text as a defect which we must overcome, by discerning, behind the individual remarks, an implicit or burgeoning theory of how language functions, of how our psychological concepts work, or of the nature of psychological states. The price of this is that we must then assume that the form which Wittgenstein was so careful to give to his work is irrelevant to his philosophical aims, and reflects nothing more than a stylistic preference, or even his inability to present his views in a more conventional format. Such an approach also means that we are no longer able to make sense of the large number of remarks in which Wittgenstein insists that 'we may not advance any kind of theory' (*PI* §109), that philosophy, 'neither explains nor deduces anything' (*PI* §126), that '[a]ll *explanation* must disappear, and description alone must take its place' (*PI* §109).

Some interpreters have clearly been willing to pay this price. For example, A.C. Grayling expresses the following view:

> Wittgenstein's writings seem to me not only summarizable but in positive need of summary
> ... Nor is it true that Wittgenstein's writings contain no systematically expressible theories,
> for indeed they do. It is the difference between what Wittgenstein says and the way he says
> it which is relevant here; the fact that his later writings are unsystematic in style does not
> mean that they are unsystematic in content.

> (Grayling, 1988:v–vi)

I shall, however, take the opposite view, and assume that any convincing interpretation must succeed in making sense of both the form of the *Investigations*, and Wittgenstein's remarks on the nature of his approach to philosophical problems; any other attitude is at odds, not only with his remarks on the nature of his investigation, but with the well attested care he took in both writing and arranging his remarks.

The Idea of Grammatical Investigation

Wittgenstein himself, as I've already remarked, is perfectly aware of the difficulty that faces us in trying to understand his work, and even of our resistance to his way of thinking. He sees this difficulty 'not [as] the intellectual difficulty of the sciences, but the difficulty of a change of attitude' (*BT*, p. 300). He wants us to undertake a new sort of investigation, one that directs itself, not to the construction of new and surprising theories or explanations, but to the examination of our life with language. For he believes that the problems that confront us in philosophy are rooted in 'a misunderstanding of the logic of language' (*PI* §93); they are 'not empirical problems', but are misunderstandings that 'are solved through an insight into the workings of our language, and that in such a way that these workings are recognized—*despite* an urge to misunderstand them' (*PI* §109).

Language is, for Wittgenstein, both the source of philosophical problems and the means to overcome them:

> Philosophy is a struggle against the bewitchment of our understanding by the resources
> of our language.

> (*PI* §109)

We are struggling with language. We are engaged in a struggle with language.

(*CV*, p. 11)

Philosophy, as we use the word, is a fight against the fascination which forms of expression exert on us.

(*BB*, p. 27)

The power of language to mislead through false analogies and misleading, surface similarities must be countered by our coming to see more clearly into the actual workings of language, that is, into how we *operate* with words, into how the concepts that make up the different regions of our language actually function. He suggests, in particular, that we have a general notion of the meaning of a word as something that is correlated with it, as something towards which we can direct our attention when we ostensively define a word, and that this picture of meaning 'surrounds the working of language with a haze which makes clear vision impossible' (*PI* §5). He believes that the 'fog' is dispersed by our coming to command a clear view of our employment of expressions, which we achieve through a careful study of our actual use of words in the context of our everyday lives.

In *PI* §90, he describes the kind of investigation he is engaged in, by which philosophical problems are solved through the clarification of our use of expressions, as 'a grammatical one'. The idea of a grammatical investigation is central to Wittgenstein's later philosophy, and it is the key to understanding his work. The *Investigations* can be seen as a large collection of particular grammatical investigations, which aim to resolve specific philosophical problems and paradoxes through a detailed examination of the workings of our language. These investigations of how a particular region of our language works are invariably subtle and complex, and how Wittgenstein uses them as a means to unravel philosophical problems can properly be understood only by looking at how his method works in practice. One of the principal aims of my exposition of the *Investigations* is to follow the line of Wittgenstein's particular grammatical investigations very closely, in an attempt to show exactly how his grammatical method both diagnoses, and attempts to counter, philosophical confusion, through coming to command a clear view of our use of words. The general remarks on the grammatical method that follow are, therefore, intended to provide no more than a general indication of how Wittgenstein approaches philosophical problems, and of the way his approach confronts traditional philosophy.

Wittgenstein describes a grammatical investigation as one in which 'we call to mind the *kinds of statement* that we make about phenomena' (*PI* §90). This does not mean, however, that Wittgenstein is interested in what he calls 'the construction of sentences' or 'the part of [a word's] use ... that can be taken in by the ear' (*PI* §664). His use of the concept of grammar relates, not to language considered as a system of signs for the construction of well-formed sentences, but to the actual use or application of expressions, to how words are employed in our life with language. He calls this the 'depth grammar' of a word (*PI* §664), and it is something that can be discerned only if we attend to how we operate with words; not merely to the connection between one expression and another, but to the circumstances in which we use expressions, the circumstances in which we learn to use them, to the way their use is woven in with other activities, and to the criteria by which we judge whether someone has understood them.

The idea of a grammatical investigation is intended to draw our attention to what Wittgenstein calls 'the language-game', which he describes as 'the whole, consisting of language and the activities into which it is woven' (*PI* §7). Wittgenstein's grammatical method is one in which 'we call to mind' the details of the distinctive patterns of employment—the grammar—of expressions, which constitutes their role in our life with language. The techniques that Wittgenstein uses to describe the grammar of our concepts are various. They include imagining a variety of circumstances in which we would use a given expression, asking how we teach its use to a child, asking how we know he has learned it, asking for the criteria on the basis of which we judge that it applies in a particular concrete case, looking at how it connects with other expressions, asking whether it would still be usable if certain facts of nature were different, imagining what we would say in a variety of peculiar cases, comparing our use of an expression with an example that Wittgenstein makes up, and so on. By using these techniques he attempts, not to systematize or regiment the rules for our use of words, but to evoke our life with signs; it is by making ourselves aware of the distinctive ways in which we employ expressions, as revealed in our life with language, that we clarify what Wittgenstein calls 'the grammar of our concepts'.

The purpose of Wittgenstein's evocation of the details of our practice of employing the different expressions of our language is twofold. On the one hand, he uses it to make us aware of the clash between our philosophically reflective idea of how a concept works and the way it actually functions, and on the other, he uses it to draw our attention to the profound differences in the patterns of use that characterize the expressions of our language. Wittgenstein labels the latter differences in use 'grammatical difference[s]' (*PPF* §62); making us aware of these differences is central to his grammatical method. When he speaks of our need for '*an overview* of the use of our words' (*PI* §122), he is thinking both of our need to uncover the conflict between our philosophical notions and the way our concepts actually function, and of our need to become aware of the grammatical differences between concepts.

However, while he believes that it is only by achieving this sort of clarity concerning our employment of expressions that philosophical problems are diagnosed and overcome, he also recognizes that it is difficult for us to accept this switch of attention away from the construction of theories, or a concern with explanation, towards describing the details of our ordinary practice of employing expressions. We have certain intellectual habits that stand in the way of our undertaking the detailed, grammatical investigations that he is recommending, for we simply cannot see the *point* of describing how we operate with words:

> We are not at all *prepared* for the task of describing the use of the word 'to think'. (And why should we be? What is such a description useful for?)

> (*Z* §111)

> One cannot guess how a word functions. One has to look at its application and learn from that.
>
> But the difficulty is to remove the prejudice which stands in the way of doing so. It is not a *stupid* prejudice.

(PI §340)

Wittgenstein is also aware that his idea that 'we may not advance any kind of theory' (*PI* §109), and his insistence that we are exclusively concerned with the clarification and description of our use of words, will create a sense of dissatisfaction and frustration:

> Where does this investigation get its importance from, given that it seems only to destroy everything interesting: that is, all that is great and important? (As it were, all the buildings, leaving behind only bits of stone and rubble.)

(PI §118)

The very idea that '[a]ll *explanation* must disappear, and description alone must take its place' (*PI* §109), or that philosophy 'leaves everything as it is' (*PI* §124), may seem to impose a quite unwarranted intellectual constraint on us, which we might, at least in the first instance, find unsatisfactory and chafing. Surely, we might feel, language and mental states are phenomena that cry out for philosophical explanation. There must, for example, be some explanation of what language's ability to represent the world consists in, of what our understanding of our language consists in, of what thinking is, of what an intention, or a sensation, is, and so on. How could it possibly be wrong or inappropriate to try to provide an account of the nature of these phenomena, to say what they consist in, or to offer some sort of explanation of them?

Here we come to the nub of our resistance to entering into and understanding the sort of investigation that Wittgenstein wants us to engage in; we've come to the exact point at which his style of thinking 'goes against the grain'. For we simply don't see how what appear to be completely unexceptional questions—'What is meaning?', 'What does understanding consist in?', 'What is thought?', 'What is an intention?'—could possibly be answered by anything other than a theory which explains or elucidates the nature of these phenomena. We feel that it is only by means of some sort of account of these phenomena, one which explains their nature or shows how they fit into the natural world, that our urge to understand them more clearly could possibly be met. To suggest that such an explanatory account cannot, or should not, be given, or that it is not the task of philosophy to give it, can amount, we feel, to nothing less than the absurd suggestion that these phenomena cannot be explained, that they are in some way mysterious or occult.

Wittgenstein recognizes that it is this understandable desire for some form of explanatory account which makes us resistant to the idea that our problems 'are solved through an insight into the workings of our language' (*PI* §109). It is this desire that Wittgenstein means to characterize when he says that '[w]e feel as if we had to *see right into* phenomena' (*PI* §90). It is vital to our coming to understand Wittgenstein's later philosophy that we come to understand the way in which Wittgenstein works to overcome the desire for explanation and to persuade us that '[s]ince everything lies open to view, there is nothing to explain' (*PI* §126).

The Rejection of Philosophical Theories

It is clear that Wittgenstein himself sees the concern with explanation, which is associated with our idea of the methods and aims of science, as a major obstacle to our achieving the understanding we seek when we ask questions like 'What is meaning?', 'What is thought?', 'What does our understanding of our language consist in?' He writes:

> Philosophers constantly see the method of science before their eyes, and are irresistibly tempted to ask and to answer questions in the way science does. This tendency is the real source of metaphysics and leads philosophers into complete darkness.

> (*BB*, p. 18)

> The existence of the experimental method [in psychology] makes us think we have the means of getting rid of the problems which trouble us; but problem and method pass one another by.

> (*PPF* §371)

> (One of the greatest impediments for philosophy is the expectation of new, unheard of elucidations.)

> (*BT*, p. 309)

Wittgenstein is not here expressing any general opposition to science. It is rather that the methods of science, in particular the ideas of explanation and discovery, are misleading and inappropriate when applied to questions like 'What is meaning?', 'What is thought?', and so on. There is the suggestion that when we interpret these questions as requests for an explanatory account, or as the expression of a need to discover something hitherto unknown, on analogy, say, with the question 'What is the specific gravity of gold?', then we set out on a path that leads, not to an understanding of these phenomena, but to 'complete darkness'.

In *PI* §89, Wittgenstein picks out those questions which we misunderstand when we take them as requests for explanations as follows:

> Augustine says in the *Confessions* XI.14 "quid est ergo tempus? Si nemo ex me quaerat scio; si quaerenti explicare velim, nescio." ["What, then, is time? If nobody asks me, I know well enough what it is; but if I am asked what it is and try to explain, I am baffled."]—This could not be said about a question of natural science ("What is the specific gravity of hydrogen?"

for instance). Something that one knows when nobody asks one, but no longer knows when one is asked to explain it, is something that has to be *called to mind*. (And it is obviously something which, for some reason, it is difficult to call to mind.)

Philosophical questions—'What is time?', 'What is meaning?', 'What is knowledge?'—characteristically focus on concepts that we employ, often without reflection and generally without difficulty, all the time in our everyday lives. They focus on just those things 'that one knows when nobody asks one, but no longer knows when one is asked to explain it'. Wittgenstein suggests that these characteristically philosophical questions are of a special kind:

> (Questions of different kinds occupy us. For instance, "What is the specific weight of this body", "Will the weather stay nice today", "Who will come through the door next", etc. But among our questions there are those of a special kind. Here we have a different experience. These questions seem to be more fundamental than the others. And now I say: When we have this experience, we have arrived at the limits of language.)

(*BT*, p. 304)

What we are concerned with when we ask questions of the form 'What is time?', 'What is meaning?', 'What is thought?' is to understand the nature or essence of these phenomena. Yet in the very act of framing these questions, Wittgenstein believes, we are tempted to form a conception of what will count as an answer to them that leads us to approach the problem of understanding the essence of these phenomena in the wrong way, in a way which assumes that we have to uncover or explain something. Our attempts to meet the explanatory demands that we feel we face lead us, Wittgenstein tries to show, into ever increasing difficulties. The phenomena we set out to understand and explain seem suddenly bewilderingly mysterious, for as soon as we try to account for them in the way that our questions seem to require, we find we cannot do it: we find that we 'no longer know'.

Thus, we are led deeper and deeper into a state of frustration and philosophical confusion. We think that the fault lies in our explanations and that we need to construct ever more subtle and surprising accounts. We go astray and imagine that 'we have to describe extreme subtleties, which again we are quite unable to describe with the means at our disposal. We feel as if we had to repair a torn spider's web with our fingers' (*PI* §106). The real fault, Wittgenstein believes, is not in our explanations, but in the very idea that the puzzlement we feel can be removed by means of a discovery. The puzzlement which our attempts at explanation or theory construction create can only be removed by means of a description of the workings of our language. The nature of these phenomena is not something that we discover by 'digging', but is something that is revealed in 'the *kinds of statement* that we make about phenomena', by the distinctive ways of using expressions that characterize the different regions of our language.

Our problems are, Wittgenstein believes, conceptual ones, and the method we need is the method of grammatical investigation: a careful attention to our actual use of words. It is by attending to the application of expressions—to what lies open to view in our use of language—that we will overcome our sense of philosophical perplexity concerning the phenomena that puzzle us, and achieve the understanding we seek. The difficulty, he suggests, lies, not in the method itself, but in the fact that we are so unwilling to undertake, and so unprepared for, this task of description. The real difficulty is not the one associated with the tasks of discovery and explanation, but of coming to recognize the significance of what is there before our eyes:

> The aspects of things that are most important for us are hidden because of their simplicity and familiarity. (One is unable to notice something—because it is always before one's eyes.)
>
> (*PI* §129)

One of the main obstacles to understanding the *Investigations* is that the switch, which Wittgenstein repeatedly makes, away from a concern with explanation, and towards a concern with the details of our ordinary practice of employing language, is so difficult to accept. The style of thought that is involved in undertaking a grammatical enquiry seems to go in quite the wrong direction, for its direction is the very opposite from the one we want to take. For while we feel that our question can only be answered by the construction of an account that explains what a given phenomenon consists in, Wittgenstein wants us simply to look at the intricate details of concrete examples of our practice of using expressions, or to consider various imaginary cases, or to reflect on what we'd say in a variety of circumstances, and so on, without attempting to draw any sort of general conclusion or put forward any general statement about what constitutes the essence of the phenomenon.

Wittgenstein expresses this idea that his method tries to turn us in a direction that we are unwilling to follow at a number of points:

> It is as if a man is standing in a room facing a wall on which are painted a number of dummy doors. Wanting to get out, he fumblingly tries to open them, vainly trying them all, one after the other, over and over again. But of course it is quite useless. And all the time, although he doesn't realize it, there is a real door in the wall behind his back and all he has to do is turn round and open it. To help him get out of the room all we have to do is to get him to look in a different direction. But it's hard to do this, since, wanting to get out he resists our attempts to turn him away from where he thinks the exit must be.
>
> (Gasking and Jackson, 1978:52)

> A man will be *imprisoned* in a room with a door that is unlocked and opens inwards; as long as it does not occur to him to pull rather than push it.
>
> (*CV*, p. 42)

The idea that Wittgenstein's style of investigation is to be set in opposition to the construction of philosophical theories clearly suggests that we should not look in his text for any sort of philosophical account of, say, meaning or mental states. The book is, in a sense, philosophically more radical. He is not setting out to replace one philosophical account with another, but to change the way we see philosophical questions and the sort of investigation they call for. The philosophical ideas concerning the nature of meaning, or the nature of mental states, that Wittgenstein investigates, are not seen as mistaken answers to genuine questions, but as pictures of our use of expressions, which, in our concern with explanation, we try to make the basis of a generalized, explanatory account. His aim is to get us to recognize the illusions and paradoxes which these attempts at explanation throw up, and to see that, contrary to our first impression, they really explain nothing.

Wittgenstein focuses, therefore, on the origin of these philosophical ideas in the pictures that guide our philosophical reflections, which have their source in our ways of using expressions, but which our concern with explanation tempts us to misapply. By a careful examination of the applications that we are tempted to make of the pictures which govern our philosophical imagination, Wittgenstein hopes gradually to reveal the emptiness of the accounts that our sense of a need 'to *see right into* phenomena' has led us to construct. What he opposes to the misunderstandings and philosophical illusions that he examines is not an alternative explanation or theory of what meaning or understanding consist in, but a different form of investigation, one which sets out to counter the disastrous effects of the pictures which have come to dominate our thought, by means of a careful attention to facts about our use of expressions. It is by coming to command a clear view of how we operate with expressions that Wittgenstein hopes gradually to release us from problems and paradoxes that have their roots in the misapplication of a picture, which our concern with explanation leads us to make. His ultimate aim is to reveal 'that nothing extraordinary is involved' (*PI* §94), that 'everything lies open to view, there is nothing to explain' (*PI* §126).

Thus what we see in the specific problems and pictures that form the focus of Wittgenstein's critical reflections are ideas about how the particular expressions of our language function, together with the phantasms, myths, superstitions and chimeras that these ideas give rise to when we take the questions 'What is meaning?', 'What does understanding consist in?', 'What is a sensation?', and so on, as calling for some sort of philosophical account. He does not see the temptation to misunderstand the nature of the enquiry that these questions call for, or the temptation to misapply the pictures which our forms of expression invite, as a sign of a defective intellect. The misunderstandings which Wittgenstein believes to be the source of the philosophical problems that trouble us have their roots, he believes, in the forms of our language. Language itself invites the move from unselfconscious employment of it to an attitude of reflecting on it, and once we take up the reflective attitude, language itself presents a series of traps for the understanding:

> Language has the same traps ready for everyone; the immense network of easily trodden false paths. And thus we see one person after another walking down the same paths and we already know where he will make a turn, where he will keep going straight ahead without noticing the turn, etc., etc.

> (*BT*, p. 312)

The philosophical confusions that arise, once we begin to reflect on the nature of meaning or understanding or thinking, are not, therefore, mere mistakes. They are misunderstandings which, when we become reflective about it, language itself has the power to draw us into. Wittgenstein sometimes suggests that philosophical confusions share these roots in language both with forms of human mental disturbance and with primitive styles of thought. The problems created by language are *deep* problems that arise in situations of reflection or withdrawal from a practical engagement in human life, 'when language is, as it were, idling, not when it is doing work' (*PI* §132):

> The problems arising through a misinterpretation of our forms of language have the character of *depth*. They are deep disquietudes; they are as deeply rooted in us as the forms of our language, and their significance is as great as the importance of our language.
>
> (*PI* §111)

In setting out to counter the pictures we construct, and the applications we are tempted to make of them, Wittgenstein does not see himself as out to refute doctrines, but as attempting to release us both from a particular style of thought, and from the paradoxes that it has given rise to. He does not challenge outright either the pictures or their application, but rather encourages us to explore the pictures and the applications to which we are inexorably drawn, so that we find out for ourselves that they represent 'dummy doors', that they offer no solution to the problems of understanding which confront us. Woven in with remarks that attempt to guide us in this process of discovering the emptiness of the applications we are inclined to make of the pictures we construct are remarks in which Wittgenstein tries to draw our attention towards neglected details or aspects of our concrete practice of using language. Simply by putting these details together in the right way, or by using a new analogy or comparison to prompt us to see our practice of using language in a new light, we find that we achieve the understanding that we thought would come only with the construction of an explanatory account:

> I think one reason why the attempt to find an explanation is wrong is that we have only to put together in the right way what we know, without adding anything, and the satisfaction we are trying to get from the explanation comes of itself.
>
> (RFGB, p. 30)

Philosophy as Therapy

Wittgenstein describes the above processes as 'therapies' (*PI* §133), and he speaks of treating philosopher's questions 'like an illness' (*PI* §255). These descriptions are apt for a number of reasons. First of all, they convey the idea that our concern with the construction of explanatory models is in some way itself an *obstacle* to our progress, something that holds or arrests us and prevents us from moving on. Second, they capture the fact that Wittgenstein's method is not aimed at producing new, stateable conclusions, but works on us in such a way as to change our whole style of thinking or way of looking at things. The idea of therapies, or of treating an illness, emphasizes that Wittgenstein's philosophical method aims to engage the reader in an active process of working on himself. It also underlines the fact that the reader's acknowledgement of Wittgenstein's diagnosis of the source of philosophical problems and paradoxes is a vital part of his method, for 'we can only prove that someone made a mistake if he (really) acknowledges this expression as the correct expression of his feeling' (*BT*, p. 303). If the reader is to be liberated from what Wittgenstein sees as the disastrous effects of the misapplication of pictures that have their roots in our forms of expression, then he must first of all acknowledge that Wittgenstein has indeed identified 'the source of his thought' (*BT*, p. 303).

Finally, these ideas recognize that the process by which we escape from philosophical perplexity is in its nature protracted. Therapy is essentially a slow process in which the patient is brought by degrees to a new understanding of the nature of the problems that trouble him, one which allows him to recognize that he had been seeking satisfaction in the wrong way, and which thereby brings him peace. Wittgenstein's use of an interlocutor's voice allows him to present the therapeutic process, not as a series of exchanges between a therapist and a patient, but in the form of an internal dialogue, in which Wittgenstein both gives expression to the temptations to misunderstand which our language presents to us and struggles to resist these misunderstandings. The interlocutor's voice (which is introduced both indirectly in remarks beginning 'We want to say … ', 'One would like to say … ' and directly through the use of double quotation marks) expresses our desire for explanation, and succumbs to the traps that our language presents; the therapeutic voice uses a whole series of methods which work against these inclinations, for example, by exploring what the pictures we construct actually amount to, by offering alternative analogies and pictures, by examining particular concrete examples of our use of expressions, by reflecting on how we teach a child to use it, and so on. In this way, Wittgenstein works to achieve a new way of looking at things, one in which problems which had hitherto seemed insoluble no longer trouble us.

If all this is correct, then we should not look in Wittgenstein's text for the familiar structure of thesis/refutation/counter-thesis (for example, we should not look for a precise theory of how language represents which Wittgenstein is opposing, for his arguments against it, or for his alternative account of how language functions). We should discern a rhythm of an altogether different kind. Given that we are, at the outset at least, in the grip of a concern with explanation, our first response to questions like 'What is meaning?', 'What is thought?', and so on, will be to try to model or explain what meaning, thought, and so on actually consist in. The focus of Wittgenstein's interest is, as I remarked earlier, on the very first moves that we make in response to these questions, where the pictures and ideas that guide our future approach are laid down, and a whole series of mistakes become inevitable. He wants to uncover the point of origin of our philosophical false leads, where their roots in the forms of our language can be more clearly seen and diagnosed.

He believes that many of the ideas that we use as the basis for our philosophical accounts are ones that already occur as metaphors or pictures within our everyday discourse. For example, the idea that natural language can be compared with a precise calculus, that meaning can be pictured as a word's standing for something, that understanding is a state which is the source of correct use, that pain is inner and pain-behaviour outer, all occur to us quite naturally. However, when we are intent on constructing an explanatory account of what meaning or understanding consist in, or of what sensations are, we try to give these ideas a literalness and explanatory force which we never attempt to give them in ordinary life; we try to transform what is really no more than a way of looking at things—an 'object of comparison' (*PI* §131)—into the basis for a theoretical account of the essence of these phenomena; our object of comparison becomes 'a preconception to which reality *must* correspond' (*PI* §131), even though we cannot immediately see just how it does so.

' ... The Philosophical Problems Should Completely Disappear'

In *PI* §122, Wittgenstein introduces the notion of an '*ubersichtliche Darstellung*' to describe the aim of his grammatical investigations. In the original English translation, by G.E.M. Anscombe, this was translated as 'perspicuous representation', but is translated as 'surveyable representation' by Hacker and Schulte. The accuracy of the new translation is not a matter for dispute. However, the emphasis that it places on surveyability may suggest the idea of providing a systematic representation of the grammar of our language, which can be taken in at a glance. This idea does not fit well with Wittgenstein's unsystematic reflections, which frequently focus on the investigation of a particular case, rather than on anything that might justly be described as 'an overview' of the use of a word. For these reasons, I have decided to stick with Anscombe's original translation of *PI* §122, which runs as follows:

> A main source of our failure to understand is that we do not *command a clear view* of our use of our words.—Our grammar is lacking in this sort of perspicuity. A perspicuous representation produces just that understanding which consists in 'seeing connexions'. Hence the importance of finding and inventing *intermediate cases*.
>
> The concept of a perspicuous representation is of fundamental significance for us. It earmarks the form of account we give, the way we look at things.

This makes it natural to understand a 'perspicuous representation' as one which aims to achieve 'a clear view' of our practice of using words. We do not have to understand this as a call to provide a systematic or surveyable presentation of rules for the use of expressions, which might be appealed to in order to criticize the assertions of others. Rather, we can take it that in focusing on the concept of a perspicuous representation, Wittgenstein's aim is to reveal an order in how we actually operate with expressions, which he associates with 'the understanding that consists in "seeing connexions"' (*PI* §122), and which may be achieved by the careful investigation of a particular case, or range of cases.

On this interpretation, Wittgenstein's grammatical enquiries are seen as aiming to produce a kind of understanding which consists in seeing an order in our use of expressions, in recognizing variations on a theme, in seeing one thing as a complication of another, in recognizing the significance of context, or of how things unfold over time, and so on; that is, in seeing clearly what is there before our eyes, but which we had previously neglected or overlooked. It is through an emerging sense of how we operate with expressions in our life with language that the essence of language, meaning, understanding, thinking, intending, and so on, is gradually revealed and understood. We gradually come to see that 'nothing extraordinary is involved' (*PI* §94), that no further (deeper) explanation is needed, that the essence 'lies open to view' (*PI* §126). The particular examples that Wittgenstein examines, the particular analogies and comparisons he uses, are not made the basis for formulating general claims or theories; it is not through the construction of a general account, but through the examination of the grammar of our concepts, and the light that Wittgenstein's analogies and comparisons throw on our actual employment of expressions, that we overcome an urge to misunderstand, and gradually achieve the understanding we seek.

It is clear that Wittgenstein does not conceive of the task of providing a perspicuous representation of the grammar of our language—of our everyday employment of expressions—to be one that is to be, or even could be, undertaken systematically, or as an intellectual end in itself. It is clear, moreover, that he does not conceive of such a perspicuous representation as something that could be expressed in the form of a systematic description of the rules for the use of words. One might, however, wonder why Wittgenstein is so against the idea of a systematic description of the use of the expressions of our language. If a grammatical investigation is one that goes in the opposite direction from theory construction, why shouldn't it take us in that direction systematically? The answer to this question lies, first of all, in the fact that the idea of language as a calculus that is operated according to precise rules, which this conception of a perspicuous representation presupposes, is itself a philosophical illusion. The practice of employing expressions that Wittgenstein aims to evoke is essentially concrete, context dependent, dynamic, indeterminate and shifting; the idea of a systematic representation, in the form of a surveyable system of rules for the use of expressions, of what Wittgenstein calls the grammar of our language is itself a myth.

Second, Wittgenstein's essentially unsystematic approach is linked with the fact that his method in the *Investigations* is essentially *responsive*. Thus, the anti-systematic nature of Wittgenstein's philosophy is connected with the idea that his grammatical investigation is one that 'gets its light, that is to say its purpose, from the philosophical problems' (*PI* §109). The self-conscious awareness of an order in our practice of employing language, which a grammatical investigation is intended to evoke, does not represent an increase in our knowledge of the kind we associate with science. Wittgenstein's interest in 'calling to mind', or prompting us to see, an aspect of our use of words is motivated by, and takes its light from, the problems and paradoxes he aims to resolve. Bringing these aspects of our life with language to light gives us a kind of understanding which 'consists in "seeing connexions"', and which frees us from both the false pictures which lie at the source of philosophical paradoxes, and from an inappropriate urge to explain the phenomena that puzzle us.

In *PI* §132, Wittgenstein remarks: 'we want to establish an order in our knowledge of the use of language', but he makes it clear that this order is merely 'an order for a particular purpose; one out of many possible orders; not *the* order'. This suggests that Wittgenstein acknowledges that someone with different interests might be concerned with establishing a different order; the order he discerns is only one way of looking at the phenomena, and it is of interest because of the kind of problems he is concerned with. The order that Wittgenstein wants to draw our attention to is one that will enable us to overcome the philosophical puzzlement that arises as a result of misleading pictures of how our concepts function.

Wittgenstein's aim is to evoke particular concrete cases in which we employ expression, to present alternative pictures or comparisons, and to point out connections we have overlooked, in order to help us to see more clearly how our concepts actually function, how we operate with the relevant expressions in our life with language. The order that his grammatical investigations reveal enables us to see, not only that our philosophical theories and accounts make no contact with the phenomena they are intended to explain, but that the need for explanation evaporates. Through the constant repetition of this process of grammatical investigation, Wittgenstein works to bring about a gradual shift in our understanding and in our style of thought. The cumulative effect is that we see things differently. What before had looked like an explanation is now seen to be no more than an empty construction; what before cried out for elucidation is now seen as unmysterious; our language-game can be accepted just as it is, without our feeling a need to justify it or to give it further foundations or support.

Thus we will miss the whole point of Wittgenstein's philosophical method if we attempt to extract from his remarks a series of philosophical claims about what constitutes meaning, understanding, thinking, intending, and so on. Not only is Wittgenstein not concerned with the construction or elaboration of philosophical theories, but whatever general claims we might extract from his remarks are not to be understood as the *point* of the work. The aim of the work is to escape from philosophical confusion through coming to command a clear view of our use of words. Thus Wittgenstein himself gives clear warning that any such attempt to extract 'theses' will produce, not gold, but banality: 'If someone were to advance *theses* in philosophy, it would never be possible to debate them, because everyone would agree to them' (*PI* §128).

An adequate interpretation of the *Investigations* should not, therefore, concern itself with theses, but strive to show how Wittgenstein uses the pictures and analogies he presents, and the concrete examples of our practice of using expressions that he describes, not as a source of generalizations, but as a means to overcome the particular misunderstandings and misleading pictures that our urge to explain throws up, and as a means to achieve a recognition that there is nothing that needs to be explained. Wittgenstein's philosophical aim is not to arrive at conclusions, but to bring about a gradual acceptance of the fact that our attempts at explanation are empty and that 'since everything lies open to view there is nothing to explain' (*PI* §126). It is in the detailed workings of the dialectical process through which he brings this acceptance about that Wittgenstein's philosophical method is revealed. We must, therefore, resist the attempt to sum up, or to state philosophically exciting conclusions, and allow instead for a series of clarifications to take place in which 'the philosophical problems ... *completely* disappear' (*PI* §133). In this way, we never lose sight of the fact that '[t]he work of the philosopher consists in marshalling recollections *for a particular purpose*' (*PI* §127, my italics); the dialectical structure of the work—seen in the interaction of Wittgenstein's different voices—is thereby acknowledged as an essential part of his method, and is not seen as a mere stylistic device which obscures the general views that are being surreptitiously advanced, and which our exposition must somehow draw out.

On this interpretation, the *Investigations* is not viewed as a work that concerns itself with a large number of discrete topics—names, ostensive definition, meaning, rules, understanding, sensations, and so on—and provides a corrective to our thinking on each of them. There is, rather, an attempt to produce an overall shift in how we approach philosophical questions, and respond to the desire for understanding that they express. This means that there is not only a profound unity to the work, but there is a powerful cumulative effect which is properly achieved only if we read the book as a whole. We cannot locate the understanding that Wittgenstein offers us in the dismantling of specific misunderstandings, or in the description of one or two concrete cases that help to reveal how a bit of our language functions. The shift in our understanding which he aims to bring about cannot be conveyed to a passive audience in the form of 'results' or 'conclusions', but this is not to say that the *Investigations* is in any way mystical; there is, for instance, no suggestion that the understanding that Wittgenstein offers to the individual reader cannot be communicated or shared. It is only that it cannot be communicated in the form of a statement of systematic doctrines or theories. This understanding must be conveyed to someone else in the way it is conveyed to an individual reader, through a process of guidance and persuasion, which responds to the inevitable temptations to misunderstand with an examination of particular cases, and which aims at getting someone to see things differently. It is not that the other has to guess the vital thing, but that it is actually through coming to see the particular cases in a new way that we will achieve the change of vision which constitutes the shift in understanding. This understanding is expressed, not in doctrines, but in a change of attitude which is connected with the emergence of a concern with what lies open to view in the concrete details of our practice of using expressions, and with the abandonment of the attempt to construct elucidations or speculative accounts. This not only makes the *Investigations* difficult to understand, it makes it exceptionally difficult to write about.

References and Further Reading

Anscombe, G.E.M., 1969, 'On the Form of Wittgenstein's Writing', in R. Kiblansky, ed., *Contemporary Philosophy: A Survey*, vol. 3 (Florence: La Nuova Italia), pp. 373–78

Baker, G., 2006a '*Philosophical Investigations* section 122: neglected aspects', in G. Baker, 2006:22–51

___, 2006b, 'Wittgenstein's "Depth Grammar"', in G. Baker, 2006:73–91

___, 2006c, 'Wittgenstein on Metaphysical/Everyday Use', in G. Baker, 2006:92–107

Baker, G. and Hacker, P.M.S., 2009, *Wittgenstein: Understanding and Meaning*, second edition (Oxford: Wiley Blackwell)

Binkley, T., 1973, *Wittgenstein's Language* (The Hague: Martinus Nijhoff)

Bouveresse, J., 1992, '"The Darkness of this Time": Wittgenstein and the Modern World', in A. Phillips Griffiths, ed., 1992:11–40

Cavell, S., 1966, 'The Availability of Wittgenstein's Later Philosophy', in G. Pitcher, ed., 1966: 151–85; reprinted in S. Cavell, 2002:44–72

___, 1988, 'Declining Decline: Wittgenstein as a Philosopher of Culture', *Inquiry*, vol. 31:253–64

Connant, J., 2011, 'Wittgenstein's Methods', in O. Kuusela and M. McGinn, eds, 2011:620–45

Fann, K.T., 1969, *Wittgenstein's Conception of Philosophy* (Oxford: Wiley Blackwell)

___, ed., 1978, *Ludwig Wittgenstein: The Man and His Philosophy* (Hassocks: Harvester Press)

Fogelin, R.J., 2009, *Taking Wittgenstein at his Word: A Textual Study* (Princeton: Princeton University Press)

Gasking, D.A.T. and Jackson, A.C., 1978, 'Wittgenstein as Teacher', in K.T. Fann, ed., 1978:49–55

Genova, J., 1995, *Wittgenstein: A Way of Seeing* (London: Routledge)

Grayling, A., 1988, *Wittgenstein* (Oxford: Oxford University Press)

Hacker, P.M.S., 1972, *Insight and Illusion* (Oxford: Clarendon Press)

Heal, J., 1995, 'Wittgenstein and Dialogue', in T. Smiley, ed., *Philosophical Dialogues: Plato, Hume, Wittgenstein*, *Proceedings of the British Academy* (Oxford: Oxford University Press)

Heller, E., 1978, 'Wittgenstein: Unphilosophical Notes', in K.T. Fann, ed., 1978:89–106

Hilmy, S., 1987, *The Later Wittgenstein: The Emergence of a New Philosophical Method* (Oxford: Wiley Blackwell)

___, 1991, '"Tormenting Questions" in *Philosophical Investigations* section 133', in R.L. Arrington and H.-J. Glock, eds, 1991:89–104

Hughes, J., 1989, 'Philosophy and Style: Wittgenstein and Russell', *Philosophy and Literature*, vol. 13:332–39

Kenny, A., 1984, 'Wittgenstein on the Nature of Philosophy', in *The Legacy of Wittgenstein* (Oxford: Wiley Blackwell), pp. 38–60

Kuusela, O., 2008 *The Struggle Against Dogmatism: Wittgenstein and the Concept of Philosophy*, (Cambridge, Mass.: Harvard University Press)

McGinn, M., 2011, 'Grammar in the *Philosophical Investigations*', in O. Kuusela and M. McGinn, eds, 2011:646–66

Minar, E., 1995, 'Feeling at Home in the Language (what makes reading the Philosophical Investigations possible?)', *Synthèse*, vol. 102:413–52

Rowe, M.W, 1991, 'Goethe and Wittgenstein', *Philosophy*, vol. 66:283–303; reprinted in M.W. Rowe, 2004:1–21

___, 1994, 'Wittgenstein's Romantic Inheritance', *Philosophy*, vol. 69:327–51; reprinted in M.W. Rowe, 2004:46–72

———, 2007, 'Wittgenstein, Plato, and the Historical Socrates', *Philosophy*, vol.82:45–85

Savickey, B., 1990, 'Voices in Wittgenstein's Philosophical Investigations', MPhil thesis, Cambridge University

———, 1999, *Wittgenstein's Art of Grammatical Investigation* (London: Routledge)

———, 2011, 'Wittgenstein's Use of Examples', in O. Kuusela and M. McGinn, eds, 2011:667–96

Stern, D.G., 2004, '*Wittgenstein's Philosophical Investigations* (Cambridge: Cambridge University Press)

Wittgenstein, L., 'Philosophy', in *BT*, pp. 299–318

Discussion Questions

1. What are the two principal topics of *Philosophical Investigations*?
2. According to McGinn, the peculiar form of the text reflects the unique philosophical method of Wittgenstein. How does the textual form shape the philosophical method?
3. Do you think many of philosophical problems can be examined by investigating the ways in which we use languages? What do we aim at discovering in linguistic investigation?
4. Wittgenstein's grammatical investigation employs language-game as the key component of study. Language-game is described as the whole of language and the activities involving language. Recall a time in your childhood when you first learned a word or phrase. Did you learn them by learning how to use them in a proper context accompanied with appropriate behaviors?
5. According to Wittgenstein, "philosophical problems are solved through an insight into the workings of our language." By "insight" Wittgenstein may have meant the psychology of language users in terms of the intentions and purpose of communication. Do you think language is transparent enough to mirror what is meant by the human person? Can we answer the philosophical problems by understanding the mental states of persons?

UNIT V

MAKING SENSE OF HUMANITY

In the seventeenth chapter, Peggy Jones introduces the first two hexagrams from the *I Ching*, explaining how each hexagram is constructed out of two trigrams and what each of the six lines indicates in the unceasing cycles of change. In the eighteenth chapter, chosen from the first book of the *Nicomachean Ethics*, Aristotle presents the goal of human life in terms of fulfilling the uniquely human functions throughout the entire life, suggesting that happiness is an arduous process of cumulating activities in accordance with rational human virtues. In the nineteenth chapter, Allen Wood discusses alienation as the capitalistic usurpation of human freedom in two senses—spiritual deprivation of self-determination on the one hand and political-economic deprivation as lack of control in one's social relations on the other. In the last chapter, Ray Billington offers a refreshing outlook on Taoism as an enlightening strand of spirituality that wholeheartedly embraces the here-and-now, earth-bound, heaven-gazing human life and in so doing allowing us to embody the eternal Way (Tao) and cultivate it in our spontaneous human virtues.

The Hexagrams

Peggy Jones

1. Ch'ien/The Creative, Heaven

———
———
———
———
———
———

Primary Trigrams
above *Ch'ien* / The Creative, Heaven
below *Ch'ien* / The Creative, Heaven

Nuclear Trigrams
above *Ch'ien* / The Creative, Heaven
below *Ch'ien* / The Creative, Heaven

In human life, the Creative works to activate, to engender, to inspire. It raises our energy level and expands and extends our capacities. This energy is bright and sharp, often impatient with the requirements or details of a process. In fact, when we or the atmosphere around us are charged with this pure, yang energy, there may be a sense almost of invulnerability, even God-likeness. For this reason, there may well be a considerable degree of resistance to the limits imposed by human life and the conditions of the world. The process of transformation may have its roots in the Creative, but unless our awareness also undergoes an expansion the net result of such a time could be no more than the after-glow of a beautiful fireworks display.

The construction of the hexagram consists of the trigram *Ch'ien* repeated in both upper and lower positions. Both nuclear trigrams are also *Ch'ien*. This construction represents the timeless, undivided, unconditioned force of creativity. As such, it is not any thing, and is unable to become some thing without being received, modified, and given form. At that point time enters the picture as the medium, the dimension through which creativity and transformation occur. The Creative is continuous; it does not have a resting state. It is a dynamic constant, the energy of which finds expression in the innumerable finite forms that have arisen since the universe came into being. Thus, it permeates, activates, and is identical with every living thing, every process, every experience. The Creative, seamlessly and dynamically embracing and embraced by the Receptive (see *K'un,* below), each carrying the seed of the other within, constitutes Life, eternal and unopposed.

As noted above, this hexagram is constructed of six yang lines. While no balance exists in this structure, the powerful dynamic at its heart constitutes the process of life seeking manifestation. We cannot know what came before, or what will follow, whether 'constructive' or 'destructive'. Our part in the overall picture is also an unknown. None the less, when we are gripped by the need to express our creativity—to allow the Creative to express itself through us—it is unlikely to be either easy or comfortable. Whatever the area to which we feel drawn, compromise is not an option and will never satisfy us. We express our humanity and our individuality most fully in the creative act and the lack of a connection to, or channel for, our creativity can be deeply distressing.

Ch'ien is a calendar hexagram representing the fourth month of the Chinese year, May–June. In the northern hemisphere the sun is at its height and the daylight hours are at their maximum. The calendar hexagram that follows *Ch'ien* is 44, *Kou/Coming To Meet,* where a yielding line re-enters at the bottom of the hexagram indicating the beginning of the darkening of the light as the year's cycle turns towards autumn.

The Changing Lines

Dragons are associated with the trigram *Ch'ien,* and the six places of the hexagram are seen as the six dragons, or steps, that lead to wisdom and the fulfilment of the Tao. Dragons are fabulous and dangerous, wonderful, fascinating, potentially arrogant, and charismatic. They represent the untamed condition of raw energy. The changing lines picture the taming of the dragon in that they reflect the process of transformation from yang to yin. The interaction of the Receptive (see the next hexagram, *K'un)* and the Creative creates a powerful dynamic; consequently, each of the changing lines represents an exceptional time.

9/1st   In order for the tremendous potential of the Creative to be realized, it must be channelled through a form, an individual, a life. We could almost say it must open itself to doubt about its own perfection or purity; it must open to the Other. It is when we are most self-assured and confident of our direction and our goals that we are most vulnerable to the entry of radical challenge from the least expected direction—and most in need of it.

9/2nd   Too much agreement or homogeneity leaves no space for the creativity that derives from variety and challenge. Where a lively dialectic exists, there is the possibility of wholly new ideas emerging. We must be prepared to welcome dissent, passion, argument, and frustration if we wish for new visions to arise and inspire or teach us.

9/3rd   At the growing edge of our lives there is so much to learn and we have so little experience that we may find ourselves faced with the choice between dissembling, which can require a lot of energy to sustain, and simply throwing ourselves into the moment, admitting our ignorance and accepting guidance when it is genuinely offered. The lack of pretension and freshness of this path, as long as it is not contrived or calculated to elicit a particular response, is unlikely to meet with rejection or rebuff. This is not a counsel for lack of consideration of others; rather, it is for the release of any attachment we might have to our self-image or self-importance.

9/4th   In the context of this hexagram, the fourth position represents an opportunity for a conscious re-balancing of our priorities. There are times in life when we have little freedom of choice, particularly when we are children; but we rarely imagine or recognize how open the world is to us and how much effect we can have if we are prepared to work hard. The clue is to start now, with quiet determination, to take the first small step and then the next and the next, trusting that the strength to carry on will be there when we need it

9/5th   The image associated with this line is that of a dragon flying in the sky. For the Chinese, the dragon represented all things charged with mystery and extraordinary potency. The dragon was one of the four magic animals capable of transformation and was associated with great good fortune. Its abode was the heavens. If we attempt to translate this into human terms it is bound to be difficult, as it reaches beyond all ordinary boundaries and definitions. It suggests a wild and glorious capacity for life, freed from the burden of fear, and limitless in its joy. How we apply this to ourselves is for each of us to discover.

9/top   While this firm line at the highest point of the hexagram of Heaven has been associated with arrogance, a more thoughtful reading might consider the significance of finding oneself as far from the dark of earth as it is possible to be. There is no further one can go in this direction, the only way forward is down into just the area where our deepest fears reside, the realm of the physical, of earth, of ordinary collective existence. If a person does not know how to let go and be re-absorbed, but insists on always pressing forward, there will be a hard lesson to learn. All things turn into their opposite in time; that is how time and transformation work, and learning this lesson is a first step towards wisdom.

When all the lines are nines: the hexagram will then change into *K'un*, Earth, The Receptive. By its very nature *Ch'ien* is a guiding and moving force, but is not itself visible or manifest; its effect is made visible, made manifest through the birth of all forms and creatures out of its union with *K'un,* Earth, The Receptive.

2. K'un/The Receptive, Earth

```
== ==
== ==
== ==
== ==
== ==
== ==
```

Primary Trigrams
above *K'un*/The Receptive, Earth
below *K'un*/The Receptive, Earth

Nuclear Trigrams
above *K'un*/The Receptive, Earth
below *K'un*/The Receptive, Earth

K'un is a calendar hexagram representing the ninth month, November–December. In the northern hemisphere it is the season of the year when the days are shortest and growth appears to have ceased. All is quiet. All four trigrams that constitute the hexagram are *K'un*. There are no light yang lines. This is the opposite of the month represented by *Ch'ien,* May–June, where there are no dark, yin lines remaining in the hexagram. (See Hexagram 1, *Ch'ien*/The Creative, above.)

The relationship of the Receptive to the Creative is best illustrated not by words, but by the Taoist symbol, t'ai chi (Wilhelm, 1989, p. lv), which represents the complementarity of the two within an overall unity: a circle encloses two interlocking embryonic forms, one black, the other white. Within the black lies a white 'eye' and within the white lies a black 'eye'. The Creative and the Receptive, Yang and Yin, interpenetrate each other and are indivisible. Therefore, if we wish to discuss them we should always strive to remember that the separation is artificial, a necessary dualistic trick to enable us to explore the two energies.

If *Ch'ien* is Life as infinite creative energy, *K'un* is Life as limitless capacity, boundless receptivity. As the vessel, albeit a limitless one, *K'un* forms a bridge to the temporal. Everything we can sense or measure, think or touch, space, and the relationships between, and juxtaposition of, objects, animals, people, events, all of this is shaped within the vessel of the Receptive. However, it is the interpenetration of *Ch'ien* and K'un that gives rise to these forms. The hexagrams, with their undifferentiated and homogenous structure, must effect an exchange for the six foundation trigrams, the representatives of all possible forms, to come into being and, from them, the sixty-two hexagrams that follow.

This hexagram represents a particular energy (which is more like a field or a principle) in its pure state, a state that does not exist in nature, as emphasized above. It cannot exist in human beings either, because human life is conditioned and conditioned life is shaped by the opposites.

However, with these provisos in mind, we can consider how the time and conditions reflected in the hexagram might affect our lives. The season represented is late autumn, early winter, a time when the processes of the earth, which is represented by *K'un,* continue out of sight. When such a time occurs in our lives we must learn to trust the health of the 'seeds' that have been planted within us, to be patient with gradual growth and development, to be content, for the time being, with nurturing ourselves and the world in a very grounded way, using our intuition and feelings to perceive where our efforts are best directed, not wearing ourselves out with trying to make something happen.

On the other hand, the lack of differentiation in the hexagram may point to a lack of balance, excessive passivity or an absence of complementarity. Life cannot begin, leave alone thrive, without intercourse and, if we are over-identified with the Receptive position, we may resist the focusing and choosing that is necessary if we are to advance on our particular, individual path.

The Changing Lines

In the context of a time of rest and receptivity, the changing lines introduce an altogether different energy, representing or reminding us of the dynamic process of transformation. In each position, the penetration of a yang line and yang energy into the situation pictured in the hexagram creates an opportunity for greater consciousness and awareness of self and cosmos.

6/1st   Initial conditions, the beginnings of things, are critical to how events proceed and their outcome. The times require receptivity and complete openness, and the more we can put to one side our ideas about how things should be or what we want from the future, the more ripe will we be to receive fresh ideas or to recognize new possibilities. We forget so quickly that every moment is a 'first-time' moment that has never existed before; the seeds we plant today have never been planted before. If we did remember, we would act and choose with more care and more joy. But every moment also offers us a new opportunity to wake up. In the words of Rumi (Barks & Moyne, 1995):

> The breeze at dawn has secrets to tell you.
> Don't go back to sleep.

6/2nd   All things natural fulfil themselves by becoming what they are. This may seem obvious, but if we reflect upon it further it leads us deeper and deeper into the question of what we truly are. The Zen *koan*—What is your original face?—leads to the same area of paradox and mystery. When we talk about our personal 'flow' or 'journey' we are in the same area. How do we know what it is? How do we find it? How do we become, each of us, that which we are?

6/3rd   The human mind is remarkable; we have no idea how much it is capable of as we only use a fraction of it. The uses we do make of it are potentially more within our control than we are generally aware. Calming the mind, focusing it, expanding its field of awareness, disciplining it, exercising it: we can all learn ways of owning and managing the movements of our minds and increasing our consciousness if we apply ourselves.

6/4th   This yielding line in a yielding position signifies a time when the energies of Earth are most deeply at rest and impenetrable, a time of contraction and darkness appropriate to the moment. Under these circumstances, if we feel suddenly moved to strong action, we should consider our motives and goals. The attraction of activity and focus is great when there is not much going on; sustained commitment to a particular course requires more than just temporary enthusiasm.

6/5th   The fifth position holds a particular prominence in the hexagrams, often representing the ideal response to a given set of conditions. In this case, yielding and remaining open is exemplary; however, nothing remains the same for long and when a different—firmer, more clearly defined or determined—course of thought or action is indicated it will be important to recognize how far-reaching the effects of our choice might be. We should not allow ourselves to choose in a superficial or reckless way.

6/top   Change is inevitable; how we respond to it is infinitely variable. No matter how many times we go through the cycle of beginnings, middles, and ends in life, we will still find ourselves balking at change when it pushes us into the unknown or forces us to accept that which feels unacceptable. Each of us represents a small but unique part of the whole of creation at every moment. The significance of our choices may be unfathomable, but it is not inconsequential.

Discussion Questions

1. A hexagram is a pair of two trigrams out of eight. What does each of the eight trigrams represent?
2. How is primal arrangement of the trigrams different from inner-world arrangement? How are the complementary but opposing forces of yin and yang explained in each arrangement?
3. What are the two trigrams that make up the first hexagram Ch'ien (the heaven)? How does this hexagram represent the creative force of the universe?
4. What are the two trigrams that make up the hexagram K'un (earth)? How does this hexagram represent the boundless receptivity?
5. How reasonable is the ancient thought that the changes in the universe can be represented in terms of the patterns of the sixty-four hexagrams? Is change the only invariable law of the universe, of which the course we humans can hardly fathom?

Nicomachean Ethics

Book I

Aristotle; trans. Terence Irwin

[Happiness]

1

[Ends and Goods]

§1 Every craft and every line of inquiry, and likewise every action and decision, seems to seek some good;* that is why some people were right to describe the good as what everything seeks.* §2 But the ends [that are sought] appear to differ; some are activities, and others are products apart from the activities.* Wherever there are ends apart from the actions, the products are by nature better than the activities.

§3 Since there are many actions, crafts, and sciences, the ends turn out to be many as well; for health is the end of medicine, a boat of boat building, victory of generalship, and wealth of household management. §4 But some of these pursuits are subordinate to some one capacity; for instance, bridle making and every other science producing equipment for horses are subordinate to horsemanship, while this and every action in warfare are, in turn, subordinate to generalship, and in the same way other pursuits are subordinate to further ones.* In all such cases, then,* the ends of the ruling sciences are more choiceworthy than all the ends subordinate to them, since the lower ends are also pursued for the sake of the higher. §5 Here it does not matter whether the ends of the actions are the activities themselves, or something apart from them, as in the sciences we have mentioned.

2

[The Highest Good and Political Science]

§1 Suppose, then, that the things achievable by action have some end that we wish for because of itself, and because of which we wish for the other things, and that we do not choose everything because of something else—for if we do, it will go on without limit, so that desire will prove to be empty and futile. Clearly, this end will be the good, that is to say, the best good.*

§2 Then does knowledge of this good carry great weight for [our] way of life, and would it make us better able, like archers who have a target to aim at, to hit the right mark?* §3 If so, we should try to grasp, in outline at any rate, what the good is, and which is its proper science or capacity.

§4 It seems proper to the most controlling science—the highest ruling science.* §5 And this appears characteristic of political science. §6 For it is the one that prescribes which of the sciences ought to be studied in cities, and which ones each class in the city should learn, and how far; indeed we see that even the most honored capacities—generalship, household management, and rhetoric, for instance—are subordinate to it. §7 And since it uses the other sciences concerned with action,* and moreover legislates what must be done and what avoided, its end will include the ends of the other sciences, and so this will be the human good. §8 For even if the good is the same for a city as for an individual, still the good of the city is apparently a greater and more complete good to acquire and preserve. For while it is satisfactory to acquire and preserve the good even for an individual, it is finer and more divine to acquire and preserve it for a people and for cities.* And so, since our line of inquiry seeks these [goods, for an individual and for a community], it is a sort of political science.*

3

[The Method of Political Science]

Our discussion will be adequate if we make things perspicuous enough to accord with the subject matter; for we would not seek the same degree of exactness in all sorts of arguments alike, any more than in the products of different crafts.* §2 Now, fine and just things, which political science examines, differ and vary so much as to seem to rest on convention only, not on nature.* §3 But [this is not a good reason, since] goods also vary in the same way, because they result in harm to many people—for some have been destroyed because of their wealth, others because of their bravery.* §4 And so, since this is our subject and these are our premises, we shall be satisfied to indicate the truth roughly and in outline; since our subject and our premises are things that hold good usually [but not universally], we shall be satisfied to draw conclusions of the same sort.

Each of our claims, then, ought to be accepted in the same way [as claiming to hold good usually]. For the educated person seeks exactness in each area to the extent that the nature of the subject allows; for apparently it is just as mistaken to demand demonstrations from a rhetorician as to accept [merely] persuasive arguments from a mathematician.* §5 Further, each person judges rightly what he knows, and is a good judge about that; hence the good judge in a given area is the person educated in that area, and the unqualifiedly good judge is the person educated in every area.

This is why a youth is not a suitable student of political science; for he lacks experience of the actions in life, which are the subject and premises of our arguments. §6 Moreover, since he tends to follow his feelings, his study will be futile and useless; for the end [of political science] is action, not knowledge.* §7 It does not matter whether he is young in years or immature in character, since the deficiency does not depend on age, but results from following his feelings in his life and in a given pursuit; for an immature person, like an incontinent person, gets no benefit from his knowledge. But for those who accord with reason in forming their desires and in their actions, knowledge of political science will be of great benefit.

§8 These are the preliminary points about the student, about the way our claims are to be accepted, and about what we propose to do.*

4

[Common Beliefs]

Let us, then, begin again.* Since every sort of knowledge and decision* pursues some good, what is the good that we say political science seeks? What, [in other words,] is the highest of all the goods achievable in action?

§2 As far as its name goes, most people virtually agree; for both the many and the cultivated call it happiness, and they suppose that living well and doing well are the same as being happy.* But they disagree about what happiness is, and the many do not give the same answer as the wise.*

§3 For the many think it is something obvious and evident—for instance, pleasure, wealth, or honor. Some take it to be one thing, others another. Indeed, the same person often changes his mind; for when he has fallen ill, he thinks happiness is health, and when he has fallen into poverty, he thinks it is wealth. And when they are conscious of their own ignorance, they admire anyone who speaks of something grand and above their heads. [Among the wise,] however, some used to think that besides these many goods there is some other good that exists in its own right and that causes all these goods to be goods.*

§4 Presumably, then, it is rather futile to examine all these beliefs, and it is enough to examine those that are most current or seem to have some argument for them.

§5 We must notice, however, the difference between arguments from principles and arguments toward principles.* For indeed Plato was right to be puzzled about this, when he used to ask if [the argument] set out from the principles or led toward them*—just as on a race course the path may go from the starting line to the far end,* or back again. For we should certainly begin from things known, but things are known in two ways;* for some are known to us, some known without qualification. Presumably, then, *we* ought to begin from things known to *us*.

§6 That is why we need to have been brought up in fine habits if we are to be adequate students of fine and just things, and of political questions generally. §7 For we begin from the [belief] that [something is true]; if this is apparent enough to us, we can begin without also [knowing] why [it is true].* Someone who is well brought up has the beginnings, or can easily acquire them.* Someone who neither has them nor can acquire them should listen to Hesiod:* 'He who grasps everything himself is best of all; he is noble also who listens to one who has spoken well; but he who neither grasps it himself nor takes to heart what he hears from another is a useless man.'

5

[The Three Lives]

But let us begin again from the point from which we digressed.* For, it would seem, people quite reasonably reach their conception of the good, i.e., of happiness, from the lives [they lead]; §2 for there are roughly three most favored lives: the lives of gratification, of political activity, and, third, of study.*

The many, the most vulgar, would seem to conceive the good and happiness as pleasure, and hence they also like the life of gratification. §3 In this they appear completely slavish, since the life they decide on is a life for grazing animals.* Still, they have some argument in their defense, since many in positions of power feel as Sardanapallus* felt, [and also choose this life].

§4 The cultivated people, those active [in politics], conceive the good as honor, since this is more or less the end [normally pursued] in the political life. This, however, appears to be too superficial to be what we are seeking;* for it seems to depend more on those who honor than on the one honored, whereas we intuitively believe that the good is something of our own and hard to take from us.* §5 Further, it would seem, they pursue honor to convince themselves that they are good; at any rate, they seek to be honored by prudent people, among people who know them, and for virtue. It is clear, then, that—in their view at any rate—virtue is superior [to honor].

§6 Perhaps, indeed, one might conceive virtue more than honor to be the end of the political life. However, this also is apparently too incomplete [to be the good]. For it seems possible for someone to possess virtue but be asleep or inactive throughout his life, and, moreover, to suffer the worst evils and misfortunes. If this is the sort of life he leads, no one would count him happy, except to defend a philosopher's paradox.* Enough about this, since it has been adequately discussed in the popular works* as well.

§7 The third life is the life of study, which we shall examine in what follows.*

§8 The moneymaker's life is in a way forced on him [not chosen for itself];* and clearly wealth is not the good we are seeking, since it is [merely] useful, [choiceworthy only] for some other end. Hence one would be more inclined to suppose that [any of] the goods mentioned earlier is the end, since they are liked for themselves. But apparently they are not [the end] either; and many arguments have been presented against them.* Let us, then, dismiss them.

6

[The Platonic Form of the Good]

Presumably, though, we had better examine the universal good, and puzzle out what is meant in speaking of it.* This sort of inquiry is, to be sure, unwelcome to us, because those who intro-duced the Forms were friends* of ours; still, it presumably seems better, indeed only right, to destroy even what is close to us if that is the way to preserve truth. We must especially do this as philosophers, [lovers of wisdom]; for though we love both the truth and our friends, reverence is due to the truth first.

§2 Those who introduced this view did not mean to produce an Idea for any [series] in which they spoke of prior and posterior [members];* that was why they did not mean to establish an Idea [of number] for [the series of] numbers. But the good is spoken of both in what-it-is [that is, substance], and in quality and relative;* and what exists in its own right, that is, substance, is by nature prior to the relative,* since a relative would seem to be an appendage and coincident of being. And so there is no common Idea over these.

§3 Further, good is spoken of in as many ways as being [is spoken of]:* in what-it-is, as god and mind;* in quality, as the virtues; in quantity, as the measured amount; in relative, as the useful; in time, as the opportune moment; in place, as the [right] situation; and so on. Hence it is clear that the good cannot be some common and single universal; for if it were, it would be spoken of in only one [of the types of] predication, not in them all.

§4 Further, if a number of things have a single Idea, there is also a single science of them; hence [if there were an Idea of good] there would also be some single science of all goods. But, in fact, there are many sciences even of the goods under one [type of] predication; for the science of the opportune moment, for instance, in war is generalship, in disease medicine. And similarly the science of the measured amount in food is medicine, in exertion gymnastics. [Hence there is no single science of the good, and so no Idea.]

§5 One might be puzzled about what [the believers in Ideas] really mean in speaking of the So-and-So Itself,* since Man Itself and man* have one and the same account of man; for insofar as each is man, they will not differ at all. If that is so, then [Good Itself and good have the same account of good]; hence they also will not differ at all insofar as each is good, [hence there is no point in appealing to Good Itself].

§6 Moreover, Good Itself will be no more of a good by being eternal; for a white thing is no whiter if it lasts a long time than if it lasts a day.

§7 The Pythagoreans would seem to have a more plausible view about the good, since they place the One in the column of goods. Indeed, Speusippus seems to have followed them. §8 But let us leave this for another discussion.

A dispute emerges, however, about what we have said, because the arguments [in favor of the Idea] are not concerned with every sort of good. Goods pursued and liked in their own right are spoken of as one species of goods, whereas those that in some way tend to produce or preserve these goods, or to prevent their contraries, are spoken of as goods because of these and in a different way. §9 Clearly, then, goods are spoken of in two ways, and some are goods in their own right, and others goods because of these.* Let us, then, separate the goods in their own right from the [merely] useful goods, and consider whether goods in their own right correspond to a single Idea.

§10 But what sorts of goods may we take to be goods in their own right? Are they the goods that are pursued even on their own—for instance, prudence, seeing, some types of pleasures, and honors?* For even if we also pursue these because of something else, we may nonetheless take them to be goods in their own right. Alternatively, is nothing except the Idea good in its own right, so that the Form will be futile?* §11 But if these other things are also goods in their own right, then, [if there is an Idea of good,] the same account of good will have to turn up in all of them, just as the same account of whiteness turns up in snow and in chalk.* In fact, however, honor, prudence, and pleasure have different and dissimilar accounts, precisely insofar as they are goods. Hence the good is not something common corresponding to a single Idea.

§12 But how, then, is good spoken of? For it is not like homonyms resulting from chance.* Is it spoken of from the fact that goods derive from one thing or all contribute to one thing? Or is it spoken of more by analogy? For as sight is to body, so understanding is to soul, and so on for other cases.*

§13 Presumably, though, we should leave these questions for now, since their exact treatment is more appropriate for another [branch of] philosophy.* And the same is true about the Idea. For even if there is some one good predicated in common,* or some separable good, itself in its own right, clearly that is not the sort of good a human being can achieve in action or possess; but that is the sort we are looking for now.

§14 Perhaps, however, someone might think it is better to get to know the Idea with a view to the goods that we can possess and achieve in action; for [one might suppose that] if we have this as a sort of pattern, we shall also know better about the goods that are goods for us, and if we know about them, we shall hit on them. §15 This argument certainly has some plausibility, but it would seem to clash with the sciences. For each of these, though it aims at some good and seeks to supply what is lacking, leaves out knowledge of the Idea; but if the Idea were such an important aid, surely it would not be reasonable for all craftsmen to know nothing about it and not even to look for it.

§16 Moreover, it is a puzzle to know what the weaver or carpenter will gain for his own craft from knowing this Good Itself, or how anyone will be better at medicine or generalship from having gazed on the Idea Itself. For what the doctor appears to consider is not even health [universally, let alone good universally], but human health, and presumably the health of this human being even more, since he treats one particular patient at a time.*

So much, then, for these questions.

7

[An Account of the Human Good]

But let us return once again to the good we are looking for, and consider just what it could be.* For it is apparently one thing in one action or craft, and another thing in another; for it is one thing in medicine, another in generalship, and so on for the rest. What, then, is the good of each action or craft? Surely it is that for the sake of which the other things are done; in medicine this is health, in generalship victory, in house-building a house, in another case something else, but in every action and decision it is the end, since it is for the sake of the end that everyone does the other actions.* And so, if there is some end of everything achievable in action, the good achievable in action will be this end; if there are more ends than one, [the good achievable in action] will be these ends.*

§2 Our argument, then, has followed a different route to reach the same conclusion.* But we must try to make this still more perspicuous.* §3 Since there are apparently many ends, and we choose some of them (for instance, wealth, flutes, and, in general, instruments) because of something else, it is clear that not all ends are complete.* But the best good is apparently something complete. And so, if only one end is complete, the good we are looking for will be this end; if more ends than one are complete, it will be the most complete end of these.*

§4 We say that an end pursued in its own right is more complete than an end pursued because of something else, and that an end that is never choiceworthy because of something else is more complete than ends that are choiceworthy both in their own right and because of this end. Hence an end that is always choiceworthy in its own right,* never because of something else, is complete without qualification.

§5 Now happiness, more than anything else, seems complete without qualification.* For we always choose it because of itself,* never because of something else. Honor, pleasure, understanding, and every virtue we certainly choose because of themselves, since we would choose each of them even if it had no further result; but we also choose them for the sake of happiness, supposing that through them we shall be happy.* Happiness, by contrast, no one ever chooses for their sake, or for the sake of anything else at all.

§6 The same conclusion [that happiness is complete] also appears to follow from self-sufficiency. For the complete good seems to be self-sufficient.* What we count as self-sufficient is not what suffices for a solitary person by himself, living an isolated life, but what suffices also for parents, children, wife, and, in general, for friends and fellow citizens, since a human being is a naturally political [animal].* §7 Here, however, we must impose some limit; for if we extend the good to parents' parents and children's children and to friends of friends, we shall go on without limit; but we must examine this another time.

Anyhow, we regard something as self-sufficient when all by itself it makes a life choiceworthy and lacking nothing; and that is what we think happiness does. §8 Moreover, we think happiness is most choiceworthy of all goods, [since] it is not counted as one good among many.* [If it were] counted as one among many,* then, clearly, we think it would be more choiceworthy if the smallest of goods were added; for the good that is added becomes an extra quantity of goods, and the larger of two goods is always more choiceworthy.*

Happiness, then, is apparently something complete and self-sufficient, since it is the end of the things achievable in action.*

§9 But presumably the remark that the best good is happiness is apparently something [generally] agreed, and we still need a clearer statement of what the best good is.* §10 Perhaps, then, we shall find this if we first grasp the function of a human being. For just as the good, i.e., [doing] well, for a flautist, a sculptor, and every craftsman, and, in general, for whatever has a function and [characteristic] action, seems to depend on its function,* the same seems to be true for a human being, if a human being has some function.

§11 Then do the carpenter and the leather worker have their functions and actions, but has a human being no function?* Is he by nature idle, without any function?* Or, just as eye, hand, foot, and, in general, every [bodily] part apparently has its function, may we likewise ascribe to a human being some function apart from all of these?*

§12 What, then, could this be? For living is apparently shared with plants, but what we are looking for is the special function of a human being; hence we should set aside the life of nutrition and growth.* The life next in order is some sort of life of sense perception; but this too is apparently shared with horse, ox, and every animal.*

§13 The remaining possibility, then, is some sort of life of action* of the [part of the soul] that has reason.* One [part] of it has reason as obeying reason; the other has it as itself having reason and thinking.* Moreover, life is also spoken of in two ways [as capacity and as activity], and we must take [a human being's special function to be] life as activity since this seems to be called life more fully.* §14 We have found, then, that the human function is activity of the soul in accord with reason or requiring reason.*

Now we say that the function of a [kind of thing]—of a harpist, for instance—is the same in kind as the function of an excellent individual of the kind—of an excellent harpist, for instance. And the same is true without qualification in every case, if we add to the function the superior achievement in accord with the virtue; for the function of a harpist is to play the harp, and the function of a good harpist is to play it well.* Moreover, we take the human function to be a certain kind of life, and take this life to be activity and actions of the soul that involve reason; hence the function of the excellent man is to do this well and finely.

§15 Now each function is completed well by being completed in accord with the virtue proper [to that kind of thing].* And so the human good proves to be activity of the soul in accord with virtue,* and indeed with the best and most complete virtue, if there are more virtues than one.* §16 Moreover, in a complete life.* For one swallow does not make a spring, nor does one day; nor, similarly, does one day or a short time make us blessed and happy.

§17 This, then, is a sketch of the good; for, presumably, we must draw the outline first, and fill it in later.* If the sketch is good, anyone, it seems, can advance and articulate it, and in such cases time discovers more, or is a good partner in discovery. That is also how the crafts have improved, since anyone can add what is lacking [in the outline].

§18 We must also remember our previous remarks, so that we do not look for the same degree of exactness in all areas, but the degree that accords with a given subject matter and is proper to a given line of inquiry.* §19 For the carpenter's and the geometer's inquiries about the right angle are different also; the carpenter restricts himself to what helps his work, but the geometer inquires into what, or what sort* of thing, the right angle is, since he studies the truth. We must do the same, then, in other areas too, [seeking the proper degree of exactness], so that digressions do not overwhelm our main task.

§20 Nor should we make the same demand for an explanation in all cases. On the contrary, in some cases it is enough to prove rightly that [something is true, without also explaining why it is true]. This is so, for instance, with principles, where the fact that [something is true] is the first thing, that is to say, the principle.*

§21 Some principles are studied by means of induction, some by means of perception, some by means of some sort of habituation, and others by other means.* §22 In each case we should try to find them out by means suited to their nature, and work hard to define them rightly. §23 For they carry great weight* for what follows; for the principle seems to be more than half the whole,* and makes evident the answer to many of our questions.

8

[Defense of the Account of the Good]

We should examine the principle, however, not only from the conclusion and premises [of a deduction], but also from what is said about it;* for all the facts harmonize with a true account, whereas the truth soon clashes with a false one.*

§2 Goods are divided, then, into three types, some called external, some goods of the soul, others goods of the body.* We say that the goods of the soul are goods most fully, and more than the others, and we take actions and activities of the soul to be [goods] of the soul. And so our account [of the good] is right, to judge by this belief anyhow—and it is an ancient belief, and accepted by philosophers.

§3 Our account is also correct in saying that some sort of actions and activities are the end; for in that way the end turns out to be a good of the soul, not an external good.

§4 The belief that the happy person lives well and does well also agrees with our account, since we have virtually said that the end is a sort of living well and doing well.

§5 Further, all the features that people look for in happiness appear to be true of the end described in our account.* §6 For to some people happiness seems to be virtue; to others prudence; to others some sort of wisdom; to others again it seems to be these, or one of these, involving pleasure or requiring it to be added;* others add in external prosperity as well. §7 Some of these views are traditional, held by many, while others are held by a few men who are widely esteemed. It is reasonable for each group not to be completely wrong, but to be correct on one point at least, or even on most points.

§8 First, our account agrees with those who say happiness is virtue [in general] or some [particular] virtue; for activity in accord with virtue is proper to virtue. §9 Presumably, though, it matters quite a bit whether we suppose that the best good consists in possessing or in using—that is to say, in a state or in an activity [that actualizes the state].* For someone may be in a state that achieves no good—if, for instance, he is asleep or inactive in some other way—but this cannot be true of the activity; for it will necessarily act and act well. And just as Olympic prizes are not for the finest and strongest, but for the contestants—since it is only these who win—the same is true in life; among the fine and good people, only those who act correctly* win the prize.

§10 Moreover, the life of these active people is also pleasant in itself.* For being pleased is a condition of the soul, [and hence is included in the activity of the soul]. Further, each type of person finds pleasure in whatever he is called a lover of; a horse, for instance, pleases the horse-lover, a spectacle the lover of spectacles. Similarly, what is just pleases the lover of justice, and in general what accords with virtue pleases the lover of virtue.

§11 Now the things that please most people conflict,* because they are not pleasant by nature, whereas the things that please lovers of the fine are things pleasant by nature. Actions in accord with virtue are pleasant by nature, so that they both please lovers of the fine and are pleasant in their own right.

§12 Hence these people's life does not need pleasure to be added [to virtuous activity] as some sort of extra decoration; rather, it has its pleasure within itself.* For besides the reasons already given, someone who does not enjoy fine actions is not good; for no one would call a person just, for instance, if he did not enjoy doing just actions, or generous if he did not enjoy generous actions, and similarly for the other virtues.

§13 If this is so, actions in accord with the virtues are pleasant in their own right. Moreover, these actions are good and fine as well as pleasant; indeed, they are good, fine, and pleasant more than anything else is, since on this question the excellent person judges rightly, and his judgment agrees with what we have said.

§14 Happiness, then, is best, finest, and most pleasant, and the Delian inscription is wrong to distinguish these things: 'What is most just is finest; being healthy is most beneficial; but it is most pleasant to win our heart's desire.'* For all three features are found in the best activities, and we say happiness is these activities, or [rather] one of them, the best one.*

§15 Nonetheless, happiness evidently also needs external goods to be added, as we said, since we cannot, or cannot easily, do fine actions if we lack the resources.* For, first of all, in many actions we use friends, wealth, and political power just as we use instruments. §16 Further, deprivation of certain [externals]—for instance, good birth, good children, beauty—mars our blessedness. For we do not altogether have the character of happiness* if we look utterly repulsive or are ill-born, solitary, or childless; and we have it even less, presumably, if our children or friends are totally bad, or were good but have died.

§17 And so, as we have said, happiness would seem to need this sort of prosperity added also. That is why some people identify happiness with good fortune, and others identify it with virtue.

9

[How Is Happiness Achieved?]

This also leads to a puzzle: Is happiness acquired by learning, or habituation, or by some other form of cultivation? Or is it the result of some divine fate, or even of fortune?*

§2 First, then, if the gods give any gift at all to human beings, it is reasonable for them to give us happiness more than any other human good, insofar as it is the best of human goods. §3 Presumably, however, this question is more suitable for a different inquiry.

But even if it is not sent by the gods, but instead results from virtue and some sort of learning or cultivation, happiness appears to be one of the most divine things, since the prize and goal of virtue appears to be the best good, something divine and blessed. §4 Moreover [if happiness comes in this way] it will be widely shared; for anyone who is not deformed [in his capacity] for virtue will be able to achieve happiness through some sort of learning and attention.

§5 And since it is better to be happy in this way than because of fortune, it is reasonable for this to be the way [we become] happy. For whatever is natural is naturally in the finest state possible. §6 The same is true of the products of crafts and of every other cause, especially the best cause; and it would be seriously inappropriate to entrust what is greatest and finest to fortune.*

§7 The answer to our question is also evident from our account. For we have said that happiness is a certain sort of activity of the soul in accord with virtue, [and hence not a result of fortune]. Of the other goods, some are necessary conditions of happiness, while others are naturally useful and cooperative as instruments [but are not parts of it].

§8 Further, this conclusion agrees with our opening remarks. For we took the goal of political science to be the best good; and most of its attention is devoted to the character of the citizens, to make them good people who do fine actions.*

§9 It is not surprising, then, that we regard neither ox, nor horse, nor any other kind of animal as happy; for none of them can share in this sort of activity. §10 For the same reason a child is not happy either, since his age prevents him from doing these sorts of actions. If he is called happy, he is being congratulated [simply] because of anticipated blessedness; for, as we have said, happiness requires both complete virtue and a complete life.*

§10 It needs a complete life because life includes many reversals of fortune, good and bad, and the most prosperous person may fall into a terrible disaster in old age, as the Trojan stories tell us about Priam. If someone has suffered these sorts of misfortunes and comes to a miserable end, no one counts him happy.

10

[Can We Be Happy during Our Lifetime?]

Then should we count no human being happy during his lifetime, but follow Solon's advice to wait to see the end?* §2 But if we agree with Solon, can someone really be happy during the time after he has died? Surely that is completely absurd, especially when we say happiness is an activity.

§3 We do not say, then, that someone is happy during the time he is dead, and Solon's point is not this [absurd one], but rather that when a human being has died, we can safely pronounce [that he was] blessed [before he died], on the assumption that he is now finally beyond evils and misfortunes.* But this claim is also disputable. For if a living person has good or evil of which he is not aware, a dead person also, it seems, has good or evil, if, for instance, he receives honors or dishonors, and his children, and descendants in general, do well or suffer misfortune.*

§4 However, this conclusion also raises a puzzle. For even if someone has lived in blessed-ness until old age, and has died appropriately, many fluctuations of his descendants' fortunes may still happen to him; for some may be good people and get the life they deserve, while the contrary may be true of others, and clearly they may be as distantly related to their ancestor as you please. Surely, then, it would be an absurd result if the dead person's condition changed along with the fortunes of his descendants, so that at one time he would turn out to have been happy [in his lifetime] and at another time he would turn out to have been miserable.* §5 But it would also be absurd if the condition of descendants did not affect their ancestors at all or for any length of time.

§6 But we must return to the previous puzzle, since that will perhaps also show us the answer to our present question. §7 Let us grant that we must wait to see the end, and must then count someone blessed, not as now being blessed [during the time he is dead] but because he pre-viously was blessed. Would it not be absurd, then, if, at the very time when he is happy, we refused to ascribe truly to him the happiness he has?* Such refusal results from reluctance to call him happy during his lifetime, because of its ups and downs; for we suppose happiness is enduring and definitely not prone to fluctuate, but the same person's fortunes often turn to and fro.* §8 For clearly, if we take our cue from his fortunes, we shall often call him happy and then miserable again, thereby representing the happy person as a kind of chameleon, insecurely based.

§9 But surely it is quite wrong to take our cue from someone's fortunes. For his doing well or badly does not rest on them.* A human life, as we said, needs these added, but activities in accord with virtue control happiness, and the contrary activities control its contrary. §10 Indeed, the present puzzle is further evidence for our account [of happiness]. For no human achievement has the stability of activities in accord with virtue, since these seem to be more enduring even than our knowledge of the sciences.* Indeed, the most honorable among the virtues themselves are more enduring than the other virtues, because blessed people devote their lives to them more fully and more continually than to anything else—for this continual activity would seem to be the reason we do not forget them.

§11 It follows, then, that the happy person has the [stability] we are looking for and keeps the character he has throughout his life. For always, or more than anything else, he will do and study the actions in accord with virtue, and will bear fortunes most finely, in every way and in all conditions appropriately, since he is truly 'good, foursquare, and blameless'.*

§12 Many events, however, are subject to fortune; some are minor, some major. Hence, minor strokes of good or ill fortune clearly will not carry any weight for his life. But many major strokes of good fortune will make it more blessed; for in themselves they naturally add adornment to it, and his use of them proves to be fine and excellent.* Conversely, if he suffers many major misfortunes, they oppress and spoil his blessedness, since they involve pain and impede many activities. And yet, even here what is fine shines through, whenever someone bears many severe misfortunes with good temper, not because he feels no distress, but because he is noble and magnanimous.*

§13 And since it is activities that control life, as we said, no blessed person could ever become miserable, since he will never do hateful and base actions. For a truly good and prudent person,* we suppose, will bear strokes of fortune suitably, and from his resources at any time will do the finest actions, just as a good general will make the best use of his forces in war, and a good shoe-maker will make the finest shoe from the hides given to him, and similarly for all other craftsmen.

§14 If this is so, the happy person could never become miserable, but neither will he be blessed if he falls into misfortunes as bad as Priam's.* Nor, however, will he be inconstant and prone to fluctuate, since he will neither be easily shaken from his happiness nor shaken by just any misfortunes.* He will be shaken from it, though, by many serious misfortunes, and from these a return to happiness will take no short time. At best, it will take a long and complete length of time that includes great and fine successes.

§15 Then why not say that the happy person is the one whose activities accord with complete virtue, with an adequate supply of external goods, not for just any time but for a complete life? Or should we add that he will also go on living this way and will come to an appropriate end, since the future is not apparent to us, and we take happiness to be the end, and altogether complete in every way? §16 Given these facts [about the future and about happiness], we shall say that a living person who has, and will keep, the goods we mentioned is blessed, but blessed as a human being is.* So much for a determination of this question.

Discussion Questions

1. Why does Aristotle believe that youths are not suitable students of political science? What kind of experiences are required to study this subject?
2. How does Aristotle define human function? What is the uniquely human faculty that we are expected to develop throughout life?
3. Aristotle says that happiness is complete without qualification because we always choose to be happy because of itself not for something else. Do we pursue happiness for its sake, or do we want to be happy for something else?
4. Aristotle considers happiness as a certain sort of activity of the mind in accord with virtue. What are the virtues that are contributing to happiness? How should we use our mind in a way to promote happiness?
5. Can we be happy during our lifetime? Why or why not?

Alienation and Capitalism

Allen Wood

1 The Capitalist Division of Labor

In Chapter 1, I suggested that we should look on alienation in Marx's mature thought not as an explanatory concept but as a descriptive or diagnostic one. More specifically, I suggested provisionally that we view it as describing the condition of a person who lacks a sense of self-worth or of meaning in life, or else preserves such a sense only by being the victim of illusions or false consciousness. Chapters 2 and 3 have expounded Marx's concept of humanity or the human essence, with a view to extracting his ideas about what people require to lead meaningful or fulfilled lives, and thus about the circumstances which might cause them to be alienated in practical life. The present chapter attempts to say something about Marx's views concerning the social causes of alienation under capitalism.

Marx's thinking on this topic is rich and resists neat systematization. The account we have been developing in previous chapters, however, provides us with one route of access to it. According to Marx, what is vital for the self-worth of human beings and the meaningfulness of their lives is the development and exercise of their essential human powers, whose focus is labor or production. Because these powers are historical in character, varying from society to society and (on the whole) expanding in the course of history, the degree to which alienation is a systematic social phenomenon also varies, as a function both of what society's productive capacities are and of the extent to which the human potentialities they represent have been incorporated into the lives of actual men and women. Generally speaking, the degree of systematic, socially caused alienation in a society will be proportional to the gap which exists in that society between the human potentialities contained virtually in society's productive powers and the actualization of these potentialities by the society's members. Thus the possibilities for alienation increase along with the productive powers of society. For as these powers expand, there is more and more room for a discrepancy between what human life is and what it might be. There is more and more pressure on social arrangements to allow for the lives of individual human beings to share in the wealth of human capacities which belong to social labor.

Marx's criticisms of capitalism make it clear that he regards it as a social system in which social arrangements have failed utterly to accommodate the potentialities for self-actualization which the social powers of production have put within people's reach. According to the *Communist Manifesto*:

> The bourgeoisie during scarcely a hundred years of its rule has created productive powers more massive and colossal than all past generations together. The subjection of nature's powers, machinery, application of chemistry to industry and agriculture, steam navigation, railways, ... –what earlier century dreamed that such productive powers slumbered in the womb of social labor?[1]

In contrast to this unprecedented progress at the level of social production, capitalism has utterly failed to translate its expanded powers into expanded opportunities for individual self-actualization. It has diminished rather than increased the extent to which individual laborers, their intelligence, skills and powers, participate in the potentialities of social production, as well as sharply limiting the extent to which the laboring masses share in its fruits. As Marx puts it in *Capital*:

> Within the capitalist system all methods of raising the productive power of labor are effected at the cost of the individual laborer; ... they mutilate the laborer into a fragment of a human being, degrade him to an appendage of a machine, annihilate the content of this labor by turning it into torture; they alienate from him the mental and spiritual potentialities of the labor process in the same measure as science is incorporated into it as an independent power.[2]

How do capitalist social relations frustrate the human need for self-actualization? In the present chapter, I intend to identify two related themes in Marx's account of the way capitalism leads to alienation. But there is some risk at this point of putting too much emphasis on the philosophically interesting evils, and not enough on the drabber ones. Self-actualization and spiritual fulfillment usually do not mean much to people whose more basic physical needs are still unsatisfied. And it is an important tenet of Marx's theory that capitalism cannot exist without imposing a brutalizing poverty on a sizeable proportion of the human race. There are a number of passages in which Marx appears to be saying that the downfall of capitalism is inevitable not because under capitalism people are alienated or spiritually unfulfilled, but simply because beyond a certain point capitalism will prove incapable of supplying the working population with the basic conditions for physical survival. The bourgeoisie, he says, becomes 'incapable of ruling because it is incapable of securing its slaves even their existence within their slavery'. The proletariat will overthrow capitalism (and with it alienation) not in order to lead more fulfilling lives but merely in order to be certain of survival: 'Things have now come so far that individuals must appropriate the present totality of productive powers not only in order to achieve self-activity, but even to make their existence itself secure.'[3]

Marx does, however, identify some features of capitalist social relations which lead specifically to the crippling of people's powers and the frustration of their needs for self-actualization. One principal theme in Marx's account of the way capitalism 'robs workers of all life content' is the special manner in which it accentuates the division of labor. Modern capitalist manufacture, says Marx, is carried on increasingly by a 'collective laborer', whose actions are the carefully engineered result of the activities of many men, women and children. The labor process is carefully analyzed, its various operations are 'separated', 'isolated', 'rendered independent', and then 'laborers are classified and grouped according to their predominant properties. If their natural specificities are the basis for grafting them onto the division of labor, manufacture, once it is introduced, develops labor powers which are by nature fitted only to a one-sided special functioning.' In this way, 'the individual laborers are appropriated by a one-sided function and annexed to it for life ... The habit of a one-sided function transforms them into its unfailing organ, while their connection with the collective mechanism compels them to operate with the regularity of the parts of a machine.' Yet 'the one-sidedness and even the imperfection of the detail laborer comes to be his perfection as a member of his collective laborer.'[4]

But the process of capitalist manufacture not only deprives people of the well-rounded variety of powers and activities which they need to be full human beings; it also tends to render their specialities themselves more and more mechanical, dehumanizing in nature, less and less a matter of developed skills or powers: 'Every process of production is conditioned by certain simple manipulations of which every human being who stands and walks is capable. They too are cut off from their fluid connection with the content-possessing moments of activity and ossified into exclusive functions.'[5] Consequently, capitalist manufacture creates a positive need for mechanical, 'unskilled' labor, a need unknown to pre-capitalist handicraft manufacture: 'If it develops a one-sided specialty into a virtuosity at the cost of the whole laboring faculty, [capitalist manufacture] also makes the absence of development into a specialty.... In [capitalist] manufacture the enrichment of the collective laborer, and hence of capital, is conditioned by the impoverishment of the laborer in his individual productive powers.'[6]

It is plain that Marx blames capitalist social relations, and not the technical requirements of modern industry, for the fragmentation of human beings and the impoverishment of their individual powers. Why? Capitalist society is characterized fundamentally by the fact that the means of production are privately owned by a minority of the members of society who, acting largely independently of one another, tend to employ these means in such a way as to maximize the profit each earns on the investment. The nature of the means of production, moreover, is to a considerable extent at the discretion of this capitalist class, since their investment choices ultimately determine the selection of these means from the range of possibilities afforded by the technical capabilities of society, and even exercise a certain influence on the rate and direction of technical developments. These choices, moreover, are in the long run not arbitrary or at the mercy of individual capitalists, but are tightly constrained through competition with other capitalists by the requirement of profit maximization. Those capitalists who choose methods of production which maximize profits will survive and flourish; those who make different choices will lose their capital and the social power it represents. But the division of labor and the nature of individual laboring activity are largely determined by the means and techniques labor must employ. Hence under capitalism the factors which determine the life activities of the laboring majority are not in its hands but in the hands of a minority whose interests are opposed to its own; and the choices made by this minority are constrained by a principle (profit maximization) which is indifferent to the question whether the lives of wage laborers are rich and fulfilled or degraded and alienated. Of course it might be that self-actualizing labor and maximal profits are facilitated by the same set of productive forces and techniques; but in Volume 1, Part Four, of *Capital*, Marx argues in detail that there is no such happy coincidence, that it is just the kind of production dictated by profit maximization which has led to the alienating division of labor he describes.

Marx believes that far from being incompatible with the technical requirements of modern industry, the potentiality for varied, well-rounded human activity is inherent in modern scientific manufacture itself, and will begin to appear naturally as soon as production comes to be regulated consciously by the workers instead of being driven blindly by dead capital's vampire-like thirst for profit at the expense of human life. 'The nature of large industry', he says, 'conditions change of labor, fluidity of function, all-sided mobility of the laborer.' Every step in technical progress demonstrates this fact, by changing the laboring function required for manufacture, thus rendering whole categories of detail laborers (who have been trained only for one function) productively superfluous, and (under capitalist conditions) doing away with their only marketable skill. 'Change of labor' and 'fluidity of function' are not, however, inherently destructive or crippling. On the contrary, they represent precisely the potentiality for all-sided human development whose suppression under capitalism is a chief cause of alienation:

> But if change of labor now imposes itself as an overpowering natural law, ... large industry through its catastrophes makes it a question of life or death to recognize the change of labor and hence the greatest possible many-sidedness of the laborer as a universal law of social production, and adapt its relation to the normal actuality of this law; ... to replace the partial individual, the mere carrier of a detail function, with the totally developed individual, fit for the changing demands of labor, for whom different social functions are only so many modes of activity relieving one another.[7]

2 Capitalism and Freedom

One cause of alienation cited by Marx is the frustration or abortion of human potentialities by the capitalist division of labor. Another, perhaps even more prominent and fundamental in

Marx's account, is the way in which people under capitalism are placed in a condition of degrad-ing servitude, not merely to other human beings, but even more basically to impersonal and inhuman forces of their own creation. *The German Ideology* describes 'alienation' as 'the positing of social activity, the consolidation of our product as a real power over us, growing out of our control'.[8] *Capital* speaks of the conditions of wage labor as 'alienated from labor and confronting it independently', and of capital as 'an alienated, independent social might, which stands over against society as a thing (*Sache*)'.[9]

This use of 'alienation' is clearly an extension of Feuerbach's notion of religious alienation. In religion, according to Feuerbach, the human essence has come to be thought of by people as an alien (divine) being, which dominates them and makes them worthless (sinful) in their own eyes. The difference is that for Marx the human essence is not merely species consciousness but social labor; the alien being, the dominion and the state of worthlessness are thus not unhappy illusions but monstrous realities. In *Capital*, Marx makes the parallel with Feuerbach quite explicit: 'As in religion the human being is ruled by a botched work (*Machwerk*) of his own head, so in capitalist production he is ruled by a botched work of his own hand.'[10]

Under capitalism, production and distribution are not regulated collectively but determined by the interaction of independent individuals as private owners of commodities. This system, its apologists tell us, insures the maximum freedom of individuals to dispose of themselves and their property as they choose. Yet in capitalism, the large scale consequences of all this 'free' behavior, the market mechanism and economic system resulting from it, will fall outside anyone's control, and may react catastrophically on each or all of us in a manner which we are powerless, both individually and collectively, to prevent. This powerlessness is most noticeable in a trade crisis, when many capitalists are suddenly ruined, workers thrown out of employment, not through any natural disaster or any failure on the part of society's productive capacities, but simply by the social disaster inherent in the capitalist trade cycle. The alienating feature, however, is not just that the market system leads periodically to disastrous results. What is alienating is more basically that under capitalism human beings cannot be masters, whether individually or collectively, of their own fate, even within the sphere where that fate is a prod-uct solely of human action. As *The German Ideology* puts it: 'Their own conditions of life, their labor and with it all the conditions of existence of modern society, have become something accidental for them, over which individual proletarians have no control and over which no *social* organization can give them control.'[11]

The two themes I have identified (alienation as frustration of human self-actualization by the division of labor and alienation as the domination of social conditions over their creators) are closely related in Marx's thinking. For one thing, Marx counts the division of labor as one of the inhuman conditions over which people lack control: 'As long as there exists a cleavage between the particular and the common interest, as long, therefore, as activity is divided not freely but naturally (*nicht freiwillig, sondern naturwüchsig*), the human being's own deed becomes an alien might standing over against him, subjugating him instead of being dominated by him.'[12] People are forced into stunting and degrading forms of activity only because they lack control over the social conditions which determine the way labor is divided. From this point of view alienation as frustrated self-actualization through the capitalist division of labor can be regarded as a special case of alienation as the degradation of human beings through subjection to their own creations. But from another point of view, this subjection can also be regarded as a special case of frustrated human self-actualization. The Paris manuscripts complain that under capitalism the worker's life activity is not 'his own activity', not 'self-activity' (*Selbsttätigkeit*) but is rather the 'loss of his self' (*Verlust seiner selbst*).[13] *The German Ideology*, using a slightly different terminology, declares that the proletarian revolution will 'transform labor into self-exercise' (*Selbstbetäti-gung*), by 'producing the form of intercourse', 'the conditions of [people's] self-exercise will be produced by this self-exercise'.[14]

What does Marx mean by 'self-activity' or 'self-exercise'? I think at least part of what Marx intends to designate by them is a kind of activity or a mode of life which is consciously determined by the agent's own understanding and choice rather than being forced on him or her by alien external factors. I 'activate' or 'exercise' my 'self' when I exercise my essentially human capacity to be practically conscious of my humanity in my activity, giving the form of self-understanding and rational choice to the life I live, and making my plans and deliberations effective in shaping my life. When I do this, I 'make my life activity its own object', in that I bring that activity under my conscious control. At the same time, I 'appropriate' my own life, it comes to belong to me instead of belonging to alien forces which master me instead of being mastered by me. By subjecting human beings to the socially produced conditions of their labor, capitalism frustrates the exercise of these powers of self-understanding and self-determination, and this is part of the way in which it frustrates their self-actualization.

If this interpretation is correct, then Marx's emphasis on 'self-activity' or 'self-exercise' involves an affirmation of the value of human freedom, and belongs to a definite tradition of thinking about what this value consists in. Freedom for Marx is self-determination, the subjection of one's self and its essential functions to one's own conscious, rational choice. This concept of freedom, in such philosophers as Spinoza, Rousseau, Kant and Hegel, is given such names as 'spontaneity', 'moral liberty', 'autonomy' and 'being with oneself' (*Beisichselbstsein*). For these thinkers, as for Marx, freedom in the 'negative' sense, the absence of constraint or coercion on individuals, has value mainly because it provides the opportunity for the exercise of freedom in this deeper, 'positive' sense. Marx's adherence to this notion of freedom is explicit: to be free 'in the materialistic sense' is to be 'free not through the negative power of avoiding this and that, but through the positive might of making one's true individuality count'.[15]

In most modern thinkers before Marx, however, the conception of positive freedom is given a predominantly individualistic and moralistic interpretation. To be sure, they note that the exercise of this freedom requires the satisfaction of certain social (especially political) conditions. But they conceive self-determination itself chiefly as the inner volitional disposition of individual human agents, their mastery over their impulses and passions through rational self-knowledge and moral fortitude. Given Marx's materialist conception of human beings as socially productive beings, he cannot be content with an introverted, spiritualistic sort of self-determination. For Marx, true self-determination must rather consist in the imposition of human control on the social conditions of human production.

Marx often insists that social institutions and relations of production are not facts of nature but historically transient social forms which are the products of human activity every bit as much as wheat, cloth or machinery.[16] He does so in part to give the lie to those who would defend existing institutions by declaring them unalterable; but his purpose is also to make clear how much is required if human beings are to have genuine freedom or self-determination. If social relations are human products, then people cannot be accounted free until they create these relations with full consciousness of what they are doing. Human freedom requires not only that people should not be (as Locke says) subject to the arbitrary will of others; it requires also that the social relations in which they stand should be products of their own will. To recognize this fully is already to see through the sophistry which represents capitalist society as free because its relationships result not from coercive laws or the will of rulers but (apparently) by accident, from unregulated economic decisions made by individuals. As Marx puts it: 'In imagination (*Vorstellung*), individuals under the dominion of the bourgeoisie are freer than before, because their conditions of life are accidental to them; but in reality they are more unfree, because they are more subsumed under a reified social power (*sachliche Gewalt*).'[17]

Because freedom for Marx requires the conscious production of people's social relations, it is something which can be achieved only in community with others, and cannot be attained by retreating into oneself or by the exercise of one's self-determination within the confines of a jealously guarded 'private domain' in which society does not interfere. Yet Marx does not neglect to emphasize the complementary point that no society can be free unless it 'gives to each the social room for his essential life expression'.[18] There can be no genuine freedom unless men and women have the opportunity to exercise choice over their own lives and develop their individuality fully and freely. Marx is the consistent foe of political repression, press censorship, and other such measures which curb the free development and expression of individuals. He has only contempt for any brand of communism which would turn the state or community into 'the universal capitalist' by imposing a uniform, impoverished mode of life on all members of society alike.[19] There can be no doubt that for Marx individual liberty is necessary to a free society. But it is equally evident, to Marx at least, that the liberty proclaimed by bourgeois liberalism is not sufficient for genuine (that is, positive) freedom.

Human freedom can be attained only when people's social relations are subject to conscious human control. Therefore, it is only in communist society that people can be truly free, because human control over social relations can only be collective control, and only in communist society can this control be exercised by and for all members of society: Communism, says Marx, 'consciously treats all natural (*naturwüchsig*) presuppositions as creations of earlier human beings, divesting them of their natural character (*Naturwüchsigkeit*) and subjecting them to the might of the united individuals'. Only communist society can do this, because communist society will be a classless society, in it people will 'participate in society just as individuals. For it is the unity of individuals (of course within the presupposition of developed productive powers) which gives individuals control over the conditions for their free development and movement.'[20] Up to now, the class character of society has precluded the possibility of this unity, and hence of the freedom which can be attained only through it: 'The apparent community in which individuals have united themselves up to now always made itself into something independent over against them, and since it was always a unity of one class standing over against others, it was at the same time for the dominated class not only an illusory community, but a new fetter as well.' Further, because individual self-expression and self-actualization are possible only through the capitalist division of labor, even individual freedom will become possible only with the collective human control over people's conditions of life:

> The transformation of personal power (relations) into reified (*sachliche*) ones, ... can only be abolished by individuals subsuming these reified powers again under themselves and abolishing the division of labor. This is not possible without the community. Only within the community has each individual the means of cultivating his abilities on all sides; hence personal freedom becomes possible only within the community.[21]

Marx does not conceive of social control over the means of production as the exclusion of individuals from ownership of what they produce and use. On the contrary, it is capitalism which involves such an exclusion, since it delivers the means and objects of production over to a class of nonworkers. Communism, as Marx sees it, will be a system of 'individual property for the producer', based on 'cooperation and the possession in common of land and the means of production'.[22] The means of production must be owned collectively, because in modern industry labor is directly social, and the disposition of the means of production is always an act affecting society as a whole. Such acts, in Marx's communism, will be performed consciously. Decisions about them will be made democratically, by society as a whole, and not by a privileged class, acting contrary to the interests of the laboring majority and subject to the alien constraint of profit-maximization.

Marx's critique of capitalism is based on some familiar philosophical value conceptions, such as self-actualization and positive freedom. But it is wrong to conclude from this, as some writers on Marx appear to do, that his denunciations of capitalist alienation invoke or presuppose a conception of a future communist lifestyle or future social arrangements, and 'ideal' of what human beings could, would and should be. Marx never describes future social arrangements in detail, and the main point he makes about them is that they are bound to change in ways we cannot now foresee. Further, Marx often explicitly repudiates the intention of formulating 'ideals' of future society. As early as 1843 Marx writes to Ruge that any honest social reformer 'must admit to himself that he has no exact view about what ought to be. But again this is just the advantage of the new trend, that we do not dogmatically anticipate the world but only want to find the new world through a critique of the old one.' *The German Ideology* denies that 'communism' is an 'ideal' or 'state of affairs which ought to be brought about'. Communism rather is 'an actual movement which is abolishing the present state of affairs'. 'The workers', says *The Civil War in France*, 'have no fixed and finished utopias to introduce by popular decree, ... no ideals to realize.' The task of the working class is 'only to posit freely the elements of the new society which has already developed in the womb of the collapsing bourgeois society'.[23]

The plain import of these passages (and others like them) is that Marx does not pretend to know what the lifestyle or social arrangements of future society will be like. He evidently believes that these matters are dependent largely on the further growth of our knowledge, and hence beyond our power to forecast. Marx's desire to overthrow capitalist society is not motivated by any ideal picture of communist society, but by the real alienation and deprivation of people in capitalist society, together with the conviction that these conditions result from capitalist social arrangements. Marx views his task not as one of concocting 'recipes for the cookshops of the future', but rather one of identifying the historical tendencies and social movements which promise to bring down the outmoded society and point the way to a future in which people will enjoy more of such goods as self-actualization and freedom.[24] It is wrong to think that Marx's judgment that the victory of the proletarian movement will bring about a world which is richer in these goods commits him to having some more definite conception of what this world will be like.

3 Assessing Marx on Capitalist Alienation

The issues involved in assessing Marx's thoughts about alienation under capitalism are difficult and complex. I think in the end most of these issues are empirical ones, but this does not mean that they are clear cut or easily resolved. Any adequate assessment of Marx's views at this point would certainly take up far more space than I have already used in expounding them. Even then, I suspect, any assessment seasoned with the proper scholarly caution would probably be inconclusive. It is unlikely that anyone, in Marx's time or today, knows enough to be entitled to a strong opinion for or against what Marx says about alienation and its social causes. If many people (the present writer included) do hold strong opinions, this is largely because the only alternative to committing oneself in practice for or against Marx would be to take no effective stand whatever on the social reality around us. In the present section I will try to identify (but not to resolve), some of the main issues raised by Marx's account of alienation as it has been expounded here.

Marx's account of alienation in capitalist society aims at substantiating three principal theses:

(1) The vast majority of people living under capitalism are alienated.
(2) The chief causes of this alienation cannot be removed so long as the capitalist mode of production prevails.
(3) Alienation as a pervasive social phenomenon can and will be abolished in a postcapitalist (socialist or communist) mode of production.

These three theses are obviously interrelated. (1) is more or less presupposed by both (2) and (3). But (1) itself, as Marx understands it, is also dependent on (2) and (3), and on his grounds for holding them. In support of (1), a Marxist might cite widespread feelings of disorientation and dissatisfaction among people living in capitalist societies, or he might point to the preoccupation of philosophers, artists, social thinkers and popular consciousness with the problem of alienation, whether in an overtly Marxian or in various non-Marxian forms. But these consider-ations, however well substantiated, would not strictly show that alienation, as Marx understands it, exists in capitalist society. By the same token, a critic of Marx cannot successfully rebut (1) merely by arguing that people in capitalist societies are on the whole satisfied with their lives, even if a convincing case for this could be made out. Alienation, as Marx conceives of it, is not fundamentally a matter of consciousness or of how people in fact feel about themselves or their lives. Alienation is rather a state of objective unfulfillment, of the frustration of really existing human needs and potentialities. The consciousness people have of this unfulfillment is merely a reflection of alienation, at most a symptom or evidence of it. Marx's real grounds for believing that people in capitalist society are alienated is not that they are conscious of being alienated, but rather the objective existence of potentialities for human fulfillment that must be frustrated as long as the capitalist mode of production prevails.

As we saw in section 2, Marx has no very definite conception of postcapitalist society or of the possibilities for fulfillment which he believes will be actualized in it. Hence Marx does not believe (3) because he has some clear idea of the ways in which socialism or communism will provide people with opportunities for self-actualization. Rather, he seems to believe (3) because he is confident that people can achieve a fulfilling life when the main obstacles to it are removed, and because he thinks he has identified these obstacles: they are the outmoded social relations of bourgeois society.

The most direct way of attacking Marx's theory would be to deny that people really are alienated under capitalism, that people in capitalist society really do fall far short of actualiz-ing their human potentialities. We could do this and still admit that many people in capitalist society are dissatisfied with their lives, so long as we hold that this dissatisfaction is due to causes other than the actual frustration of genuine potentialities of the sort Marx believes in. We could even go so far as to admit that people's dissatisfaction is due to their belief that they are being prevented by capitalism from actualizing their essential powers, so long as we hold that this belief is mistaken, perhaps that it is a tantalizing illusion disseminated by dangerous social malcontents.

It is often said that Marx is too optimistic about the inevitability of historical progress, and that the twentieth century's bitter experiences have taught us that the potentialities for human fulfillment in mass society under industrial technology are not nearly as great as nineteenth century thinkers (including Marx) believed them to be. These common opinions can easily be pressed into service against Marx's account of capitalist alienation. For if they are correct, then Marx's belief that most people in capitalist society are alienated is based on an exaggerated estimate of the human potentialities of modern society.

Marx certainly does not defend his nineteenth century optimism against twentieth century objections. Nothing he says (perhaps nothing he could say) rules out the possibility that he is wrong to believe that the colossal and unprecedented expansion of society's productive powers during the capitalist era has created comparably colossal and unprecedented potentialities for human self-actualization. But it is not so obvious as many of Marx's critics might like to suppose that his belief is unrealistic or excessively optimistic. Modern technology increases people's ability to exercise control over nature, over themselves and over their relations with each other. It shortens the time required for people to produce the necessaries of life, and thus gives people at least potential mastery over time, over the hours, days and years which are the substance of human life. If technology also adds to people's needs, it is evident (at least to Marx) that some of these needs expand and enrich human life, and that freed from the influences of an alienating social order, people could exercise rational control even over the creation of new needs.

Further, modern science has increased our knowledge both of ourselves and of nature outside us, providing us with what we apparently need most to make wise use of our increased powers. Modern society has become mass society just because science and industry have increased people's powers of communication with each other, and intensified the web of human interdependence. Marx's confidence in the human potential of modern science and technology is initially plausible. To reject it is to embrace the paradox that increasing people's powers, their self-understanding and their interdependence has no tendency to enrich their lives, their freedom and their community. The burden of proof seems to be on anyone who would defend such paradoxes. It is not obvious that events in our century have rendered them more defensible than they were in Marx's time.

Especially important for Marx's conception of our potentialities for freedom is his belief that the values of individuality and community are reconcilable, that postcapitalist society can simultaneously achieve greater individual autonomy and greater social unity than people's productive powers and social relations have hitherto permitted. Marx's critics have been particularly suspicious of his silence concerning the social decision procedures through which free individuals are to achieve the rational collective regulation of their associated labor. At least since Rousseau, philosophers and political theorists have set themselves the problem of finding a form of human association which could unite individuals, putting the common might of society at the disposal of each while at the same time leaving all completely free to follow a self-chosen plan of life. To many it has seemed highly questionable whether such an association is possible even in theory, let alone in practice. They are bound to be skeptical of Marx's apparent presumption that modern technology puts the goal within reach, and the abolition of capitalism is all we require to attain it.

Marx does say very little about the political or administrative structure of postcapitalist society, beyond insisting that it will be democratic, and will involve control by 'society itself' rather than by a separate political mechanism or state bureaucracy. Fundamentally, however, he does not see the problem as a procedural one at all. For Marx, the chief obstacle both to individual freedom and social unity is the division of society into oppressing and oppressed classes. Of course as long as we tacitly assume a class society, the goals of freedom and community will look both separately unattainable and diametrically opposed. In a society where one individual's freedom is not necessarily another's servitude, and where people have no motives to use community as a pretext for advancing some people's interests at the expense of others, questions of social decision making will not appear to people in the form of theoretical paradoxes or insoluble technical problems.

Marx also refuses to address himself to procedural questions because he regards them as premature. Such questions presuppose that we who ask them are all people of good will, pursuing a disinterested search for the right way to live together. They presuppose also that the object of such a search is, at least in its fundamentals, something which can be determined independently of detailed information about the technical resources available to society as regards its material production. Both presuppositions, in Marx's view, are false. As long as class society persists, the viability of any political mechanism will necessarily be a function not of its suitability for promoting genuine liberty or community, but only of the class interests it serves. Only after the abolition of class society can people begin to decide, on the basis of the productive capacities then at their disposal, how they will live together as free individuals.

We have been considering challenges to Marx's account of capitalist alienation based on the denial that people in capitalist society are really alienated. But many of Marx's critics might be prepared to admit that alienation is a serious problem of modern society. The question remains whether it is capitalist social relations as such which are responsible for it. Most political moderates and reformists live on the hope that the evils of modern society can be abolished, or at least greatly mitigated, without abandoning the framework of commodity production and private ownership of the means of production. These hopes are often matched with the fear that a socialist revolution would do little or nothing to abolish alienation, and might even undermine such freedom and productivity as capitalism has.

Other critics, even more pessimistic, sometimes wonder whether alienation can be abolished at all, at least within the framework of a modern, sophisticated and technologically developed society. Existentialists have in effect interpreted alienation as an ineradicable fact of the human condition, built into the ontology of our existence or the transcendental structure of consciousness. Their views are sometimes continuous with older religious ones which treat alienation as a consequence of our sinful nature, remediable only by supernatural means. Social pessimists (such as Freud) have seen alienation as the inevitable result of subjecting our animal nature to the confinement of a social order. Others (in a manner reminiscent of Rousseau) have viewed alienation as the price we must pay for living in a society which is too far from nature: a society too large and sophisticated, too developed scientifically and technologically, too dependent on complex forms of human cooperation.

Marx does believe that alienation can be overcome in a modern, complex and industrialized society. But he is not necessarily committed to denying that there might be causes of alienation other than those specifically identified by his theory. The main burden of Marx's message is that capitalist social relations are the most pervasive and obvious cause of alienation, which must be abolished first, before lesser or more hidden causes can be dealt with. But there is no reason why Marx might not grant that such traditional social ills as religious fanaticism, racism and sexual oppression also contribute to alienation, and would have to be fought against even under socialism.

Marx's explanation of alienation might also be challenged in some of its details. It is arguable, for instance, that Marx's views about the capitalist division of labor, whatever truth they might have had in his own century, are now obsolete. Certainly it would be difficult to maintain that capitalism still exhibits a tendency to turn all labor into the unskilled mechanical sort, to 'make the absence of development into a specialty'. But even if this point is no longer defensible, Marx's explanation of alienation in terms of the capitalist division of labor may still be tenable. For the constraint of profit-maximization may still exercise a powerful (and harmful) effect on the nature of laboring activity, and inhibit the development of a well-rounded humanity on the part of workers. If this is so, then Marx's explanation of alienation in terms of the capitalist division of labor may still be essentially correct, even if the specific details of his account are not. Marx is always the first to insist that capitalism is not an immutable system, but one which is undergoing constant change. It would not be inconsistent with his views to recognize that his account of alienation in nineteenth century capitalist society might not be applicable in detail to its descendants in later centuries.

Notes

All translations from the German and French are my own. In such cases I have provided citations both to the original text and to an English translation. Where no direct translation is involved, I have normally cited only the English text.

The German edition I have used is the *Marx Engels Werke* published by the Dietz Verlag (Berlin, 1961–66). (This edition will be abbreviated throughout the notes as MEW. Erg. stands for *Ergänzungsheft*.) In a few places, it has been necessary to cite the older *Marx Engels Gesamtausgabe* or other texts; fuller references are provided below.

My source for Marx's writings in French is Maximilien Rubel's *Oeuvres de Karl Marx*, published by Editions Gallimard (Paris, 1963). (Abbreviated as *Oeuvres*.)

Where possible, I have cited English texts from the *Marx Engels Collected Works* published by International Publishers (New York, 1975–). (Abbreviated as CW.) Because this edition is still incomplete, this was not always possible. Where it was not, I have favored other editions published by International Publishers or by the Foreign Languages Publishing House, Moscow (fuller references are provided below). I have made especially frequent use of the International Publishers' *Marx Engels Selected Works in One Volume* (New York, 1968). (Abbreviated as SW.)

For Marx's *Grundrisse*, I have cited the German text from the edition of the *Europäische Verlagsanstalt*, Frankfurt, and the *Europa Verlag*, Vienna, which is a photographic reproduction of the Soviet edition (Moscow, 1939). English citations of the *Grundrisse* are to Martin Nicolaus' translation published by Penguin Books (Harmondsworth, 1973). In citing this work, the German pagination will be indicated by a 'g' and the English pagination by an 'e'. (Thus a citation of p. 12 in the German—which is p. 90 in the English—would read: *Grundrisse* 12g, 90e.)

Marx and Engels, *Selected Correspondence: 1846–1895* (New York, 1965), is abbreviated as *Selected Correspondence*.

Alienation and Capitalism

1 MEW 4:467, CW 6:489.
2 MEW 23:674, *Capital* (New York, 1967) 1:645.
3 MEW 4:475, CW 6:495; MEW 3:67, CW 5:87.
4 MEW 23:369–70, *Capital* 1:349.
5 MEW 23:370, *Capital* 1:350.
6 MEW 23:383, *Capital* 1:361.
7 MEW 23:511–12, *Capital* 1:487–8; cf. CW 6:190.
8 MEW 3:33, CW 5:47.
9 MEW 25:832, *Capital* 3:824; MEW 25:274, *Capital* 3:264; cf. *Capital* 1:432, *Grundrisse*, 358g, 454e, CW 3:272.
10 MEW 23:649, *Capital* 1:621.
11 MEW 3:77, CW 5:79.
12 MEW 3:33, CW 5:47.
13 MEW Erg. 1:514; CW 3:274.
14 MEW 3:67, CW 5:88; MEW 3:71, CW 5:82.
15 MEW 2:138, CW 4:131.
16 See CW 6:165–6; *Capital* 1:578.
17 MEW 3:76, CW 5:79.
18 MEW 2:138, CW 4:131.
19 CW 3:295. For example, see Marx on freedom of the press: CW 2:109–31, 311–30. In the same vein, note Engels' praise for English law as 'the only one which has preserved through ages, and transmitted to America and the Colonies, the best part of that old Germanic personal freedom, local self-government and independence from all interference but that of the law courts which on the Continent has been lost during the period of absolute monarchy, and has nowhere been as yet fully recovered' (SW 392).
20 MEW 3:70, CW 5:81; MEW 3:75, CW 5:80.
21 MEW 3:74, CW 5:77–8.
22 MEW 23:791, *Capital* 1:763.
23 MEW 1:344, CW 3:142; MEW 3:35, CW 5:49; MEW 17:343, SW, 294–5. In the Paris writings, where Marx's readers usually pretend to find his 'ideal' of nonalienated society, he says: 'Communism is the necessary form and actualizing principle of the immediate future, but communism is not as such the goal of human development' (MEW Erg. 1:546, CW 3:306). See also SW 690, *Grundrisse*, 387g, 488e.
24 MEW 23:25, *Capital* 1:17.

Discussion Questions

1. What is alienation of human labor and why is it inevitable under capitalism?
2. What are the three principal theses that Marx's account of alienation aims at grounding?
3. On what ground does Marx believe in human potential to free themselves from the inhuman practice of bourgeoise economy?
4. According to Marx, "because freedom requires the conscious production of people's social relations, it is something which can be achieved only in community with others, and cannot be attained by retreating into oneself." Is freedom intrinsically social in the sense Marx understands?
5. Can alienation be abolished in a modern, sophisticated, and technologically developed society? Argue your position, thoughtfully reflecting on your experiences in a digital era of civilization.

Taoism

Ray Billington

> The Tao is like a well: used but never used up.
>
> It is like the eternal void: filled with infinite possibilities.
>
> It is hidden but always present.
>
> I do not know who gave it birth.
>
> It is older than God.
>
> (*Tao Te Ching*, 4, trans. S. Mitchell)

Taoism stands alongside Confucianism and Buddhism as one of the three philosophies/religions which have stamped Chinese thought and culture over the past two and a half millennia. When Bodhidharma brought Ch'an (Zen) Buddhism to China around the sixth century CE, he found that the ground had been well prepared by Taoist teachers to receive the message he brought, and throughout subsequent centuries the two schools have not found it difficult to function harmoniously alongside each other

Although in general the Chinese, like the teachers of India, do not make as clear-cut a distinction between philosophy and religion as we do in the West, with our stronger analytical traditions, Taoism does in fact fork unambiguously in two directions: *Tao-chia,* philosophical Taoism; and *Tao-chiao,* religious Taoism, though the latter is often translated as magical Taoism. Our main concern is with Tao-chia, but, since Tao-chiao has always been its most popular expression (and is so even in the British Taoist Society), we should not overlook it.

Its basic aim is the attainment of immortality, and religious Taoists designate their great teachers of the past as 'immortals' *(hsien),* whom they believe to be still among us in one guise or another. The immortals are often depicted in Chinese art as covered with feathers, symbolising their rising and ascension into the air to the highest stages of self-realisation. W. Bauer (*China und die Hoffnung auf Gluck,* 1974 p. 157) draws on this description of them by a fourth-century Taoist scholar, Ko Hung:

> Some immortals ascend to the clouds, their body upright, and they fly among the clouds without beating of wings; some glide across the cloudy vapour by harnessing a dragon and ascend up to the very steps of Heaven ... Their kind has attained an eternal life, free from death; but before they reach their goal they have to shed all human emotions and all ambitions about fame and glory ... They have abandoned their former nature and are pervaded by a new life energy.

There are, according to Tao-chiao, a number of ways to achieving the status of a hsien. These include: first, various alchemic practices, the most powerful of which involves the use of cinnabar, sulphide of mercury, symbolising what Philip Rawson (*Tao,* p. 263) termed the 'nuclear energy of joined yin and yang' (though there is a cautionary tale here, as many Chinese went beyond the symbolic to the literal use of cinnabar, and died from mercury poisoning after consuming it—the ultimate in irony for anyone seeking longevity); second, embryonic breathing *(hsing-ch'i)* and other exercises to stretch the body and allow the breath to circulate more freely (Tao-yin), a much more intense and prolonged process than *pranayama,* the rhythmic control of the breath practised in yoga; third, meditation, especially the form which is becoming increasingly popular in the West, T'ai chi chu'an, whereby the practitioner seeks to align his or her body, through subtle and graceful movements, with the natural, though invisible, energies of the locality; and fourth, certain sexual practices *(fang-chung shu),* during which it is believed that the male yang is nourished by the female yin, and vice versa, thus mirroring the marriage of the masculine heaven with the feminine earth which, they believed, brought all things into being. As in both Hindu and Tibetan Buddhist Tantrism, though with a different aim in mind, the physical act of sex, particularly the exchange of bodily fluids, was viewed as a supremely efficacious way of bringing about longevity.

All these practices had, it was believed, one virtue in common: they enabled the practitioner to extend his or her life-span, and possibly become an immortal. What this essentially required was harmony with the *Ch'i,* and for an understanding of this concept we must turn to Tao-chia.

Philosophical Taoism is concerned not with longevity, but with the achievement and enjoyment of the eternal here and now; and here the link with Ch'an (Zen) Buddhism in unambiguous. Both Tao-chia and Ch'an teach the virtues of simplicity, naturalness, and the discovery of the intuitive side of one's nature. However, whereas teachers of Ch'an exhort followers of its path to turn away from the tangible world, a process exemplified by Bodhidharma's 'nine years facing the wall', Taoism encourages its followers to discover the intuitive side of their natures by enjoying the natural world around them so as to experience a harmony with it that is beyond self-consciousness. Once again we have encountered the advocacy of mysticism, but in Taoism there is an important and unique emphasis: the key is to be *natural.*

> When you are content to be simply yourself
> and don't compare or compete,
> everybody will respect you.

(Tao Te Ching, 8)

What, then, does 'Tao' mean? To be able to give a direct answer to this seemingly straightforward question would, paradoxically, be to fall into error, since, as the opening verse of the most famous of all Taoist classics states unambiguously,

> The tao that can be told is not the eternal Tao;
> The name that can be named is not the eternal Name.

This couplet is from the *Tao Te Ching*, the 'classic of the way and its power'. According to Chinese tradition, it was written by Lao Tzu, a famous teacher and mystic of the sixth century BCE, just before he removed himself from civilisation in order to become a recluse. It is now generally agreed by sinologists that the work is the product of many hands (Lao Tzu means 'great master', which is more a title than a name); that it was compiled over some centuries; and was finalised in its present form around the second century BCE.

According to the *Tao Te Ching*, the Tao is *the first principle of the universe, the all-embracing reality from which everything else arises*. Although the Tao remains eternally unknowable, its power (Te) can enter into every human being, so that the test of one's commitment to Taoism is viewed as the extent to which one's life is in harmony with the Tao. (The Chinese hieroglyphic for 'philosophy' depicts a hand and a mouth, symbolising a condition where words are consistent with deeds.)

While one should be cautious about establishing cross-cultural likenesses, some commentators on Taoism have compared the concept of the Tao with that of Brahman in Hinduism. Brahman as the (unknown) ground of being certainly presents a parallel, but the immediacy of Brahman illustrated in the belief in the possibility of a union between it and the Atman is out of harmony with Taoist teaching, which accepts that, while a person may reflect the Tao in his or her life, nobody can possibly *know* the Tao. Other commentators, including George Chryssides (*Journal of Religious Studies* 19, pp. 1–11), find it not inapposite to view the Tao as having the same place in Taoist thought as the Godhead has in the thinking of (my example) Meister Eckhart: it is unknowable, but there could be nothing in the universe without its prevenient creative energy. This is a fair comment, but an important rider must be added: Taoism does not proceed to make any case for God, or gods, as divine powers operating under the Tao's auspices, so to speak. Section 42 of the *Tao Te Ching* puts the matter rather differently:

> The Tao gives birth to One.
> One gives birth to Two.
> Two gives birth to Three.
> Three gives birth to all things.

The 'One' to which the Tao gives birth—and was mentioned in relation to Taochiao—is Ch'i, or primordial breath (wind, spirit, energy, like the Hebrew word *Ruach* as used in Genesis 1:2: 'The spirit of God moved upon the face of the waters'). It is the life-force that pervades and vitalises all things, the cosmic energy which brought the universe into being and continues to sustain it. Chryssides suggests that if the Tao is unknowable, Ch'i is the Tao that can be known—like God, the origin of all things even if, like God, it is not the unknown and unknowable origin of the origin. He argues that, while the Judaeo-Christian tradition certainly presents images of a 'hands-on' God, there are throughout their scriptures signs of development, leading, for example, to St John's link between Jesus, the Son of God, and the logos in Greek philosophy (John 1: 1 ff.). This is certainly a more advanced concept than that of a God who helps Adam to name the animals in the Garden of Eden, but it remains the case that the God who is involved with his people in all their doings is so fundamental to the theistic tradition that the idea of a 'Godhead' remains, at best, marginalised. The concept of the logos as defined in Greek thought is probably the nearest we have to that of the Tao outside China: but the concept must remain pure if the comparison is to be valid. To tinge it with Christian mythology, as in 'Son of God', is to undermine the comparison.

For Taoists even the Ch'i remains remote. It can be experienced, but only with time and dedication. If the Te, the power of the Tao in each individual life, is to be evinced, a force is needed which can be experienced more immediately. It is here that Taoists turn to the 'Two' to which the Ch'i gives birth. These are the twin forces of yin and yang, the polar opposites by which the universe functions, such as negative and positive, cold and heat, darkness and light, intuition and rationality, femininity and masculinity, earth and heaven. Neither of these can be without the other, and neither has any meaning without the other. We know the meaning of 'hot' only in relation to 'cold', of 'wet' to 'dry', of 'tall' to 'short', of 'dark' to 'light', of 'life' to 'death'. (We know that we are alive only because we know that we were once, and shall again be, dead. If we were eternal, there would be no word either for 'eternal' or for 'living'.)

These twin forces, the yin and the yang, operate throughout the world, giving us day and night, summer and winter, seedtime and harvest. As the symbol of yin and yang, the *T'ai-ch'i-tu* (diagram of the supreme ultimate) illustrates, there is, however, some light (yang) in the dark yin, and vice versa. This indicates two important features of life, which are often lost sight of. First, no living creature is entirely one or the other: there is some feminine yin in every male and some masculine yang in every female, and the wisest couple will recognise this and live together accordingly, with neither claiming to be the dominant partner (yang) in every aspect of their relationship. Second, and more importantly, neither yin nor yang is ever motionless; each is continuously moving into the other, which means that one must learn to recognise when to apply yin, and when yang, energies. This again means allowing the intuition to exert itself: to know when to speak out and when to remain quiet; when to be gentle and when to be violent; when to be active and when to stand and stare. Both the workaholic and the playboy are, according to the yin-yang doctrine, living distorted and incomplete lives because only half of their natures is being allowed expression. Neither the ant nor the grasshopper in Aesop's fable would receive Taoism's stamp of approval.

The 'Three' to which the Two give birth are heaven, earth and humanity. As we shall see, it is when there is harmony between these three—the yang of heaven, the yin of earth, and the human occupants of the arena which between them they bring into being—that the Te can be identified in people's lives. The final stage is the creation of 'all things' which we encounter and experience, for which 'the Three' are responsible.

The important consideration with Taoism, however, as with the concept of nirvana in Buddhism, is not to speculate on the meaning of the idea of the Tao, but to find out how to respond to its power (Te) in one's own life. The aim, as already mentioned, is to be natural, and the *Tao Te Ching* gives many hints about how this state may be achieved. One way is to practise *wu-wei*. This is often translated as living a life of 'non-action', but a more accurate translation would be not to take any *inappropriate* action. The most famous exponent of Taoism who was unquestionably a historical figure was the teacher of the third century BCE, Chuang-Tzu (Master Chuang). He argued that many of the things we do and the words we speak are simply a waste of time and breath, since the situation we are discussing or trying to affect cannot be changed by our efforts: all we're actually doing, he said, was 'flaying the air'. Or worse: our frenetic efforts may actually lead to the loss of what was wholesome and acceptable in itself. We destroy a lily by gilding it; a snake is no longer a snake if we paint legs on it; we shall not help young wheat to grow by tugging at it. We must practise patience and learn how, in the words of the religious existentialist Tillich, 'to read the signs of the times', acting only at the right time and with the minimum amount of effort. In fact, if we learn how to wait, we shall frequently find that no action is necessary in any case. The *Tao Te Ching* (15) states:

> Do you have the patience to wait
> till your mud settles and the water is clear?
> Can you remain unmoving
> till the right action arises by itself?

There is a skill involved in such behaviour, which few people raised in Western cultures have learned (and perhaps not many modern Chinese: although Confucianism has been restored in their school syllabuses, Taoism has no place). A Western equivalent might be, 'Never do today what you can possibly leave till tomorrow', where the operative word is *possibly*. It sounds like a policy of procrastination, and therefore heinous, and is condemned in the German couplet, 'Morgen, Morgen, nur nicht heute/Sagen alle faule Leute' ('Tomorrow, tomorrow, anything but today/That's what lazy people say'). This may be the case; but it may also be the case that a person recognises what is essential to be completed today and what can preferably be left till later, bearing in mind that, when it is later, the job may no longer be necessary. Chuang-Tzu was, in fact, active in public life and must have been widely respected since he was offered the prime ministership of his province. Wu-wei means striking only when the iron is hot, sowing one's seed—whether in deed or word—and leaving it time to burgeon. Where disagreement with another person occurs, its approach is to present one's viewpoint unambiguously, then leave it time to germinate—if there is any worth in the idea—in the mind of the other, rather than to overcome the other with decibels or, worse, to force him to accept a viewpoint or an activity against either his will or his personal assessment of the situation. Wu-wei is the way of the diplomat, not the dictator; of the philosopher, not the proselytiser.

Another concept in Taoism with which wu-wei is linked is *fu*, meaning 'returning'. This could be interpreted as aligning oneself with the yin and yang by understanding that seasons, whether in nature or in a nation's culture and values, arrive and pass, only to return again and pass away again, so that the wise person will accommodate his living to the eternal process of change. More basically Taoist is the concept of fu as returning, or, at any rate, remaining loyal, to one's roots:

> If you let yourself be blown to and fro,
> you lose touch with your root.
> If you let restlessness move you,
> you lose touch with who you are.

(op. cit., 26)

Fu is one example among many in Eastern philosophy of an idea which is mirrored in existentialist thought, with its emphases on, for example, authenticity, avoiding bad faith, even autonomy. (See my *East of Existentialism*.)

The same is true of another Taoist virtue which reflects but antecedes Zen. This is *p'u*, literally an unhewn block, and is an image used to denote simplicity, even innocence: not arising from ignorance, but from a backcloth of full awareness of the human condition: childlikeness without being childish. It means being oneself, avoiding what Sartre was to term 'bad faith' or living behind a mask. To live according to p'u is to speak as one feels, to behave according to the person one is, or has become; in other words, to act naturally. The *Tao Te Ching* (25) states:

> Man follows the earth.
> Earth follows the universe.
> The universe follows the Tao.
> The Tao follows only itself.

That final phrase has also been translated as 'suchness', the spontaneous and intuitive state of *tzu-yan*, meaning 'being such of itself', 'being natural'. In human beings, it includes everything which is free of human intention or external influences: that which is in harmony with itself. It may therefore be linked with wu-wei with its call for action only when it is appropriate—that is, when it is the natural action for those particular circumstances. When a person achieves this condition (which is not easy), he or she can be described as being at one with the Tao. It will not be achieved by academic research, or the study of sacred texts, or through a correct observance of ritual: like Zen, Taoism relegates all these activities to a low ranking on the scale of spiritual aids. It will be gained by living one's life in accordance with the natural forces of the universe, expressed both in nature itself and in human nature. As one of the contributors to G. Beky's *Die Welt des Tao* ('The World of Tao'), Akira Ohaima, states (p. 126):

> The Tao acts like an immanent energy, a mysterious presence within the world of the ten thousand things. Therefore the individual effects of the ten thousand things—if they are not prevented from following their own nature—are in accordance with the *tzu-jan* [tsu-yan] of the Tao. What matters is not the self-conscious intentional striving for oneness with the Tao, but rather the fact that human action is identical with the Tao that is present and acting in man. That is *tzu-jan*.

While there are parallels between Taoism and Indian thought, it is important to recognise its distinctiveness, especially because of issues raised in Chapter 9. One could call the Tao the 'ground of being'; but unlike the Hindu view of Brahman, which can be known through being awakened to the Atman, the Tao must be preceded, tacitly at least, by the epithet 'unknowable': which implies that there really is no counterpart. The Zen experience of satori, entry into the void, is probably closer to Taoist ontology, but there remains a difference between Taoism and Zen in relation to the world, the 'ten thousand things'. Zen can be compared with Taoism in its treatment of the natural world as a mystery, which emerges through the haiku (and sometimes in a koan); and Chinese rural paintings often create the same sense of mystery in the presence of something awesome and inexplicable. Both encourage an intuitive approach to nature, which results in a sense of deep respect for that with which we should always be co-operating rather than exploiting. For Taoism, however, (and in this it exemplifies one of the major differences between Indian and Chinese philosophy) this is enough: to be at one with nature is a sign of being in harmony with the Tao. I shall discuss shortly the significance of this oneness with reference to Taoist art, but it is immediately clear that we are here engaged on a different quest from that followed by either Buddhists or Hindus. For them, while nature may be a valuable and often-sought context for enlightenment, it remains no more than that. The experience of moksha, or satori, are ultimately independent of anything which the tangible world provides, and can just as well be gained by facing a wall (though a Zen garden provides a context and can create a mood which is easily conducive to a spiritual experience). For Taoists, however, the relationship with nature is at the heart of the mystical experience, and this is illustrated continually in Taoist paintings.

The beauty of these paintings is being increasingly appreciated in the Western world, but it is not with their beauty alone that the artists have been concerned. Their primary purpose is to express Taoist values. The seventeenth-century painting by K'un-ts'an, *Among Green Mountains I build a House,* is typical, if not archetypical, and has countless imitators whose works today adorn living-room walls in Western homes. To begin with, there is a sense of deep tranquillity pervading the entire scene, providing the assurance of how easy it will be for anyone to be becalmed in such surroundings, and to share in its unhurried, if not entirely soundless, completeness. Then there is the sense of unity in the whole, with its various features blending into one another so that no one aspect protrudes. The river and its banks are at one with the trees alongside, and these in their turn harmonise with the mountain, so that its heights do not appear to impose on the valley below. Above all, the simply structured house merges with its natural surrounding—it could even be overlooked with a cursory glance—and the figure gazing from its unglazed window is not expressing ownership of what he surveys, but a reverence towards this manifestation of the Tao, of which he—or she—is privileged to be part. There is no sense of 'me', 'me', about either the house or its owner, any more than there is about the river, the trees, or the mountain. It is as far removed as one can imagine from the Western attitude to the natural world, as exemplified in the triumphalism of its newspapers after the first successful climbing of Mt Everest: 'Everest Conquered!' they proclaimed. A Taoist would see this attitude as typical human conceit, preferring to describe the event along the lines of permission to visit the mountain peak for a brief period before the guests scuttled off back down to the safety of the lower levels.

Equally important in the picture is the manifestation of the yin and the yang. As these move back and forth towards and away from each other, so we find a sense of movement between the various features. The yin of the river and the foliage merges with the yang of the trees and the mountain, while remaining distinctive entities in themselves. The yang sky and the yin earth are in partnership together, light and shade combine to give clarity and contrast. Yet overall there is, as in so many Taoist landscapes, a brooding sense of mystery. There is what Wordsworth described (and will be further discussed in Chapter 9) as 'a presence', a living spirit which pervades and unifies the whole, and with which the human participant is in communion. The mystery is given direct expression by the depiction of clouds and mist which pervade one side of the house. One senses that the hermit is experiencing an absorption in the whole which can be described only in mystical terms, on a par with the mysticism of Meister Eckhart and others of the theistic traditions; with the absorption of Atman and Brahman in the Hindu tradition; and the experience of the void, satori, in Zen. *Among Green Mountains I build a House* is, in fact and in short, a religious painting.

Even the food we eat can, as a balance of yin and yang, be evidence of this natural harmony and therefore a spiritual experience, and on this issue Taoism parts company with its Indian counterparts. While neither Hinduism nor Buddhism expresses the extreme suspicion of all foods as found in the Jainite tradition (because for them eating means the expression of *ahimsa,* violence, towards living entities and is therefore detrimental to the spiritual quest), there remains the whiff of self-denial in all their different schools. The view frequently propounded in both Hinduism and Buddhism is that, on the whole, abstinence is more spiritually beneficial than indulgence (and this applies to sex as well as food). This is a moot point, of course, but most Taoists would view this attitude as a straightforward example of acting unnaturally.

Taoists seek enlightenment through what heaven and earth provide, rejoicing in their glories and discovering through them the deepest mysteries of the universe. So it is seen as unnatural to deny oneself that which is both health-giving and enjoyable; in fact, anyone who knows how to balance his diet is at one with the Tao, so that a chef could well be described as the Chinese equivalent of the Hindu guru.

Taoism's ideal is to balance yin and yang forces, an aim which is expressed in the teachings of Confucius, who was—and still is—often viewed as a rival to the Taoists, but saw himself as one who was seeking to apply their ideas and ideals in the practical world of family, social and political life. He indicated, for example, how nations could experience the harmony of the Tao in the world of politics; his *Analects* reverberate with admonitions for rulers to rule with a light hand so that their subjects will not feel threatened or intimidated—and will thus be more co-operative with them in their enterprises.

Furthermore, and coming closer to home than politics, Taoism reaches out into regions which Hindu mystics leave virtually unexplored—the sexual harmony between a man and a woman, when give and take, assertion and submission, hardness and softness, fierceness and tenderness, mirror the yin-yang forces, the twin pillars of the Ch'i, the vital breath by which the Tao is known. Much Taoist art, whether paintings or other artifices, features the yin and yang in openly sexual terms, abounding with images of male and female genitalia expressed not only in scenes of human sexuality, but as images in stones, fruits, plants, or any other natural object which resembles a vulva or a lingam. A mutually fulfilling sex life is viewed as a sign that those concerned have discovered the harmony and completion of the yin and yang, and so are sharing what may be without apology called a religious experience.

Western attitudes on this matter have been sadly distorted, perhaps terminally, by the fear of sex which runs virtually unmodified throughout Christian scriptures and traditions. It is still expressed in high places, as is exemplified by a member of the British Upper House who objected to sex education in schools on the grounds that it 'gave children wrong ideas'. Ray Monk records in his *Ludwig Wittgenstein* that the philosopher's friend and disciple, Maurice Drury, expressed disgust over the bas-relief on the wall of one of the Luxor temples which depicted the god Horus with an erect phallus in the act of ejaculating and collecting the semen in a bowl. Wittgenstein rejected Drury's disapproval:

> Why in the world shouldn't they have regarded with awe and reverence that act by which the human race is perpetuated? Not every religion has to have St Augustine's attitude to sex.

> (op. cit., p. 454)

(For further reflections on this theme, see Chang's *The Tao of Love and Sex*.)

The harmony of the Tao, then, is seen as reflected in a healthy body, a reciprocal relationship, a fine balance of work and leisure, of committed time and spare time. A Taoist's diary will have enough engagements to fulfil the yang side of his life with enough free time not to leave the yin incomplete. Both the lack of responsible commitment reflected in an empty diary, and the furious round of unsatisfactorily completed duties in one that is overcrowded, would be viewed as unlikely to lead its owner into the joy of being at ease with himself, an ease which is one of the sure indicators of being in harmony with the Tao, and possessing the Te. The *Tao Te Ching*, 27 states:

> A good traveller has no fixed plans
> and is not intent upon arriving.
> A good artist lets his intuition
> lead him wherever it wants.
> A good scientist has freed his mind of concepts
> and keeps his mind open to what is.
>
> Thus the Master is available to all people
> and doesn't reject anyone.
> He is ready to use all situations
> and doesn't waste anything.
> This is called embodying the light.

In the Taizé Community in France, this virtue is described as being *disponible*—available. I should describe it also as being religious, which leads to our final consideration.

To the untutored mind, Taoism may well appear to be a philosophy of life rather than a religion. It makes no distinction between the sacred and the secular, has no dedicated buildings, no liturgy, no holy books, no moral code except to be natural, no forms of prayer and, above all, no God in any sense in which that concept is expressed in other religions. While Tao-chiao, religious Taoism, aims for longevity in this life, it affirms no belief in a life beyond and has no conception of reincarnation. To be sure, Chuang-Tzu, who evinced no signs of mourning after the death of his beloved wife, said to his critics:

> How do I know that loving life is not a delusion? How do I know that in hating death, I am
> not like a man who, having left home in his youth, has forgotten the way back?

But this was a cryptic question rather than an affirmation of belief, on a par with the anti-anthropomorphism of his famous remark after dreaming that he was a butterfly:

> Now I don't know whether I'm a man dreaming he is a butterfly, or a butterfly dreaming
> it is a man.

As mentioned on p. 13, Confucius—if we can take him according to his own self-description and number him among the Taoists—often referred to 'the way of heaven', but he used this phrase to mean no more than the ideal as we perceive it—the ideal way of ruling, of relating to other people, of achieving fulfilment. He was Nietzschean, in fact, in his insistence on being concerned with the problems of this world rather than using our energies preparing for the next. Asked about how we should serve the gods, he peremptorily replied that the service of our fellow men was enough of a challenge to anyone without wasting time on this vacuous consideration.

The *Tao Te Ching* is a more spiritual book than the writings of Confucius, but its reverence is certainly not directed towards any kind of divine architect or heavenly father, analogies which are typical in overtly religious organisations. In place of these it presents the natural world, the world of the 'ten thousand things', as both the context for living, and the catalyst of whatever philosophy we may embrace. To live naturally means to accept other people as, potentially at least, fellow-witnesses to the Tao, and consequently to accept them for their own sakes. This is the way of nature, with checks and balances which, on the whole, ensure that no single species plays too dominant a role. The wise person is therefore one who accepts his or her place in the natural order by co-operating with it, and so gaining the fulfilment of living in harmony with the Tao. It is pointless to try to alter or control nature: that is a form of megalomania which will bring inevitable disaster in one form or another—a disaster of the perpetrator's own making.

So the image we receive from the heart of Taoism is of a life lived without guile, without pretence, in tune with the natural forces of yin and yang, which are manifested in all that exists or occurs. The follower of what Alan Watts characterised in his translation of the *Tao Te Ching* as 'the Watercourse Way' learns how to adapt herself intuitively to any situation, to breathe in strength from what nature provides, so that, contented with her own self and with her role in life, she is able naturally to enrich the lives of those she encounters. According to the *Tao Te*

Ching, this apparent ideal can become anyone's norm. If it means abandoning the rat race for a simpler way of living, then this is a change worth making, and many, in the West as well as in the East, are making that choice.

With this brief account of Taoism we reach the end of this overview of mysticism as experienced in selected religions of the world. It is difficult not to sympathise with Taoists' own assessment of their philosophy as one that, in its acknowledgement of an ultimate spiritual power which cannot be known or named, but is affirmed by the manifest world which we all encounter, is, in fact, a unifying factor between all religions. Confucians, Buddhists, Hindus, theists, have their own terms for the mystery, but in the end all are discussing the same thing. This may well be a valid assessment of Tao-chia; and if its religious or magical expression, Tao-chiao, remains fundamentally related to Chinese culture, even there (for example, in its forms of meditation) it may have a contribution to make in the quest for religion without God. The universal appeal of Taoism is expressed in an inscription on a Ming rock, dated 1556, and it sums up Taoism's central affirmation:

> Vast indeed is the Ultimate Tao,
> Spontaneously itself, apparently without acting,
> End of all ages and beginning of all ages,
> Existing before Earth and existing before Heaven,
> Silently embracing the whole of time,
> Continuing uninterrupted through all eons,
> In the East it taught Father Confucius,
> In the West it converted the 'Golden man' [the Buddha]
> Taken as pattern by a hundred kings,
> Transmitted by generations of sages,
> It is the ancestor of all doctrines,
> The mystery beyond all mysteries.

Discussion Questions

1. In what sense is Taoism a form of religion despite its disregard for any deities or prospect for a disembodied afterlife?
2. What are the Taoist religious practices that are done to achieve immortality?
3. What is the goal of philosophical Taoism and how does Ch'an Buddhism play a part in shaping a distinct school of Taoism?
4. The first chapter of *Tao Te Ching* goes: "The Tao that can be told is not the eternal Tao; the name that can be named is not the eternal name." What is your interpretation of this opening verse?
5. Taoist ideal of *wu-wei* (non-action) is captured in the *Tao Te Ching*: "Do you have the patience to wait; till your mind settles and the water is clear? Can you remain unmoving; till the right action arises by itself?" What is the meaning of *wu-wei*, and how can it be a mark of wisdom that makes all things in order?

EPILOGUE

Philosophy simply puts everything before us, and neither explains nor deduces anything.—Since everything lies open to view there is nothing to explain.

Wittgenstein, Philosophical Investigations, §126

Socrates left a legacy with his trenchant admonition: "The unexamined life is not worth living." I interpret "examination" as an observation with a detached and impartial outlook on the one hand and a deep empathetic concern on the other. In a nutshell, an impartial and empathic observation of life. Most of us find it challenging to be impartial because we are engaged in life with a vested interest. It is why philosophy appears to be difficult; we take it for granted that we are biased and prejudiced. Can we observe our biased and prejudicial tendency? Certainly! "Philosophy does not explain nor deduce anything but simply puts everything before us," says Wittgenstein. We do not, however, observe life as if it were a pastime but as a serious endeavor, a puzzling conundrum, an endless series of projects, and what have you. We can be contemplatively detached but never be disinterested. We all seek the best way to live by being able to respond to the variety of frames we see our life through.

Understanding how life works is at the same time understanding ourselves because we are nothing but a host of life experiences. Knowing who we truly are is indeed a perennial subject of human being's spiritual quest. What drives human beings in this quest from time immemorial? I find the answer in the hallmark of human nature: We think wisdom and good life are synonymous. We have a natural desire to reach out far beyond what we think we are here and now and understand our life from the specter of eternity (*sub specie aeternitatis*). Life is well lived when we strive to transcend the confines of what we think we are and aspire to be free. I believe this urge to transcend what we think we are is the spiritual DNA of humanity and certainly the meaning of human life.

Philosophy is inherently a spiritual practice in its Socratic provenance however varied the subsequent philosophical developments have been since then. Our desire for self-understanding is an expression of our pursuit of freedom. We can practice these two aspects of intrinsically human vocation by cultivating compassion. Compassion is not a sentimental feeling directed to the pain and agony of others, nor a momentary act of kindness. Compassion is the grounding human characteristic that empowers us to see life and ourselves intently and insightfully, offering us a penetrating wisdom which is vital for a good life. In this regard, Socratic wisdom in all its intellectual and critical tour de force must be accompanied with compassion-powered infrastructure. Philosophy is a valuable instrument we can practice in the pursuit of wisdom and compassion. A life well lived is truly a superb philosophical performance. I offer my share in this philosophical performance by creating an anthology comprising core subjects in the humanities, so students and readers alike can play a part, as if part of a humanist quartet, and carry out a philosophical examination in an accentuated form of human experience.

I wish this anthology may afford you a chance to rethink the function of philosophy as an academic discipline and seek promising ways in which philosophy classes can thrive in the age of profound chaos and undervalued human spirit. I feel deeply grateful for those readers who approach this anthology with the spirit of compassionate Socrates.

CPSIA information can be obtained
at www.ICGtesting.com
Printed in the USA
FSHW010743180122
87673FS

9 781516 598700